Joining the Dots:

uniting Salisbury's past through holes in the ground

by Phil Harding

with Lorrain Higbee and Lorraine Mepham

Belfry

Cathedral Church of StMary

Joining the Dots: uniting Salisbury's past through holes in the ground

Phil Harding

with Lorrain Higbee and Lorraine Mepham

Illustrations by

Linda Coleman, Liz James, Kitty Foster, Will Foster,
Elizabeth Garwood and Tom Westhead

Wessex Archaeology Occasional Paper
2022

Published 2022 by Wessex Archaeology Ltd
Portway House, Old Sarum Park, Salisbury, SP4 6EB
www.wessexarch.co.uk/

British Library Cataloguing in Publication Data
A catalogue record for this book is available from the British Library

ISBN 978-1-7391876-0-6

Designed and typeset by Will Foster
Cover design by Elizabeth James, Elizabeth Garwood and Will Foster
Copy-edited by Tess Millar

Front cover
A map of Salisbury about 1500 by Elizabeth James and Elizabeth Garwood
Back cover
Excavations on Brown Street in the 1980s
Printed by Lightning Source

Wessex Archaeology Ltd is company limited by guarantee registered in England,
company number 1712772. It is also a Charity registered in England and Wales number 287786, and in
Scotland, Scottish Charity number SC042630. Our registered office is at Portway House, Old Sarum Park,
Salisbury, Wiltshire, SP4 6EB

Contents

List of Figures

List of Plates

Chapter 3

List of Tables

Acknowledgements

This project was initiated to celebrate both the 800th anniversary of the foundation of the new city in Salisbury and the 40th anniversary of Wessex Archaeology.

Thanks must be extended to Wessex Archaeology for their commitment not only to complete the long-overdue publication of back-log excavations, undertaken in the 1980s, but also to discuss these results along with those of subsequent work. Appreciation is especially due to Linda Coleman for encouraging the completion of the work. The opportunity to compile this study has been an enjoyable experience, not least for the fact that the principal author actually saw most of these embryonic excavations at first hand. Acknowledgement must also be given to David Algar, John Chandler, Richard Deane and Peter Saunders for reading and commenting on the preliminary draft of the text. These individuals have been involved with the archaeology and history of Salisbury for longer than the principal author. Discussions have also taken place with a number of people who have shared their accumulated knowledge of Salisbury and its architecture, including Jamie Wright, who has extensive knowledge of the local brickfields; Sarah Wyles, for information regarding production and consumption of oysters; and Bob Davis, who advised on construction and detail of timber-framed buildings. Lorraine Mepham also benefited from discussions with Duncan Brown and Ben Jervis regarding the dating framework of the Laverstock kilns and with Penny Copland-Griffiths for sharing results of research on the products of the Crockerton kilns. Marek Lewcun kindly provided detail to the lives of local clay pipe makers.

Thanks are due to Linda Coleman, who compiled many of the original graphics and especially to Liz James, Elizabeth Garwood and Will Foster for the cover. Kitty Foster and Will Foster have added more recent graphics, with additional illustrations added from a 3D model produced by Jonathan Sutton, Tristan Bradburn and Will Foster. Many of the photographs formed part of the excavation archive and were taken by personnel on the excavation. Additional images have been taken by the author, supplemented by material supplied by Tom Westhead. Photos of the excavations at the Dominican friary in 1978 by John Hadley are reproduced by courtesy of David Algar. Will Foster undertook typesetting of the manuscript and Philippa Bradley supplied invaluable editorial skills, a task completed by Tom Wells who worked tirelessly to accommodate interminable changes to the text without complaint. Tess Millar copy-edited the final draft. Gratitude is also extended to staff at The Salisbury Museum, notably Megan Berrisford, Wessex Museums Collections Manager, for making much of the original archive accessible for study and for supplying permission to photograph and reproduce images of objects from the museum collections.

A belated thankyou is due to all those who contributed to the excavations undertaken between 1984 and 1990, especially Duncan Coe, Peter Cox, John Hawkes, Mike Heaton, Vince Jenkins, Jo Mills and Roland Smith, authors of the individual site summary reports without which this publication would have been more difficult to compile. Rosamund Cleal, Andrew Fitzpatrick and Catherine Underwood should also be acknowledged for individual specialist reports, which remain in the archive. Finally, the work could not have been completed without the efforts of the 'diggers' and supervisors who have toiled in Salisbury to recover and record the primary archive of these excavations. Their labour has not been in vain.

Preface

In 2020, I was approached with a request to consider revisiting a series of archives created by archaeological excavations in Salisbury, with the aim of allowing them to be published.

These reports were outstanding from the early 1980s, when excavations had been commissioned under the Job Creation Scheme operated by the Manpower Services Commission, but no contingencies had been put in place to address the issues of post-excavation analysis and publication of the results. As such, the archive represented a skeleton in the cupboard at Wessex Archaeology, one we were keen to eliminate to coincide with an anniversary celebrating 40 years as an archaeological company. I'm not sure why this opportunity should have been placed on my shoulders; possibly because I was the only surviving employee from those fledgling beginnings at Wessex Archaeology or perhaps because in the intervening period I have led excavations in different parts of the city. These projects have allowed me to experience the archaeology of Salisbury at first hand and to appreciate the associated challenges offered for interpretation. Whatever the reason behind the request, I accepted the opportunity with enthusiasm.

Once the draft stratigraphic reports for each site had been completed, I began to explore the threads that could bring these sites together and relate them to the broader development of the medieval city. In the process, I became aware of the vast array of archaeological work, available in grey literature and published accounts, that had taken place since those early excavations in Salisbury. The resulting map provided a scatter-gun distribution of individual projects; hence Joining the Dots was initiated to use this material and tell the previously untold story of medieval Salisbury and its earlier communities from an archaeological perspective, and so the text expanded to create this volume.

The story has drawn on summaries of the principal finds by my colleagues Lorraine Mepham and Lorrain Higbee, who have studied respectively the collections of pottery and animal bones that add detail to the lives of former residents. I do not claim that this account is definitive or flawless; nevertheless, it contains our best efforts and, hopefully, provides a sufficiently broad narrative that can be visited by those interested in the story of our city. If it motivates others to improve on the approach, that, in itself, will justify the work that has been undertaken, but until that point arrives, this version will have to do!

Phil Harding

Chapter 1
Introduction

by Phil Harding

Salisbury was established as a planned medieval city incorporating a gridded chequer system that survives to this day (**Fig. 1.1**), and which at its height (Chandler 1983) constituted one of the foremost cities of medieval England.

The fabric of the city has been well described by the Royal Commission on the Historical Monuments of England (RCHME 1980) yet sadly, research of the city's archaeological remains has lagged behind that of other cathedral cities, most notably York (Hall *et al.* 1988; Richards *et al.* 1989) and Winchester (Biddle 1967; 1975a; 1975b; Cunliffe 1964; Ottaway 2017; Ottaway and Qualmann 2018). This omission is not unique; long overdue research into the back-log of excavation work undertaken in the 1970s at Exeter was completed only belatedly (Rippon and Holbrook 2021a; 2021b). Investigations into Salisbury's archaeological past were begun by Salisbury Museum Archaeology Rescue Group (SMARG), who valiantly undertook rescue excavations during construction of the Inner Ring Road in the 1960s and early 1970s; however, numerous episodes of redevelopment within the city centre in these decades, including demolition of medieval structures, took place with only limited record, and opportunities were missed.

Interest in the archaeological potential of the city increased after 1980; between 1984 and 1990 The Trust for Wessex Archaeology (TWA) and subsequently Wessex Archaeology (WA) undertook excavations at 11 locations in Salisbury (**Fig. 1.2**), both within the medieval city limits and the outlying suburbs. Some of these projects, prefixed by 'W' and funded by English Heritage, District and County Councils, and the Manpower Services Commission (MSC) with supplementary funds from individual developers, were of limited area, scope and detail but nevertheless contributed data to the archaeological record of the city. Attempts were made to incorporate public outreach, including school visits, which were unconventional measures at the time. Limited post-excavation analysis was undertaken and preliminary stratigraphic matrices were compiled. Summary stratigraphic reports (Wessex Archaeology 1992a), containing details by phase, were prepared, together with a synthesis (Hawkes nd) of the various projects, which included details of artefact assemblages; neither document reached publication. Cave-Penney (2005, 292) noted the omission and considered that 'publishing material from these excavations would be of considerable benefit to the study of Salisbury'. This request has finally been heard; details of the unpublished excavation back-log form the basis of this volume.

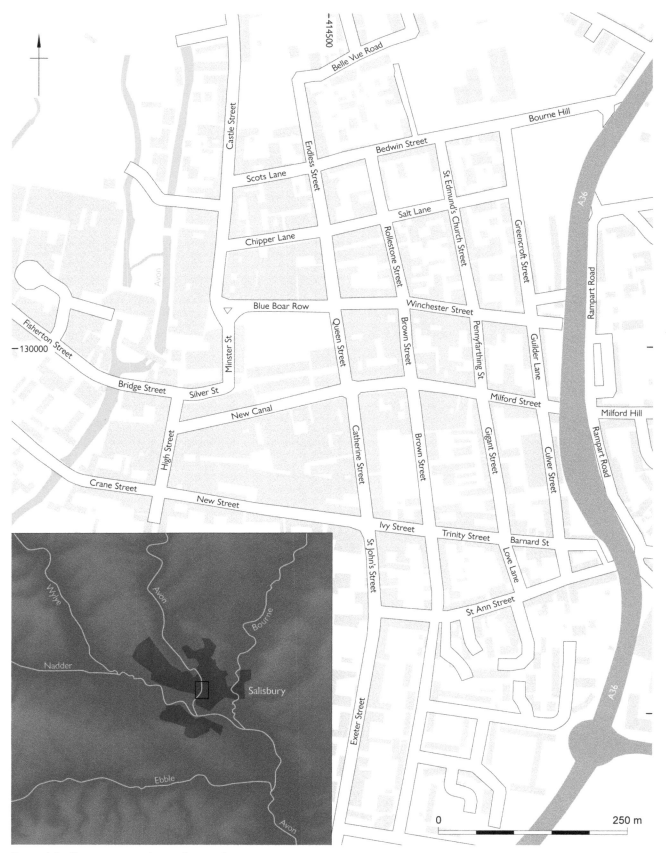

Figure 1.1 Current street plan and natural watercourses

Archaeological work has not stagnated; projects funded by developers under the present planning process have now allowed a more systematic approach to be adopted. This work includes both large- and small-scale fieldwork but, most importantly, contingency for post-excavation reporting. The results, of which Wessex Archaeology alone has undertaken 45 projects at 28 different locations within the boundary of the medieval city, have generated a wealth of literature. This includes unpublished client reports by Wessex Archaeology (2013; 2014a; 2014b) and other archaeological contractors (TVAS 2014a; 2014b; Cotswold Archaeology 2017), which have been prepared to meet the requirements of planning consent, together with final (Barber 2005; Chaffey and Fitzpatrick 2015; Currie and Rushton 2005; Harding 2016) and summary reports (Butterworth 2005a; 2005b; 2005c; Garland *et al.* 2021), which have appeared in the county journal. Other back-log excavation reports, undertaken by SMARG (Algar and Saunders 2014; Saunders and Algar 2015; 2017) have also been published.

The first section of this study covers the previously unpublished detail from excavations spanning the period 1984–90. The section concludes with a review of the combined results of evaluation (Wessex Archaeology 2014a) and excavation (Cotswold Archaeology 2017; Garland *et al.* 2021) at the Salisbury Bus Station. This site forms a significant location at the heart of medieval Salisbury containing data that is essential to the wider discussion of the city. Summary discussions follow, describing excavated pottery assemblages and faunal remains with smaller comments on other artefact groups. The volume concludes by using this impressive level of available data from the city to consider the development of Salisbury from an archaeological perspective.

The back-log excavations

The catalogue of unpublished work from the period 1984–90 comprises 11 sites (**Table 1.1**) which were situated at various locations across the city (**Fig. 1.2**). They were conducted at varying levels of detail, and included, what are now termed, watching briefs, evaluations and area excavations. The standard of recording was also variable between each project; however, in many cases detail can be extrapolated from the better recorded excavations and applied to those that were less fully documented.

Although archaeological work was undertaken across all parts of the city, five sites, W129A–D, W139, W192 and W227 (**Fig. 1.3**), were located within Trinity Chequer. These excavations, when viewed with those at Anchor Brewery (Barber 2005), Milford Street/Gigant Street (Currie and Rushton 2005) and the Elim Chapel (Butterworth 2005b), collectively constitute the largest concentration of work within a single chequer at the heart of the medieval city. This accumulated corpus of work offers sufficient material to compile a synthesis representing the spread of urbanisation within the heart of medieval

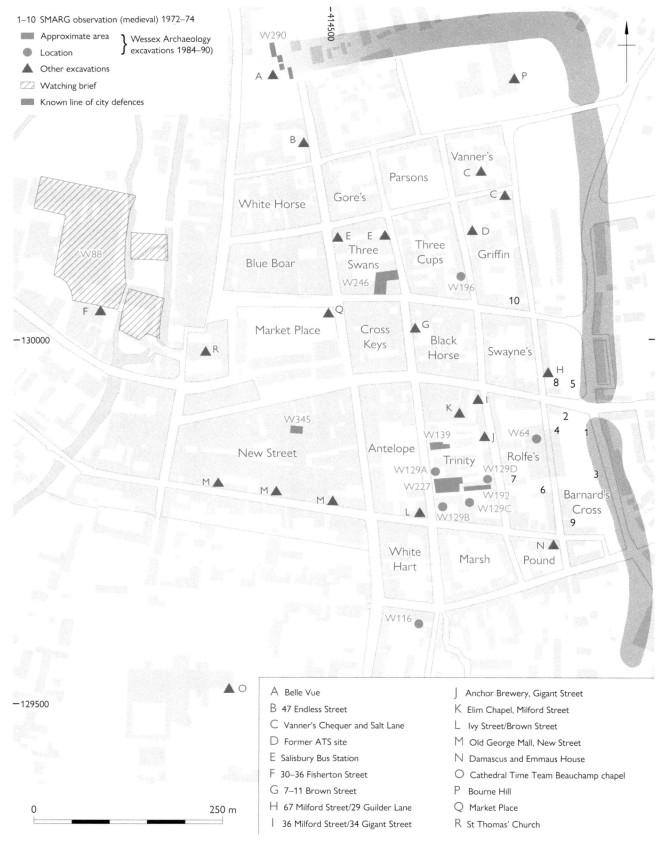

1–10 SMARG observation (medieval) 1972–74

■ Approximate area ⎫ Wessex Archaeology
● Location ⎬ excavations 1984–90)
▲ Other excavations ⎭
▨ Watching brief
■ Known line of city defences

A Belle Vue
B 47 Endless Street
C Vanner's Chequer and Salt Lane
D Former ATS site
E Salisbury Bus Station
F 30–36 Fisherton Street
G 7–11 Brown Street
H 67 Milford Street/29 Guilder Lane
I 36 Milford Street/34 Gigant Street

J Anchor Brewery, Gigant Street
K Elim Chapel, Milford Street
L Ivy Street/Brown Street
M Old George Mall, New Street
N Damascus and Emmaus House
O Cathedral Time Team Beauchamp chapel
P Bourne Hill
Q Market Place
R St Thomas' Church

0 _____ 250 m

Figure 1.2 Principal excavations cited in the text

Salisbury and to contrast it with similar development in other chequers. The detailed summary reports for each of the previously unpublished sites now form part of the site archive (Wessex Archaeology 1992a; Hawkes nd) and, together with the primary records, have been deposited with Salisbury Museum. These reports are now available online at: *www.wessexarch.co.uk/our-work/ salisbury-sites-40-years-wessex-archaeology-excavations*.

This report attempts to address the back-log of work, which remains otherwise unpublished from the period 1984–90, in more detail. It has been compiled using the summary reports, plans and sections. No additional analysis of the archive or artefact assemblages to validate the detail of individual site records has been possible. The content comprises a broad chronological reappraisal of each site and concludes by attempting to assimilate the accumulated data with that of subsequent work within Trinity Chequer
(Barber 2005; Butterworth 2005b; Currie and Rushton 2005) and the broader city of Salisbury.

All excavations were opened using mechanical excavators with hand-dug samples or more detailed areas examined as conditions, survival of deposits or time allowed. Structural remains were encountered in most trenches, although none exposed the street front elevations. These frontages undoubtedly remain beneath the fringes of the modern street line; extant medieval buildings in the city suggest that this has remained largely unaltered.

Site	Code	Author
Culver Street	W64	P W Cox
The Maltings	W88	J W Hawkes
Nos 8–10 St Ann Street	W116	J W Hawkes and M J Heaton
Gigant Street Car Park	W129A-D	R J C Smith
No.39 Brown Street	W139	J M Mills
Gibbs Mew, No. 68 Gigant Street	W192	D Coe
Goddard's Garage	W196	D Coe
Nos 47–51 Brown Street	W227	A V Jenkins
Winchester Street and Rollestone Street	W246	D Coe
Belle Vue House	W290	P W Williams
New Canal	W345	D Coe

Table 1.1 List of sites and summary reports (Wessex Archaeology 1992a)

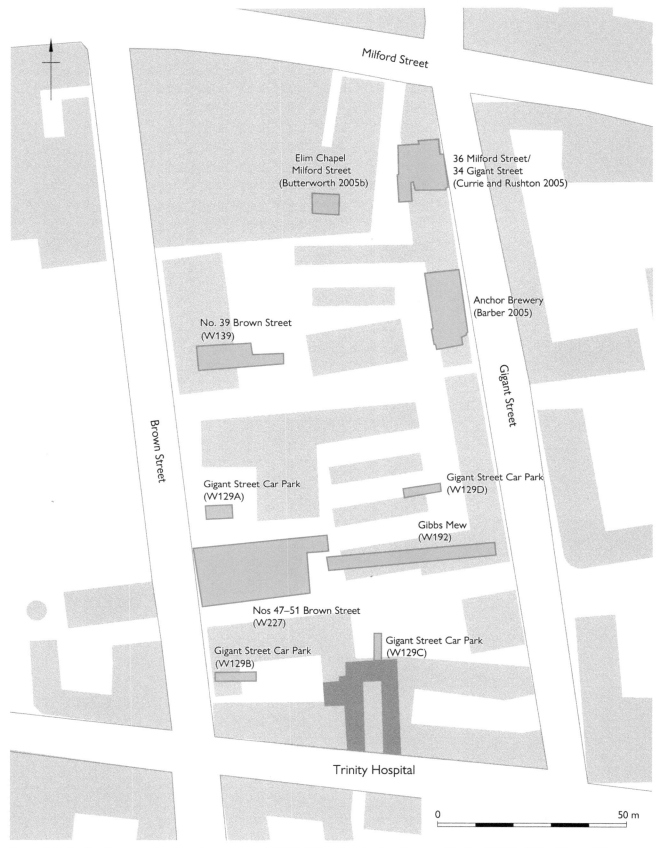

Figure 1.3 Trinity Chequer, showing sites excavated 1984–90 and at Anchor Brewery (Barber 2005), Milford Street/Gigant Street (Currie and Rushton 2005) and the Elim Chapel (Butterworth 2005b)

Chapter 2
The Excavations

by Phil Harding

Introduction

This section forms an essential part of the archaeological narrative, containing stratigraphic detail from which much of the concluding discussion, incorporating material from other published excavation reports, is presented. It describes the results of the previously unpublished excavations, many in Trinity Chequer, in the order in which they were undertaken. The text is drawn from individual summary reports (Wessex Archaeology 1992a) that were written by separate authors, supplemented by data shown in the original site graphics and photographic archives. Some of the detail is incomplete; however, the strategy has made it possible not only to provide a general description for each site but also incorporate features, where appropriate, from adjoining sites and expand and update the site-specific discussion. Opportunity has also been taken to amalgamate and reconsider the results of evaluation and excavation at the site of the former bus station.

Culver Street – W64

The Trust for Wessex Archaeology, now Wessex Archaeology, commenced work in Salisbury in 1984 when two trenches were dug at Culver Street, in Rolfe's Chequer (**Figs 1.1 and 1.2**), following a decision to construct a multi-storey car park on the site. The excavation aimed to evaluate urban development on the eastern fringes of the medieval city and investigate a ditch (Saunders and Algar 2015) that had been observed during construction of the Inner Ring Road, adjacent to the site, in 1972. The ditch was aligned north-east–south-west and measured 5 m wide and 2.3 m deep, with a V-shaped profile. Tip lines suggested that a bank had been located to the south-east. The ditch did not conform to the grid pattern of the urban chequers, suggesting that it was related to pre-conquest settlement around St Martin's Church.

The two trenches were both excavated on the projected line of the ditch. The first trench, which measured 22 m long, revealed a build-up of soil, over 3 m deep, making the base of the trench, which comprised light brown, sandy 'brickearth', inaccessible. This material probably represents a natural fluvial deposit, similar to material that occurs elsewhere in the city along the lower slopes of Milford Hill (Harding 2016). No structures or features were observed, and no explanation offered to account for the excessive depth of soil; however, Saunders and Algar (2015) demonstrated that extensive accumulations extended south from Rampart Road, much of it derived from the medieval rampart on the east edge of the city, and its spread, which may account for some of this build-up.

The second trench (**Pl. 2.1**), which measured 14 m long and 4 m wide, was placed on the Culver Street frontage where deposits were heavily disturbed by modern building foundations. No evidence of the ditch was found; however, traces of two buildings with flint and tile foundations and clay floors remained (**Pl. 2.2**), which were associated with 13th- and 14th-century pottery. Two small pits (**Pl. 2.3**), containing pottery that may predate the 13th century, and a series of disconnected postholes were observed beneath the floors. These traces apparently replicate and extend the evidence for 13th-century activity found in a series of pits that were sealed beneath the rampart (Saunders and Algar 2015).

Plate 2.1 Culver Street (W64): general working, from the south

Plate 2.2 Culver Street (W64): wall 35 and clay floor 43, from the south

Plate 2.3 Culver Street (W64): pits 1 and 3 and wall 7, from the north

The Maltings Development – W88

Preliminary work to redevelop a large block of flood plain land immediately north of Fisherton Street in 1984–5 was subjected to an archaeological watching brief (**Fig. 1.2**). This area was occupied by a Dominican friary from 1280 until its dissolution in 1538. Limited, poorly located, rescue excavations in 1978 (**Pl. 2.4**) had failed to recover any trace of the original ground plan of the friary but did locate four inhumation graves (**Pl. 2.5**), wall foundations and organic remains, including a wooden lathe-turned bowl (**Pl. 4.44**) and leather with 13th–14th-century pottery.

Plate 2.4 The Maltings: rescue excavations in 1978, showing general location

Plate 2.5 The Maltings: excavation of a medieval burial in waterlogged conditions in 1978

The watching brief by Wessex Archaeology, which was conducted under difficult, often waterlogged, conditions, revealed that much of the development area comprised ballast that formed the foundations of railway sidings. This material overlay flood plain alluvium, which was exposed in drainage trenches and boreholes. More substantial sections, approximately 2.3 m deep, which reached the water table, resulted from the removal of an air-raid shelter. This work revealed traces of a timber revetment (**Pl. 2.6**), which formed part of the river management system and was thought to be of 18th-century date.

Plate 2.6 The Maltings (W88): showing waterlogged conditions and traces of timber revetment of the 18th-century river management system

Traces of a mortar floor, which apparently overlay a layer of bricks, were found at the south end of the development, approximately 15 m from the speculated location of the 1978 excavations. The floor was not examined in detail but was attributed to malthouses recorded on the 1881 Ordnance Survey map. No evidence of the friary was found. The watching brief concluded that although additional archaeological deposits may be preserved below any proposed foundation levels, the flood plain area on the west side of the river probably remained largely undeveloped throughout the early settlement of Salisbury, a conclusion endorsed by Wright (2020).

Renewed interest in the area resulted in six test pits being monitored towards the south end of the Maltings precinct in 2019 (Clarke and Baker 2020, 328; Wessex Archaeology 2019a) when the site became available for redevelopment. These observations recovered traces of four additional inhumation graves, aligned west–east, in three separate test pits towards the north end of the development site. Layers of 20th-century make-up rubble overlay the former land surface, creating a situation where the burials were located approximately 2.5 m below the present ground surface. The burials provide additional examples to those found in 1978, which in retrospect were undoubtedly found at the base of a foundation pit for a lift shaft installed during that redevelopment. The collective results have established more precisely the location, but not full extent, of the friary graveyard, although no traces of the friary buildings were discovered, suggesting that the religious complex was located further to the north. The progress of development slowed following the Dissolution in 1538, before the construction of the malthouses in the 19th century. The test pits produced a small collection of clay pipes from the upper fills, but no medieval pottery or ceramic building material (CBM), the latter a ubiquitous feature on most sites in Salisbury. These collective, limited, results support the idea that the friary was established within an open precinct on previously unused flood plain. The final test pit was located on the Fisherton Street frontage and produced no structural evidence before the 18th century.

Nos 8–10 St Ann Street – W116

Two small trenches (**Pls 2.7 and 2.8**) measuring 10 x 4 m and 5 x 3 m respectively were excavated to examine an area that extended south from the street frontage. The results were hampered by the effects of demolition, but a number of small postholes, two areas of tiled flooring and spreads of chalk and ash were noted at the north end of the site in Trench 1, where preservation of deposits was better. The postholes were not all clearly contemporary, and the sequence could not be dated closely. No walls or foundations were noted; nevertheless, the summary report concluded that the deposits probably represented remains of a former building, the function of which could not be established. A small assemblage of pottery was found which contained coarsewares (**eg, Fig. 3.1, 5**), which could date from the 13th century or possibly the early part of the 14th century.

The results of this small excavation provided tantalising evidence of additional trends near the urban margins. The site lies immediately west of the junction of St Ann Street and the access to the Franciscan friary where the 14th-century building, which occupies the 'angle tenement', is extant. The excavated remains at Nos 8–10 St Ann Street may relate to adjoining outbuildings. It is possible that other parts of St Ann Street, which lay in the shadow of the friary precinct, remained undeveloped for residential use, as indicated on John Speed's map of 1611, until the later post-medieval period.

Plate 2.7 Nos 8–10 St Ann Street (W116): general view of Trenches 1 and 2 from the north

Plate 2.8 Nos 8–10 St Ann Street (W116): Trench 2 from the south

Gigant Street Car Park – W129

Gigant Street Car Park (subsequently Brown Street Car Park) covered an area of approximately 2300 m² between Brown Street and Gigant Street. Four separate locations (A–D) (**Fig. 1.2**), were examined, providing a combined area of 68 m² (3% of the total site). The project was designed to evaluate archaeological deposits along street frontage locations and central 'backlands' of the chequer.

Trench W129A was located on the frontage of No. 43 Brown Street (**Fig. 1.2**), approximately 5 m north of the subsequent and more extensive excavations at W227, Nos 47–51 Brown Street (**Figs 2.3–2.5, below**). The deposits at No. 43 Brown Street were extensively disturbed, which reduced the area available for excavation to 6 m² and made it impossible to recover an accurate stratigraphic or chronological record of structures and associated floors. The suggested chronological sequence shown in **Figs 2.3–2.5** is therefore extremely speculative but adopts that given in the summary report, which concluded that construction commenced in the 16th century.

The earliest deposits comprised natural gravel at 44.48 m OD, which overlay a series of clays and gravelly silts. Several layers contained charcoal with 14th–15th-century pottery. These layers included possible floor levels and suggest activity contemporary with development elsewhere in the chequer and earlier than that proposed by the summary report. A shallow U-profiled gully (1566) (**Fig. 2.3**), 0.35 m deep and possibly representing a timber beam slot, ran north–south across the trench. It followed a line that could be projected along the rear elevations of structures at Nos 47–51 Brown Street, where well-preserved foundations dated from the 13th to the 16th century. These observations reinforce the argument that the tenement at No. 43 Brown Street was occupied at an earlier date than that proposed in the summary report and that phasing should be placed as in **Figs 2.3–2.5**.

The gully was subsequently formalised by a foundation (1560) of mortared chalk blocks and tile that followed the line of the gully (**Fig. 2.4; Pl. 2.9**). The foundation was not placed within a construction trench and was therefore difficult to date but undoubtedly confirms the presence of a more substantial building in the tenement. Several discontinuous spreads of sand or silt-clay were associated with foundation 1560, which included two compacted floors, one of sand and one of chalk, which, with deposits outside the building, contained pottery of 16th-century or later date. These layers may themselves be associated with foundation 1560 or with episodes of later refurbishment.

The wall foundation was subsequently rebuilt (**Fig. 2.5**) of mortared flint with occasional limestone blocks (1524). Two sandstone ashlars at the rear of the building may have defined a doorway. A slight tile and flint wall (1519), aligned east–west and dated by pottery from floor levels and adjacent layers to the 17th–18th century, was interpreted as an internal division. An unexcavated chalk-lined well (1568) to the rear of the building (**Fig. 2.5**) was also thought to be contemporary. These deposits were capped by an 18th–19th-century brick building with an alley to the north.

Trench W129B (**Figs 1.2 and 2.1; Pl. 2.10**) was aligned on an east–west axis at No. 65 Brown Street. It initially measured 10 × 2 m, (**Fig. 2.1C and D**) but was subsequently shortened at the west end to cover an area 8 × 2 m (**Fig. 2.1A and B**). The deposits were generally well preserved and covered a basal dark grey-brown clay-silt buried soil. This deposit was exposed in a sondage, 0.5 m², which was cut through a series of overlying floor levels, which were associated with a flint and mortar wall foundation (598). This foundation was aligned north–south, parallel to the street frontage (**Fig. 2.1A**), following the projected wall line (1560/1524) identified in Trench W129A. Thirteenth-century pottery recovered from the sondage was thought more likely to have derived from the floor levels than from the buried soil.

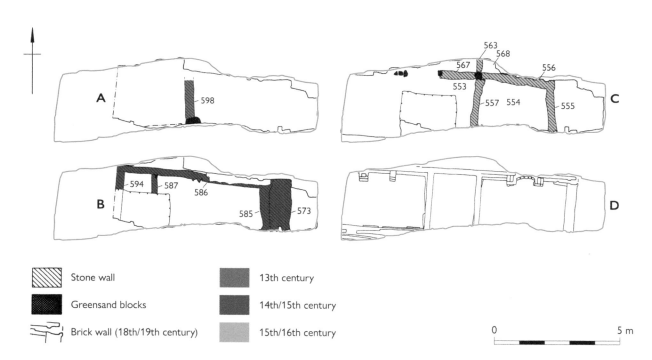

Figure 2.1 *Gigant Street Car Park/No. 65 Brown Street (W129B): phase plan showing A) 13th century, B) 14th–15th century, C) 15th–16th century, D) 18th century*

Plate 2.9 Gigant Street Car Park (W129A): well 1568 and foundation 1560/1524 with floor levels beyond, from the east

Plate 2.10 Gigant Street Car Park (W129B): site location and general working, from the east

Left: Plate 2.11 Gigant Street Car Park (W129B): 14th-/15th-century phase from the east, with wall lines 573/585 (foreground), 586 (right) and 587 and 594 (beyond)

Right: Plate 2.12 Gigant Street Car Park (W129B): excavation showing 15th-/16th-century phase from the east

The building was replaced by wall foundations (**Fig. 2.1B; Pl. 2.11**) of flint and mortar (585; apparently quickly replaced by 573), which formed the eastern wall, possibly a service range, to an extended structure with an internal partition or tenement sub-division (586). The phase included two sub-divisions defined by internal walls (594) and its replacement (587). Floor levels contained pottery of 14th–15th-century date.

The building was subsequently reconstructed on essentially the same footprint (**Fig. 2.1C; Pl. 2.12**) but incorporated Greensand blocks, which probably defined bays of a timber-framed building. Alterations were made to internal dividing walls (563/557). A heavily worn silver penny of Richard II (1377–99) from the matrix of wall 567 and associated pottery suggested a 15th–16th-century date.

This sequence of deposits was sealed by a series of poorly-dated deposits that preceded an 18th-/19th-century brick structure (**Fig. 2.1D; Pl. 2.13**), which retained the imprint of the earlier medieval buildings.

Plate 2.13 Gigant Street Car Park (W129B): foundations of 18th-/19th-century brick building, from the south-east

Trench W129C was positioned (**Fig. 1.2; Pl. 2.14**) in an area of derelict land near the northern edge of the Trinity Hospital precinct, which was founded in 1379. Extensive disturbance restricted the available area to a plot 1.5 m², in which a wall foundation (016; **Pl. 2.15**), aligned east–west and constructed of flint and mortar, was exposed. The date of construction could not be confirmed; however, late 13th–14th-century pottery was recovered from soil beneath the wall with 16th-century material associated with its demolition, supporting the possible link with Trinity Hospital or its associated buildings.

Plate 2.14 Gigant Street Car Park (W129C): general working shot, from the north-east

Trench W129D was dug using a mechanical excavator on the street frontage of Gigant Street (**Fig. 1.2**), where natural gravel was recorded at 44 m OD. Archaeological deposits were seriously disrupted by a concrete plinth, which restricted the value and extent of any investigations. Despite these limitations a series of compacted chalk floors and a wall foundation of mortared flints, aligned east–west, were recorded (**Pl. 2.16**). A sherd of probable 13th-century pottery was recovered from deposits underlying the floors, which supplemented material of similar date elsewhere along Gigant Street.

Plate 2.15 Gigant Street Car Park (W129C): wall 016, from the north

Plate 2.16 Gigant Street Car Park (W129D): concrete plinth (right) with undisturbed chalk floors exposed in section, from the south

No. 39 Brown Street – W139

The absence of modern development and the fact that, following demolition, the site had been used as part of Gigant Street Car Park, suggested that a well-preserved archaeological sequence predating the post-medieval period might be present on the site. The site also represented, together with No. 49 Brown Street, a location where late medieval building remains had been preserved. The RCHME (1980) survey noted that until 1965 – when the property at No. 39 Brown Street, together with No. 37, was demolished – these buildings comprised 18th-century ranges on the street frontage, but that No. 39 retained a 16th-century range to the rear. An initial trench (**Fig. 2.2A–C; Pl. 2.17**) measuring 15 m long and 7 m wide was located over the street frontage of No. 39 Brown Street (**Fig. 1.2**). The south-east corner of the trench was subsequently extended 5 x 3 m to the east to cover approximately 5% of the proposed development area.

Four sherds of 13th-century pottery and a fragment of glazed floor tile were collected from the basal buried soil, although the summary report conceded that this material may have been derived from overlying deposits. Primary development (**Fig. 2.2A**) was marked by a flint, tile and mortar wall foundation (127/267) of a timber-framed structure, which defined the northern boundary of the medieval tenement. Variations in the coursing and alignment between 127 and 267 suggested that more than one phase of construction or repair was represented. All other tenement boundaries lay beyond the limits of the excavation or had been removed by subsequent redevelopment.

Plate 2.17 No. 39 Brown Street (W139): general site working shot

Plate 2.18 No. 39 Brown Street (W139): excavation, view from west, showing 15th-/17th- century building, wall foundation 8 (left) with flint and tile foundations 30, 38 and 40 (right).

Two internal sub-phases were identified. The first (**Fig. 2.2A**) was defined by a flint and mortar wall foundation (199/200) capped by a course of herringbone tiles; associated build-up layers and a chalk floor contained later 13th- or 14th-century pottery. A series of spreads and discontinuous floor layers overlay wall foundation 199/200. These layers indicated not only that the building had been refurbished but also suggested that the wall did not form the rear elevation of the building, making it apparently wider than most buildings known at the time in the street. One of the earliest floors within this phase produced a silver penny of Edward I (1272–1307) or Edward II (1307–1327), which suggested deposition within the first half of the 14th century, a conclusion that was complemented by pottery of 14th- or, at the latest, 15th-century date. Twenty stakeholes, containing quantities of fish, and animal, bone fragments were excavated in the south-eastern part of the building. This relative paucity of information made it impossible to reconstruct the medieval building, although it seems probable that it conformed to the design seen elsewhere in the chequer.

Figure 2.2 No. 39 Brown Street (W139): phase plan showing A) 13th–14th century, B) 15th–17th century, C) 16th–18th century

Four individual phases/sub-phases were identified within the periods spanning the 15th–17th century (**Fig. 2.2B; Pl. 2.18**); however, deposits relating to the final phases had been disturbed by demolition in 1965, which may have blurred interpretation of the late medieval and post-medieval building phases. Irrespective of these complications the tenements undoubtedly underwent major redevelopment within this period. This included the addition of a 16th-century range to the rear of No. 39 Brown Street, which was documented in the survey undertaken by the RCHME (1980, 112). The archaeological evidence for the initial phases, possibly in the 15th century, was marked by the insertion of a new northern wall foundation (8/34), immediately north of 127/267, of which wall 34, at the eastern end, survived only as an insubstantial clay and tile foundation. Walls 27, 56, 57 and 60 were also added. This phase of construction was marked by the inclusion of Greensand blocks, which were inserted at strategic points within the foundation and may have supported uprights of a timber sub-frame. No doorways were identified, although two Greensand blocks, approximately 1 m apart in wall 56, may mark an opening. Small, shallow scoops containing fish, and animal, bone fragments were again noted within the floor/build-up levels. Pottery from foundation trenches for walls 56/57 and 27 indicated a 15th–16th-century construction date.

Pottery of 16th- or early 17th-century date was also related to wall 113/274, which formed an internal division parallel with wall 27 as well as with a peg tile hearth (128/67) (**Pl. 2.19**). Further sub-division of the front room, including walls 30, 38, 40 and 94, which may represent an internal passage, was accompanied by replacement or refurbishment of the hearth (128/67). This relatively complex sequence, within potentially ill-defined stratigraphy, suggests multiple changes over a relatively short space of time; events which may have been broadly contemporary with the construction of the 16th-century range at the rear of the property. The phase was also linked to a group of 20 stakeholes, which were cut through an ashy, organic spread, once more containing abundant quantities of fish bones with late 16th- or early 17th-century pottery. The recurring presence of quantities of fish bones from deposits apparently spanning the late medieval to post-medieval periods was tentatively ascribed to possible fish smoking; however, these later phases, which were not supported by distinct pottery assemblages, were those most affected by demolition. It is possible that this may have overcomplicated interpretation of the stratigraphy.

Plate 2.19 No. 39 Brown Street (W139): section through hearth 67, from the west

The later medieval and post-medieval development and appearance of the building at No. 39 Brown Street is open to variable interpretation, an issue complicated by the fact that the outer walls of the building were located beyond the limits of the excavation. The summary report projected wall 60 to wall 34, thereby creating a rectangular structure measuring 10 x 6 m. However, it is possible that wall foundation 34, which was constructed of clay and tiles, originally served as no more than an exterior tenement boundary, although the survey by the RCHME indicates that this foundation was ultimately incorporated into the building. Walls 27 and 60 may then have provided an embryonic service range at the rear of the medieval building, with a central ridge line defined by wall foundation remnants 113/274. This interpretation maintains the front room, defined by wall 56/57, within a medieval footprint 5.5 m wide, which matches other earlier medieval structures along Brown Street, but extends the rear of the property to a point 10 m from the street frontage, which was extended in the 16th century. The peg tile hearth (128/67) was apparently located centrally beneath both the projected ridge line of the Brown Street frontage and the early service range. Details of any associated superstructure remain unclear. It is possible that it was located in the centre of a larger open ground-floor hall that was open to the roof and was furnished with a louvre in the ridge. However, the excavated evidence indicates that the hearth was ultimately designed to heat a room to the south and that an unnumbered wall foundation, immediately north of the hearth, may have supported a plaster hood and chimney located at the intersection of ridge lines of the service range and the street frontage. This reconstructed ground plan of No. 39 Brown Street contains many comparable details that are replicated at No. 83 Castle Street (RCHME 1980, 152), where an early 16th-century jettied building with two storeys and an attic may once have formed part of the George and Dragon Inn. The 16th-century extension at No. 39 Brown Street provided two additional rooms on the ground floor, which were mirrored by additional accommodation above. The rectangular range was accessed by a doorway immediately north of the central hearth and represents a typical 16th–17th building design. It created a structure of sufficient size that it may have represented a separate modest dwelling, unattached to the street frontage building, providing additional residential use of the tenement in the 'backlands' (Bob Davis pers. comm.).

The street frontages of tenements Nos 37 and 39 Brown Street were rebuilt using bricks in the mid-18th century (RCHME 1980, 112). The two properties were divided by a through-passage, which formed part of No. 37 Brown Street, while No. 39 (**Fig. 2.2C**) retained the 16th-century range at the rear.

Gibbs Mew, No. 68 Gigant Street – W192

This small trench, for which no dimensions or final plan were provided, was also located within the limits of the Gigant Street Car Park (**Fig. 1.2**); the summary report noted this level of 'very poor recording' (Wessex Archaeology 1992a, 15). Four unsubstantiated phases were identified that largely replicated the sequence noted elsewhere in Gigant Street.

A buried soil produced small quantities of medieval pottery, including a curfew rim (**Fig. 3.2, 17**). This deposit was overlain by two clay layers, which may represent make-up deposits, and a row of stakeholes, which were aligned north–south, parallel with Gigant Street. Additional medieval pottery was collected. The phase also included a mortared flint wall foundation, internal divisions and floors. An additional flint foundation extended to the west together with a series of make-up/demolition layers. These components undoubtedly contained multiple phases of medieval and post-medieval activity that were condensed into a single phase post-dating the stakeholes.

The structure was demolished and a levelling layer overlain by a brick structure, which comprised walls, a floor and circular feature was constructed. A brick outbuilding, represented by walls, with a passage, was located in the 'backlands'. A final phase of activity contained demolition rubble, rubbish pits and service trenches.

Goddard's Garage – W196

This small excavation on St Edmund's Church Street frontage of Three Cups Chequer (**Fig. 1.2**) contained an accumulation of dark silty clay garden soil, which overlay natural clay. No building remains, or demolition rubble were noted, from which the summary report concluded that this area had remained undeveloped from the foundation of Salisbury. The site was shown as undeveloped land on the map of Salisbury compiled by William Naish in his survey of 1716.

Nos 47–51 Brown Street – W227

Excavations on this site, which was located approximately 5 m south of No. 43 Brown Street (W129A) in Gigant Street Car Park (**Fig. 1.2**), comprises the most detailed archive in this corpus of unpublished work. It included limited documentary research, which provided an unbroken list of occupiers at No. 49 Brown Street from 1614. This catalogue documented a diverse range of practical occupations, including carpenters, wire drawers, bakers and skinners – a sequence broken by only one resident who was described as a gentleman. These results supplemented the archaeological record with personal detail and endorsed Chandler's (2015) observations regarding the potentially large, untapped body of written material that remains available for future study within the city.

The earliest reference to these tenements may be that contained in a deed of 1270–80 (Wordsworth 1902). This granted a tenement belonging to John de Wich (chaplain of St Martins and John, son of William Baker (vicar)), to St Nicholas's Hospital. The description referenced the property in Brown Street between the tenement of William of Twynham and that of Sebode the Cutler. It may have been one of seven properties that the hospital received in gift towards the end of the 13th century and from which it derived rent (Pugh and Crittall 1956b). Subsequent documents locate tenements by owners, occupiers, neighbours and occupations, making it possible to speculate on the status and variability of the population within the chequer. By 1628 the name of John Leminge, a skinner in Brown Street, features in land transfer documents, while a later lease held by Thomas Spencer, a felt maker, expired in 1675. The results of the excavation at Nos 49–51 Brown Street have added to the list of former occupants. Quantities of clay pipe makers' production debris associated with Joel Sanger, who was active in the first half of the 18th century, were recovered from demolition rubble and unstratified topsoil, locating his workshop in all probability at No. 49 or No. 51 Brown Street. More recent deeds list street numbers, making identification of individual properties more accurate. A 1913 painting illustrates No. 47 Brown Street as a brick building of 18th–19th-century construction, separated from No. 49 Brown Street by a passage, which may have formed part of No. 49 Brown Street. The RCHME (1980, 112) described the latter as a 'cottage', demolished in 1972, comprising a two-storey building of 16th-century construction. As such it represented the last surviving late medieval street frontage range on Brown Street. Additional detail of the 'backlands' is provided by a 1949 sketch plan that recorded details of a 19th-century service wing, outhouses and coal bunkers (Wessex Archaeology 1992a). No. 51 Brown Street was similarly of brick construction.

The excavated area (**Figs 2.3–2.5 Pls 2.20–2.22**) measured 32 m long and 13.5 m wide with an extension of 5 x 4 m at the east end of No. 47 to locate the Town Ditch and thereby sample the entire length of the tenement. Due to time constraints the excavations concentrated on recovering detailed sections through deposits, especially those with traces of buildings on the street frontage.

Plate 2.20 Brown Street (W227): general view of work at the street frontage from the south-east

Plate 2.21 Brown Street (W227): general view of work at the street frontage from the south

Plate 2.22 Brown Street (W227): general view of site from the east. No. 51 is dominated by 18th/19th-century brick foundations

The 'backlands' of each tenement (**Pls 2.23 and 2.24**) were cleaned and subsequently examined in individual trenches 1 m wide. This methodology recovered a relatively comprehensive record of development at No. 51 Brown Street but was less extensive at No. 49 Brown Street, leaving parts of the record incomplete. This is regrettable given that the superstructure and ground plan of No. 49 remained largely unaltered from the late medieval period until the building was demolished in 1972. Archaeological deposits were extensively truncated at No. 47 Brown Street, which restricted their value and any opportunity to establish clear stratigraphic relationships to deposits in the adjoining property.

Plate 2.23 Brown Street (W227): views of site looking across the 'backlands', showing (top) site under excavation and (bottom) after subsequent development, from the south-west

Plate 2.24 Brown Street (W227): views of site looking across the 'backlands', showing (top) site under excavation and (bottom) after subsequent development, from the north-east

Plate 2.25 Brown Street (W227): presentations of the site provided outreach to local primary school classes

This excavation also included embryonic use of public outreach (**Pl. 2.25**), including school visits, to communicate the project to a wider audience.

Excavations of the Town Ditch at No. 47 Brown Street (**Pl. 2.26**) were limited but identified at least two undated phases of construction or repair. The earliest phase (**Fig. 2.3**) was present on the western side of the channel, where a wall of undressed chalk blocks (830), 0.55 m thick and set in a clay matrix, possibly to aid water retention, was recorded. No foundation trench was noted, and no comparable structure was noted on the eastern side. The culvert was replaced subsequently by two parallel walls, 1.4 m apart and approximately 0.5 m thick, the western side founded directly on the earlier chalk structure. The later walls were both constructed of alternate bands of dressed Greensand blocks and courses of brick, placing this phase in the post-medieval period. Sadly, the excavation was terminated at a depth of approximately 0.70 m.

In consequence, the lower parts of the channel were not exposed nor were primary sediments observed and sampled. The upper parts comprised bands of rubble and silt, which probably related to the final infilling of the system in the 19th century.

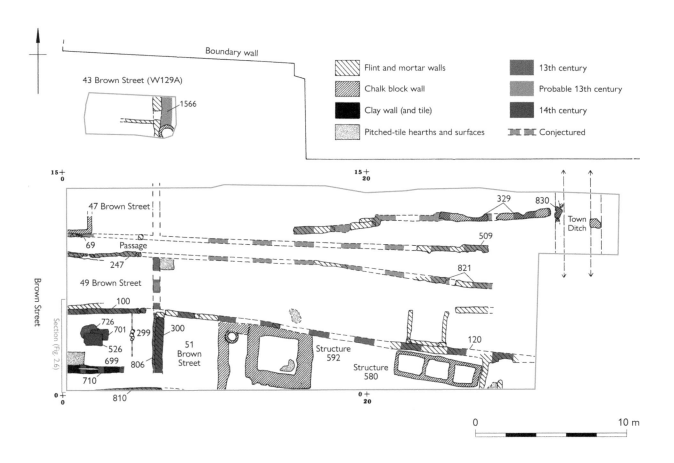

Figure 2.3 Nos 43 (W129A) and 47–51 Brown Street (W227): showing 13th–14th-century construction phases

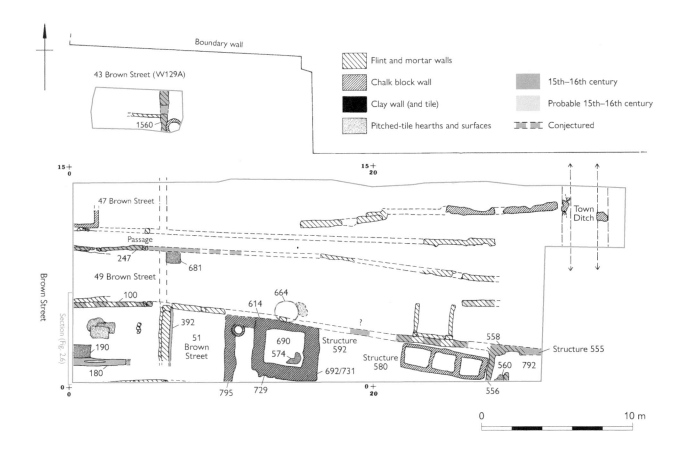

Boundary wall

43 Brown Street (W129A)

1560

Flint and mortar walls

Chalk block wall

Clay wall (and tile)

Pitched-tile hearths and surfaces

15th–16th century

Probable 15th–16th century

Conjectured

15+
0

15+
20

47 Brown Street

Passage

247

681

49 Brown Street

100

Brown Street

Section (Fig. 2.6)

392

190

180

51
Brown
Street

614

664

690
574

Structure
592

692/731

Structure
580

?

558

Structure 555

560   792

Town
Ditch

0+
0

795

729

0+
20

556

0   10 m

Figure 2.4 Nos 43 (W129A) and 47–51 Brown Street (W227): showing 15th–16th-century construction phases

Plate 2.26 No. 47 Brown Street (W227): Town Ditch from the west

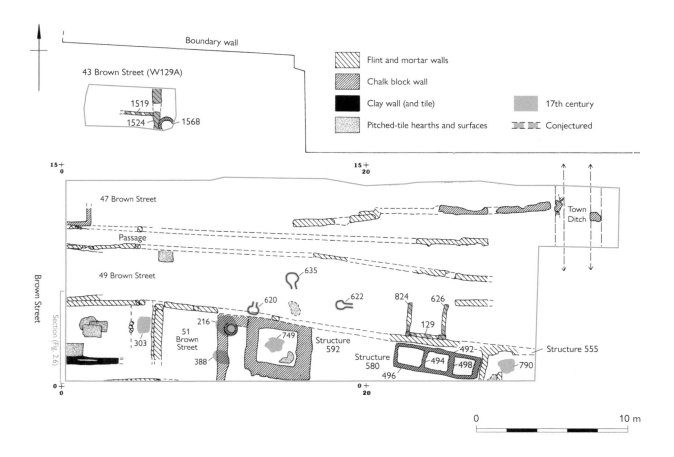

Figure 2.5 Nos 43 (W129A) and 47–51 Brown Street (W227): showing 17th-century features

Construction of the Town Ditch system was also linked to the preliminary setting out of the tenement boundaries. Wall lines (120, 329, 509 and 821) undoubtedly bear witness to the 13th-century survey but probably physically represent later reconstructions of the original line or later sub-divisions of the original tenements.

Development within tenements covered by Nos 47–51 Brown Street was principally referenced to results at No. 51 Brown Street, where a number of distinct phases and sub-phases were identified on the street frontage. The excavation failed to connect the sequence stratigraphically with the 'backlands', where deposits had been disturbed by post-medieval phases of activity.

The initial development at No. 51 Brown Street was represented by a scatter of nine postholes and stakeholes sealed beneath recognisable floors. Individual features varied in depth from 0.1 to 0.2 m but formed no recognisable pattern. The larger holes were filled with material that had slumped in from upper layers, while the smaller ones were present as hollow post voids. A roughly triangular patch of crushed chalk, 5 x 2 m, lay immediately to the south of these holes. This deposit could not be traced into No. 49 Brown Street, where similar relatively ephemeral features may have been removed by subsequent development. Comparable spreads of post and stakeholes also featured in the early development at Culver Street (W64) and Salt Lane (Harding 2016).

Small amounts of pottery suggest that construction work probably occurred at No. 51 Brown Street in the 13th–14th century, thereby substantiating the documentary records and supplementing initial phases of development elsewhere in the city and the street. The earliest structural evidence (**Fig. 2.3**) was defined by a mortared flint wall foundation (806), which measured 0.5 m wide and 0.3 m deep, and formed the rear elevation of the building. A foundation of similar construction (810) was exposed in the south edge of the trench and was separated from foundation 806 by a gap 1 m across. This space may have marked the position of a doorway giving access to a passage through the property, defined by an internal partition and perpetuated by the line of feature 710, which ran parallel to foundation 810. The west elevation probably lay beneath the present Brown Street pavement line, with the north elevation shared with No. 49 Brown Street. This arrangement provided a floor area measuring approximately 5 m north–south by 6 m deep and mirrors exactly the design, including a through-passage, and size of early buildings at the Anchor Brewery on Gigant Street (Barber 2005).

Hearths were placed in the centre of the room and included a shallow, oval fire pit, 0.8 m long, which was overlain by a hearth (726), 0.8 m wide and approximately 1.5 m long, constructed of mortared peg tiles; this was apparently enlarged and repaired (744; **Fig. 2.6**) over time. Patches of superimposed clay flooring (745; **Fig. 2.6**) abutted wall 806 and were sealed by a relatively thick layer containing dark brown/black charcoal-rich occupational debris (721; **Fig. 2.6**), from which a 13th-/14th-century pottery lamp was recovered (**Fig. 3.3, 29**). These patches of flooring suggested that occupants preferred to repair existing floors rather than install new surfaces.

The earliest structure at the adjoining tenement, No. 49 Brown Street (**Fig. 2.3**), was less securely dated but was apparently of a similar design, construction and floor area and probably contemporary. It comprised traces of a north wall foundation (69), 0.3 m thick, with a parallel wall (247) approximately 1.3 m to the south. This foundation was also of flint and mortar interspersed with Greensand blocks and defined a passageway, which became fossilised throughout the life of the building and apparently repeated the design of No. 51 Brown Street. The east wall line was absent, but was probably located along the line that, when projected through wall 806 of No. 51 Brown Street, aligns with gully 1566 and wall foundation 1560 of No. 43 Brown Street (W129A). The southern tenement boundary, which it shared with No. 51 Brown Street, was also absent.

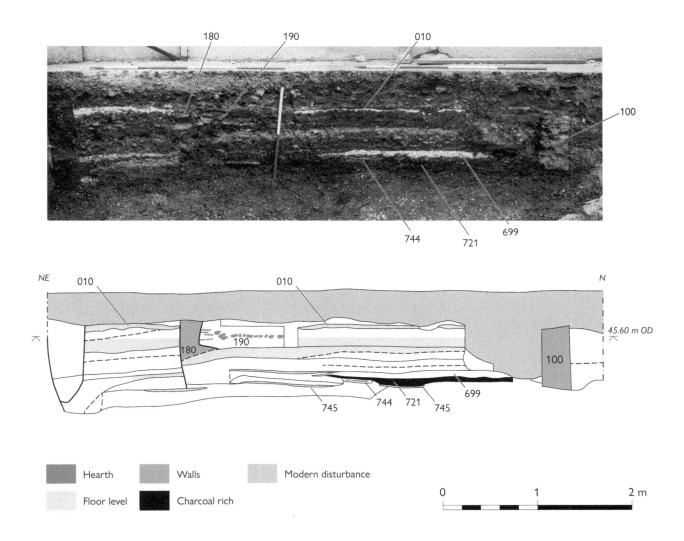

Figure 2.6 No. 51 Brown Street (W227): section showing superimposed floors and hearth features in photograph and drawing

This may indicate that Nos 51 and 49 Brown Street originally formed part of a single property which was later subdivided or that the boundary was probably represented in a 16th-century rebuilt form by foundation 100. No hearths were recorded although two crushed chalk floors survived.

No dated contemporary deposits survived at No. 47 Brown Street, although it was considered likely that structures were also erected at this tenement.

Subsequent rebuilding and renovations on the established footprint at No. 51 Brown Street were undertaken at some point in the 13th or more probably 14th century (**Fig. 2.3**). The east wall (300) was rebuilt and the south wall (810) was extensively refurbished using flint construction incorporating Greensand slabs, thereby retaining the existing passage. An internal floor was added, comprising a chalk surface (699) (**Figs 2.3 and 2.6**), which covered most of the area to the west, with sandy mortar (299) to the east. These components were separated by a row of three sandstone blocks, which may replicate internal divisions similar to those recorded (Barber 2005) in buildings dated 1350–1450 in Gigant Street. The central hearth was replaced, initially by a structure (701) that included two layers of tile, forming a fireback (reredos) (Wood 1965, 272) along the southern edge, and subsequently by hearth 526 (**Pls 2.27 and 2.28**), which was of identical size and construction. These hearths were of identical structure to hearths 128/67 at No. 39 Brown Street (W139), which were considered to be of 16th–17th-century date. The floor, which continued to respect the passage as defined by partition wall 710, was renewed using clay with tile fragments and bovine metapodials (617) (**Pl. 2.27**).

Plate 2.27 No. 51 Brown Street (W227): tile and bone floor layer 617 and hearth 526, from the west

Plate 2.28 No. 51 Brown Street (W227): hearth 526 exposed beyond temporary section, with surrounding floors, from the north

No comparable phases dating to the period 1350–1450 were identified at Nos 49 or 47 Brown Street, although it is likely that undocumented internal modifications were made.

Major alterations were apparently undertaken at both No. 51 Brown Street and No. 49 Brown Street during the 15th–16th century (**Fig. 2.4**). This may have included the reconstruction of the east elevation of No. 51 Brown Street as wall 392. The most significant archaeological evidence involved repositioning the hearth against a wall, a development which implies the appearance of chimneys on the skyline and the installation of upper storeys, if these were not already in place. The peg tile hearth (190; **Figs 2.4 and 2.6; Pls 2.29 and 2.30**), which measured approximately 1.4 m long and 0.90 m wide at No. 51 Brown Street, was relocated towards the front of the house. This revised location probably filled the internal angle formed by the front wall of the building and the passage partition (180), which was rebuilt using mortared flints to form the chimney stack. A chalk floor (010; **Fig. 2.6**) provided the final earthen floor before timber floors were laid.

Number 49 Brown Street was probably redeveloped extensively in tandem with No. 51 Brown Street. These modifications included the reconstruction of the shared tenement boundary wall, which was rebuilt as wall foundation 100. This wall, which was 0.30 m thick, was also constructed of mortared flint nodules interspersed with Greensand blocks. A clay floor was also added. Most notably a hearth (681) was inserted against wall 247. This hearth measured 2 m long and 0.8 m wide and was constructed of hand-made bricks, indicating that this occurred no earlier than the 17th century and was probably a later insertion. The summary report notes that the east end of the hearth was composed of flint nodules. Two Georgian coins, recovered from ash within the hearth, were cited to suggest prolonged use. The hearth was located in what the summary report listed as a 'back-room', the extent of which was not established in the excavation. The location of the hearth corresponds with examples noted on the street frontage of No. 51 Brown Street and at the Anchor Brewery in Gigant Street (Barber 2005), where hearths similarly occupied a corner angle. Hearths have also been recorded within service ranges on Salt Lane (Harding 2016) in the period after 1450. The trend observed in Salisbury involving the relocation of hearths to wall lines and the implied construction of chimneys mirrors similar activity across much of Britain after the 15th–16th century (Wood 1965, 196). Traces of a tiled floor, which was marked by circular imprints created by wooden barrels, added to the detail of the back-room at No. 49 Brown Street.

Plate 2.29 No. 51 Brown Street (W227): hearth 190 from the west

Plate 2.30 No. 51 Brown Street (W227): hearth 190, fill 186 removed, from the east

This phase of redevelopment probably marked the final major construction episode to the street frontage at No. 49 Brown Street as indicated by the RCHME (1980, 112). A range to the rear was built in the 19th century although the footprint of this extension or building was not included in the summary report.

Structures at the rear of No. 51 Brown Street were principally dated by relative chronology but could not otherwise be related to buildings on the street frontage. Despite these limitations the excavations (**Figs 2.3–2.5**) demonstrated that ranges, which may have been connected to the street frontage, with outhouses and wells, were present immediately behind the principal residential quarters, possibly extending to the Town Ditch. The most significant structure (**Fig. 2.4**) comprised a series of substantial wall foundations (614, 692 and 795), 0.5 m thick, which were located immediately to the rear of the main street range and were constructed of undressed chalk blocks and bonded in mortar. This structure spanned the entire width of the tenement, blocking the passage from the street frontage and making it uncertain whether it was conjoined to the street frontage as a service range or was a separate building with an intervening courtyard. No construction date was established, but wall 795 was cut by pit 388 (**Fig. 2.5**), which was filled with horn cores and sherds of 17th-century pottery. This suggests that the structure, which underwent subsequent changes, may well have been built by or within the late medieval period.

The chalk foundations were subsequently replaced by a structure (592; **Fig. 2.4; Pl. 2.31**) of similar construction, which retained elements of the earlier footprint. This rebuilt structure, for which there was no obvious hiatus between the two phases, measured approximately 3 m across internally, and was dug to the surface of the underlying natural gravel to form what was described as a small cellar, or which may have been a chalk-lined cess pit. The revised design adopted wall 614 with the addition of walls 729 on the west and south. These walls abutted wall 731 on the east, suggesting that they were later modifications.

Plate 2.31 No. 51 Brown Street (W227): structure 592, with walls 614, 729 and 731, from the south-west

The summary report considered that these two phases represented independent structures of similar construction. An alternative interpretation suggests that the combined elements represent a structure of one phase that contained a cellar or cess pit. The base of the pit was defined by a layer of organic sandy clay of the type that often characterises the primary fill of similar chalk-lined cess pits in Salisbury (Harding 2016; Rawlings 2000; TVAS 2014a; Wessex Archaeology 2014b). The deposit was, sadly, not sampled for environmental material to determine the nature of the contents. Cess pits, which typically date to the 15th–16th century, were more frequently set back from the street, often against tenement boundaries; at Endless Street (TVAS 2014a) a two-celled structure, each cell measuring over 2 m^2, straddled a tenement boundary. However, smaller examples, measuring approximately 1 m across, were found in Antelope Chequer, on the west side of Brown Street (Rawlings 2000), immediately behind street frontage properties.

The excavations at Nos 47–51 Brown Street produced very few stratigraphic benchmarks to unite adjacent tenements, but a distinctive sooty levelling-up layer, which contained fired clay fragments derived from metal casting moulds (**Fig. 3.6, 1–3**), was recorded across the 'backlands' of Nos 49 and 51 Brown Street. This layer of industrial waste reached a maximum thickness of 0.30 m and covered an area approximately 15 x 8 m. An equivalent layer in the postulated cellar/cess pit indicates that it probably extended across and post-dated the initial construction of structure 592. The summary report suggested that this levelling-up layer may have been linked to a series of small post-medieval brick-built kilns or ovens (**Fig. 2.5**) at No. 49 Brown Street. However, the majority of the layer, which included mould fragments, seems more likely to have been derived from a nearby foundry, an industry that flourished in Salisbury from the late 14th century (Algar and Saunders 2012). Production had largely ceased in the city by the end of the 17th century (Chandler 1983), hinting that the layer is of medieval or early post-medieval date and predating the small brick kilns/ovens.

The summary report indicates that structure 592 was subsequently remodelled by rebuilding wall 731 with chalk and capping the chalk foundations with three courses of flints. The possible cellar or cess pit was backfilled, a clay floor (690) installed and an L-shaped hearth (574) constructed, using mortared tiles, in the south-west corner of the structure. No function was offered for this building; however, it may represent a detached kitchen, similar to those documented by Ralph Treswell (Schofield and Vince 2003, fig. 3.5) in his Type 2 house plans for London, where the kitchen, which posed a fire hazard, was separated from the main house range by a small yard. A structure of similar design and location, of medieval or early post-medieval date, was plotted in Salisbury at Salt Lane (Harding 2016).

An additional structure (555; **Fig. 2.4**), represented by two wall foundations, 556 and tenement boundary 558, was built adjoining the Town Ditch at the end of the tenement. Both foundations of this outbuilding were constructed of mortared flints. The interior comprised a floor (792) with a hearth (560) of tiles, which was apparently located in the south-west corner of the building.

These two structures, 592 and 555, were undated and may or may not have been contemporary. Structure 592 has been tentatively assigned to a point in the later medieval or early post-medieval periods by association with the layer of foundry debris. The maintenance of traditional methods and materials, possibly of cob construction, and the absence of bricks suggests that structure 555 can be similarly dated. An outbuilding of similar design, using chalk foundations, ephemeral internal dividing walls and also with a probable hearth in a corner, was excavated in Vanner's Chequer (Harding 2016) and predated a 17th–early 18th-century well.

Equally uncertain is the date when these buildings became obsolete. Subsequent activity at No. 51 Brown Street comprised four square or irregular pits (303, 388, 749 and 790) (**Fig. 2.5; Pl. 2.32**), which all contained horn cores in the backfill, objects that are typically craft-related waste.

Plate 2.32 No. 51 Brown Street (W227): bone/horn core pit 388, from the south

The pits averaged 1 m across and were approximately 0.2–0.3 m deep. Pit 388 cut through wall 795 and was clearly later; however, the remaining pits showed no similar stratigraphic relationships to wall lines. Pit 303 was located within the front room of No. 51 Brown Street, while pits 749 and 790 were placed within structure 592, which contained the backfilled chalk-lined cess pit, and structure 555 respectively. These locations make it impossible to determine whether the buildings were extant or not when the pits were in use. It is similarly uncertain whether the pits were contemporary, but the summary report speculated that they represented craft-related activity connected to an individual or family, possibly John Leminge, a skinner, who occupied the premises after 1628. The horn core pits therefore provide a potential benchmark by which to relate phases and structures in different parts of the 'backland' at No. 51 Brown Street. The summary report subsequently suggested that a layer containing chalk and broken tile, which extended across the internal features of the structure that included pit 749, may relate to repairs by Joseph Maton, who occupied the premises between 1760 and 1766, when the property was described as being ruinous.

The chalk foundations of structure 592 were also cut by a well (216), which was not excavated and remained undated, but appears on stratigraphic grounds to be at least of 17th-century date.

The final structure (580) at the rear of No. 51 Brown Street (**Fig. 2.5; Pl. 2.33**), which was also considered to be of 17th-century date, was rectangular, measuring 5 m long, 1.5 m wide and 0.55 m deep. The structure comprised two side walls (492 and 496), which were constructed of dressed chalk blocks set in white mortar. The west end of wall 492 was composed of flints, chalk and tile fragments, which suggested that the structure was multi-phase. A timber planked floor was bedded on a deposit of gravel and was overlain by two internal cross-walls (494 and 498), which created three separate cells, each approximately 1.5 m square. The internal walls, which measured 0.3 m thick and were also constructed of dressed chalk blocks, were bonded by white creamy mortar. The summary report speculated that this triple-celled structure may have functioned as a series of fulling tanks and linked them to Thomas Spencer, a feltmaker, whose lease of the property lapsed in 1675. Fulling as part of the cloth-making process is likely to have been transferred to water-powered fulling mills by this period (Chandler 1983); however, small-scale fulling may have been retained within the confines of the chequer by specialists, including feltmakers, who served hatters.

Archaeological deposits were documented immediately to the rear of No. 49 Brown Street but were not excavated in detail. They are consequently difficult to reconstruct, although sufficient evidence survived to indicate the early presence of a service range or paved yard. Traces of a tiled floor were exposed in the side of a backfilled well (664; **Fig. 2.4**), the construction of which was accompanied by an additional tiled floor. The well was also undated; however, the presence of a truncated tiled floor suggested that it probably dated to the 16th or, more probably, 17th century.

The excavations at No. 49 Brown Street produced further insights into the use of the 'backlands' of the chequer and the potential status of the occupants. Three small, circular kilns (620, 622 and 635; **Pls 2.34 and 2.35**), with an internal diameter 0.6–0.9 m across, were preserved as two courses of bricks. Kiln 620 was constructed on a series of demolition or make-up layers that straddled the tenement boundary separating Nos 49 and 51 Brown Street and was cut by the 19th-century range at No. 51 Brown Street. Each kiln, for which no plausible function could be offered, was constructed with a narrow stoke-hole that showed no consistent orientation. The use of brick in structures of such rudimentary design suggest that they are likely to post-date the more formal use of brick in buildings, which can be placed after 1600.

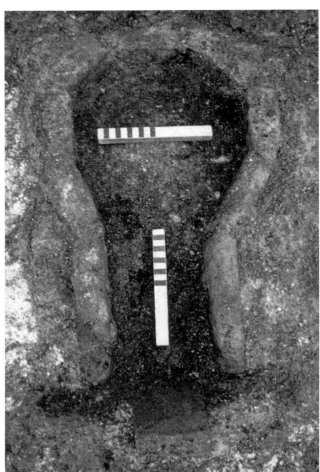

Top left: Plate 2.33 No. 51 Brown Street (W227): structure 580, from the east, with wall 556 (foreground) and tenement wall 120 (right)

Top right: Plate 2.34 No. 49 Brown Street (W227): kiln/ oven 635, pre-excavation, from the south

Right: Plate 2.35 No. 49 Brown Street (W227): kiln/ oven 620 in boundary wall, from the south

In addition, a series of wall foundations, each approximately 2 m long and 0.2 m wide, was also recorded at the extreme east end of the tenement (**Fig. 2.5**). Two of the walls (626 and 824) were constructed of chalk while the last foundation (129) comprised mortared flint and tile with Greensand blocks at the corners and was built against the tenement boundary wall. A chalk floor extended beyond foundation 626 to the limits of excavation. No construction date was established for what are probably wall foundations of an additional outhouse at the end of the tenement. The wall lines were included on the 1880 Ordnance Survey edition, although the absence of bricks in the construction suggest that they predate the mapping by some considerable time. The issue may be resolved by reference to the burnt layer, which contained industrial type waste, including mould fragments. This layer was traced across much of the site, underlay the outhouse foundations and was thought to be broadly contemporary with structure 555 at the eastern boundary of No. 51 Brown Street, which was tentatively placed within the later medieval or early post-medieval period.

Winchester Street and Rollestone Street – W246

Redevelopment work provided an opportunity to sample small areas on two sides of Three Swans Chequer (**Figs 1.2 and 2.7**). The excavation was divided into five separate areas (A–E) with Areas A and E located on the street frontages of Winchester Street and Rollestone Street respectively, which were linked by a trench that continued through the 'backlands' (B–D). The summary report offered only a limited assessment of the evidence, with no absolute chronology provided by pottery. This uncertainty resulted in individual features from each area being listed as medieval/post-medieval or post-medieval. The results considered that tenements that fronted onto Winchester Street were of medieval/post-medieval date and were constructed before properties on Rollestone Street, which were all shown as post-medieval.

Initial activity on Winchester Street was represented by a series of levelling layers, on which wall foundations 17 and 33 were constructed using flint, chalk and mortar. These walls, which probably defined the rear elevation of a building approximately 8 m wide and of comparable construction and dimensions to better-dated medieval buildings on Brown Street (W227), were aligned east–west. Two internal dividing walls, one unnumbered and wall 80, ran perpendicular to the street. Floors were of compacted chalk. Traces of an ancillary building extended to the north defined by walls 46, 305 and 312, which enclosed a floor.

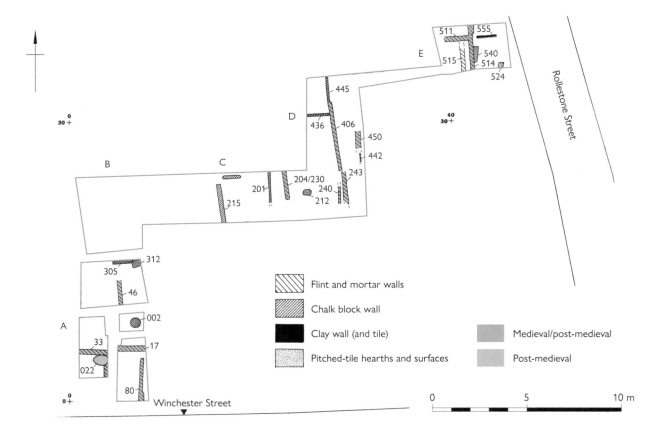

Figure 2.7 Winchester Street/Rollestone Street (W246): phase plan

A chalk-lined well (002), which was also considered to be contemporary, was located towards the rear of the building. Despite the absence of clear dating evidence, the proximity of the Market Place makes it likely that the tenement formed part of the initial development within the chequer. The span of time cannot be confirmed, but continuous, possibly long-term occupation is suggested by superimposed floors within the original building footprint.

Evidence of comparable activity on Rollestone Street (Area E), remains tenuous. The summary report noted a layer of crushed chalk that was considered to represent an early street surface but may represent a compacted chalk floor similar to those noted on Winchester Street. Two robbed wall foundations – one aligned north–south on the same alignment as subsequent wall 514 and the other, aligned east–west – were also recorded.

Activity within the 'backlands' was restricted to flint and mortar tenement boundary wall lines (442, 445 and 450), which were aligned north–south, possibly reflecting a passage between Winchester Street tenements, with wall (436) aligned east–west.

Very little evidence of post-medieval activity was assigned to the Winchester Street frontage apart from a brick-lined well (022) dug inside the footprint of the earlier building. The upper courses of the medieval well were also re-lined with brick. The scant evidence for post-medieval occupation on the tenement was considered to indicate that the plot was open at this time. This may be true, but it is also possible that post-medieval layers and structures were truncated by subsequent redevelopment.

Evidence on Rollestone Street, in contrast, was more emphatic. The summary report describes a period when the plot was abandoned and garden soils accumulated. This period of inactivity was followed by post-medieval construction of a building comprising wall 514, which was approximately 5 m from the street frontage, internal partition 555 and associated floors and surfaces. A hearth (540) was built against wall 514, confirming a probable construction date within the 15th or 16th century. The building was subsequently extended to the west as wall 511 and also included assorted floors. Wall 511 was constructed of flint and mortar but also included a large fragment of decorated window tracery or arcading from the roof of a tomb of probable Perpendicular style (14th–16th century) (**Pl. 2.36**). It is unclear where this enigmatic fragment of probable ecclesiastical stonework originated from, although a relic of the Dissolution seems possible.

Subsequent archaeological evaluation (Wessex Archaeology 2014a) suggested that buildings were probably erected further north on Rollestone Street by the 15th–16th centuries. These buildings featured flint, chalk and Greensand foundations with internal dividing walls, clay floors and external yards. This combined data suggests that development on Rollestone Street had commenced by the late medieval or early post-medieval period and possibly earlier than that indicated in the 1992 summary report. Wall 515 was listed as modern.

Plate 2.36 Rollestone Street (W246E): wall foundation 511 incorporating fragment of Perpendicular tracery, from the north

Additional walls (201, 204/230, 240, 243 and 406) were noted in the 'backlands' between Winchester Street and Rollestone Street. These walls were all aligned north–south and were associated with a hearth and floor or yard surfaces to the east of wall 201. It is unclear from this evidence whether these extensions or outbuildings, which were speculatively assigned to the post-medieval period, related to infilling of properties on Winchester Street, Rollestone Street or to the Old George Inn, on the corner of these two streets. Nevertheless, the inclusion of floor surfaces and hearths provide further valuable, if unclear, evidence of structures behind the street frontage.

Belle Vue House – W290

Four trenches, A–D, were excavated in a staggered line at the northern boundary of the city (**Fig. 1.2**) to establish or confirm whether traces of the city ramparts, which were projected to pass through the site, could be identified. Trenches A, B and C revealed a consistent series of deposits consisting of modern topsoil, which overlay late/post-medieval construction or demolition rubble, with a lower grey-brown loamy buried soil and 'brickearth' subsoil. A small number of pits, postholes and gullies were recorded, including part of an apparently linear feature (214) in Trench C (**Fig. 2.8**). This was interpreted as Hussey's Ditch, possibly named after Alderman William Hussey, who served as the mayor of the city in the 18th century and gave his name to one of the watercourses that formed a distinctive feature of the medieval and post-medieval city. Trench D, at the north end of the line, contained a more complex series of deposits. It included a layer of dark yellow-brown clay loam, which formed an intervening layer, separating the buried soil from the subsoil. The loam represented the upper fills of 21 approximately circular medieval pits and nine late medieval/early post-medieval postholes.

The pits (**Fig. 2.8**), which were dated by pottery spanning the 13th–early 14th century, represented the first phase of activity on the site and were cut with relatively steep, sloping sides and rounded or flat bases. Dimensions ranged from 2.70 m to 0.70 m (mean 1.22 m) in diameter and from 0.63 m to 0.10 m (mean 0.34 m) deep. They were filled with dark brown clay loam. The pits at Belle Vue House were succeeded by a series of late medieval or early post-medieval postholes and two shallow gullies. This sequence was sealed beneath a dump of post-medieval 'black earth', which covered the underlying 'brickearth'. It was suggested that this natural horizon had been truncated by as much as a metre since the medieval period.

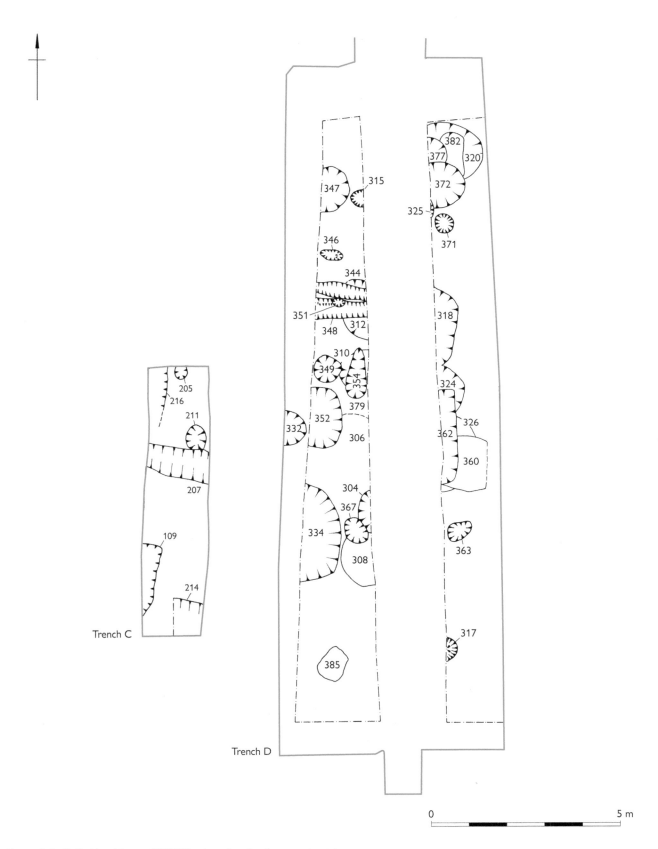

Figure 2.8 Belle Vue House (W290): plan showing intercutting pits

Subsequent archaeological evaluation at the site, documented as United Kingdom House (Wessex Archaeology 2017a), noted a similar sequence of deposits and six additional pits; in contrast to the earlier findings all were post-medieval except for one of 15th–16th-century date. The evaluation located a ditch (103; **Pl. 2.37**), 0.7 m deep, which was also aligned east–west and approximately 6 m south of, and parallel to, that found in 1987. Basal sediments were thought likely to have been water-lain. This second example, similarly undated, was also considered to be Hussey's Ditch; neither is proven, and in the absence of more compelling evidence it is possible that both ditches represent no more than parallel boundary ditches.

The project confirmed the depth of 'black earth', which the report agreed might represent subsequent dumped soil filling former 'brickearth' extraction pits. The increased amount of data from the two episodes of fieldwork, however, allows a simpler archaeological interpretation of the records. The archaeological argument for truncation or extraction of the 'brickearth' remains limited. No extraction pits were defined, and datum levels document a steady, anticipated rise of the flood plain 'brickearth' from west to east. This horizon was capped by additional dumped post-medieval soil, providing topsoil accumulations, which although exaggerated, are similar to others that have been noted in Salisbury. There was nothing to suggest that this soil was derived from the spread of a former bank nor was any evidence of a former defensive ditch discovered.

Plate 2.37 United Kingdom House: ditch 103 from the east

New Canal – W345

The excavations, on the north side of New Street Chequer (**Fig. 1.2**) comprised two trenches, A and B, which were dug during redevelopment work to extend the local branch of Marks and Spencer eastwards from the existing premises. Due to the lack of statutory planning regulations, working conditions were restricted, providing little opportunity for controlled excavation and recording. The summary report recognised that the excavation in Trench A (**Fig. 2.9**), which measured approximately 15 m north–south and 10 m east–west, was limited. A stratigraphic approach was adopted in the southern part of the trench, which produced the most clearly defined results. Excavation in the northern part of the trench was reduced to four trial sections (sondages). This methodology, while attempting to preserve a record of the stratigraphy, was intended to locate any medieval remains that were present. Features were primarily recorded in the sections. This two-dimensional approach, within restricted areas, severely limited the value of the work, making it especially difficult to define features, most notably pits, in plan. Trench B was cleaned and planned but no further work was undertaken.

The excavated areas were situated within the 'backlands', near the southern boundary of a tenement fronting onto New Canal. This tenement adjoined the 15th-century residence of John Halle, a wealthy Salisbury merchant, which was located within a large corner plot that extended eastwards to Catherine Street and south to the mid-line of New Street Chequer (RCHME 1980, 103). The residence was aligned at right angles to the street frontage and was approached through a gated entrance. It is unclear whether the remaining parts of the plot were occupied by additional buildings or remained relatively undeveloped and part of Halle's' residence. The nature and status of the property which adjoined Halle's' residence is unknown; however, additional high-status residences along the street, including a 14th-century structure at Nos 47–49 New Canal (*ibid.*, 100), suggest that this side of the chequer boasted a number of wealthy owners, which may be reflected in the character of the refuse. The site was also adjacent to the detached residence of Thomas Freeman, a wealthy 15th-century mercer, whose family retained ownership of the property into the 16th century.

The summary excavation report defined five phases of activity within Trench A (**Fig. 2.9**), of which the last phase contained three sub-phases. Most of these episodes, established by a relative chronology, were poorly dated; pits containing diagnostic pottery were frequently intercutting and poorly defined, which reduced the usefulness of their data.

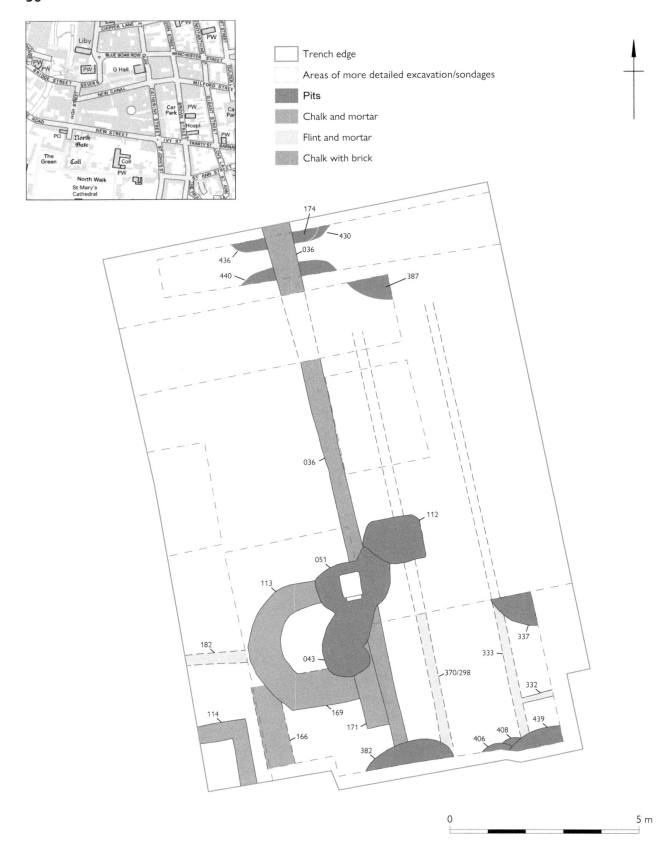

Figure 2.9 New Canal (W345): showing excavated features in Trench A and (inset) site location

The sequence developed from a basal deposit of grey-brown soil, which overlay the flood plain gravel. A pair of chalk and mortar walls (169 and 171), which formed an angled feature, were also attributed to the primary phase. The summary report makes no mention of wall 166. Both walls were extensively truncated by later activity, suggesting that they were part of the initial development but were otherwise undated. No interpretation was provided, but they may represent shallow chalk foundations for an outbuilding or be related to feature 114. This adjacent structure was of similar size and construction but was allocated to a later phase of activity. It was not completely excavated because of its depth, which suggests it was a chalk-lined cess pit similar to others in the city.

Subsequent activity comprised a pair of boundary walls (333 and 370/298), which ran north–south along the entire length of the excavation and defined a path 1.80 m wide. The walls were of two phases and the path comprised three superimposed surfaces, suggesting that it remained in use for some considerable time. Wall foundations 182 and 332 were considered to be contemporary. It is possible that this passage, which is fossilised as an archway from the present street layout, separated two adjoining tenements and allowed access to the centre of the chequer. Similar alleyways separating major tenements are known from elsewhere in the city, where they acquired the name 'abbey' (RCHME 1980, xlii), including an example at No. 19 New Canal.

The most significant findings from the excavation comprised a number of pits that cut through the path. These features were, sadly, recorded predominantly in section, which may have compromised any stratigraphic relationships and reduced the certainty with which finds could be allocated to specific features. The summary report, however, concluded that intercutting sequences could be identified.

The distribution of pits and postholes, as reconstructed from the section drawings, indicates that features were present across most parts of the site, but included a distinct intercutting concentration (382, 406, 408 and 439) towards the southern boundary of the tenement, with a similar group (174, 387, 430, 436 and 440) at the north end. Intercutting was apparently common to the extent that all traces of pit 430, one of the larger examples, were virtually obliterated by pit 174. The pits were of variables sizes, but apparently measured up to 1.5 m deep and 3 m across. Pits of this size and density are rare in Salisbury and were notable by their late 15th–early 16th-century pottery assemblages, which included 'Early Verwood', 'Tudor Green', Raeren stonewares and a sherd from a Mature Valencian lustreware bowl (**Fig. 3.4, 45**). These distinctive types remain under-represented in the city, but similar assemblages have been found subsequently in Vanner's Chequer (Mepham 2016a), where intercutting late medieval/early post-medieval pits of similar size and density were also located at the far end of the tenement.

The tenement boundary was apparently re-established by the construction of a chalk wall foundation (036), which also included a small number of bricks, signifying a site chronology within the post-medieval period. This wall was accompanied by a curving wall (113), which was also constructed from chalk and appears to overlie wall 169, although this is not stated in the summary report. The account concludes the phasing by identifying additional pits, including 043, 051 and 112 within two final sub-phases, which were separated by layers of demolition rubble. The final sub-phase also included a square pit (114), lined with chalk blocks, at the south end of the site. This pit, as outlined above, probably represents an additional cess pit, which may be paired with similar features from the earliest phase and repeating the pattern noted elsewhere in Salisbury (Wessex Archaeology 2014b).

Despite the limitations of the archive this small excavation produced a significant finds assemblage that may hint at patterns of late medieval waste disposal in pits. Furthermore, the character of these assemblages reflects the lifestyle of owners occupying high-status properties of the type known to be present along parts of New Canal. These patterns can be contrasted with those of apparently less affluent properties of the type found on the south side of New Street Chequer (Butterworth 2005a) and elsewhere across the city. Such trends help to illustrate the variable levels of occupancy within chequers.

Salisbury Bus Station

This site (**Fig. 1.2, E**) was examined in two independent projects. The results of a preliminary evaluation (Wessex Archaeology 2014a), with assessment (Cotswold Archaeology 2017) and summary (Garland *et al.* 2021) of the subsequent area excavations, have been described separately. These reports contain much useful information which, when combined and discussed in more detail, document the development of this chequer from an archaeological perspective, both on a site basis and within the broader context of the city. The site occupied a major location in medieval Salisbury – Three Swans Chequer, situated at the junction of Endless Street and Winchester Street, two of the principal thoroughfares of the city, and also adjacent to the Market Place, the economic hub of the community. In addition, the north part of the chequer, on which the bus station was situated, was owned by the Weavers' Guild, one of the wealthiest organisations in the medieval city with a guildhall in the north-west corner of the chequer. Excavation of this site therefore provided an opportunity to investigate part of the economic hub, populated by potentially more affluent residents, and allow comparisons with archaeological results from more outlying chequers. Results of the evaluation (**Fig. 2.10**, WA1–4) indicated that deposits in some areas might be relatively well preserved. Four areas (CA1–4), centred on the principal areas of redevelopment, were investigated in the subsequent excavation, which covered 685 m² (26.4%) of the total site area. The principal areas of excavation were centred on Nos 8 and 10 Endless Street (CA1) and Nos 13, 15, 17 and 19 Rollestone Street (CA2). These two areas contained a series of wall foundations, which were interpreted as Buildings A–F, of which the remains of Building A were indefinable. Areas CA3 and CA4 were heavily disturbed by post-medieval foundations.

Fragmentary wall foundations were identified (**Figs 2.10 and 2.11**) that apparently demarcated the principal tenement boundaries at the north end of the chequer. These divisions correlate with the dimensions of tenements seen elsewhere across the medieval city. The southern tenement boundary of No. 10 Endless Street was marked by wall foundation 1229, which could be projected eastwards to wall foundation 2201 apparently forming the southern boundary of No. 17 Rollestone Street. The evaluation report noted the absence of bricks in foundation 304, which ran parallel to foundation 2201, concluding that it was probably of medieval or late medieval date. Its robust construction suggested that it may have supported a load-bearing, structural wall. These tenement boundaries remained in perpetuity, as a footpath or passage demonstrates on early Ordnance Survey mapping. The proposed system of boundaries suggests that the central spine of the chequer was represented by wall foundations 204 and 2156/2171, which divided the north end of the chequer into two equal parts, each approximately 30 m north–south by 35 m east–west. This equates with four standard medieval tenements, Nos 8 and 10 Endless Street and Nos 15 and 17 Rollestone Street, as defined by Chandler (1983). Tenements to the south at No. 8 Endless Street and No. 15 Rollestone Street were extensively disturbed but could be defined on Rollestone Street by limestone foundation 3001 and a later brick extension (3025) on the same alignment.

Additional wall lines indicate that the medieval tenement forming No. 17 Rollestone Street may itself have been subdivided at some point after it was laid out. The insertion of wall foundations 2013/2097 and 2082 creates three equal parts, each 5 m wide, which may have been subjected to changes of use through time. Naish (1716) showed a building, possibly Building D of the assessment report, projecting from Building E while a building is marked on a deed plan of 1798 (WSA 1214/33) between these two wall lines. The area is shown subsequently as an open yard on early Ordnance Survey editions.

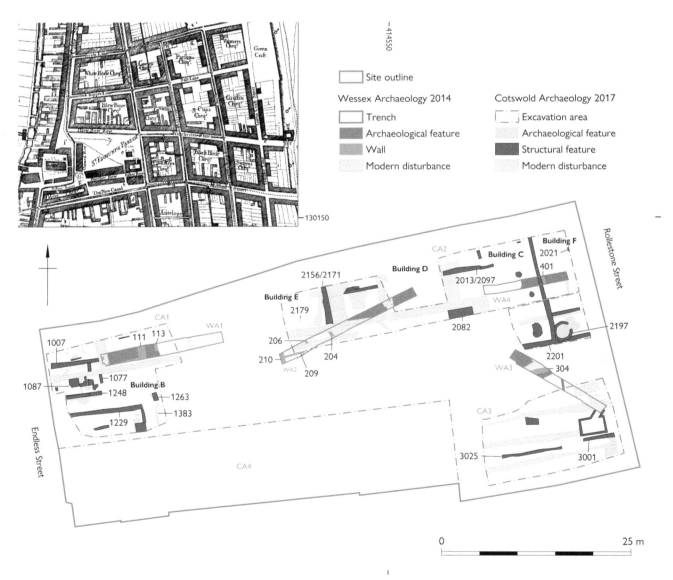

Figure 2.10 Salisbury Bus Station: showing all excavated features revealed by Wessex Archaeology evaluation and Cotswold Archaeology excavation (inset: detail from Naish's map of 1716)

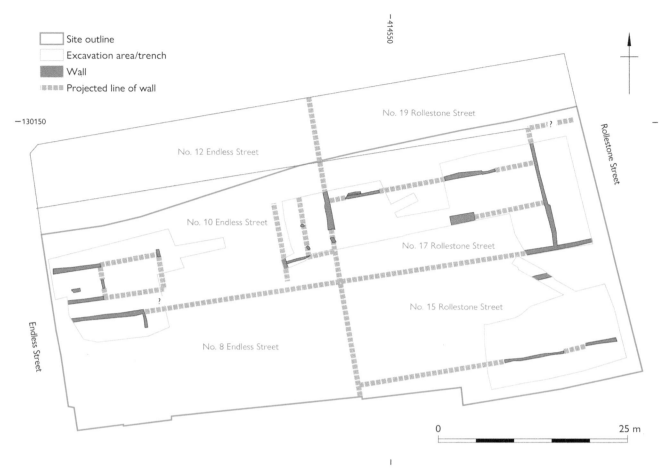

Site outline
Excavation area/trench
Wall
Projected line of wall

No. 19 Rollestone Street

No. 12 Endless Street

No. 10 Endless Street

No. 17 Rollestone Street

No. 15 Rollestone Street

No. 8 Endless Street

Endless Street

Rollestone Street

0   25 m

Figure 2.11   Salisbury Bus Station: interpretation

Plate 2.38 Salisbury Bus Station: evaluation trench (WA1) at the rear of No. 10 Endless Street showing post-medieval brick rubble overlying light-coloured medieval make-up deposits with buried soil capping river gravel

Both phases of fieldwork established that buildings fronting onto Endless Street were erected on a series of make-up deposits (**Pl. 2.38**), into which a series of shallow pits, containing 13th–14th-century pottery, were cut. The excavation in CA1 revealed traces of a preliminary building, Building A, represented by fragmentary wall foundations (1263), a robber trench (1383) and floor remnants that were associated with 13th-century pottery. There was insufficient evidence to reconstruct the extent or ground-plan of this building; however, the alignment of wall 1263 could be projected to the north, where medieval wall foundation 113 and 18th-century foundation 111 hinted at a common gable or rear elevation for buildings in the street from the earliest constructions.

Building A was replaced in the late 13th–14th century by a structure, Building B. In its simplest form this building can be reconstructed using wall foundations 1007 and 1229 to form the north and south elevations with foundation 113 possibly forming the east gable, providing a footprint extending approximately 12–14 m east–west from the street frontage and 7 m north–south. These walls were of flint and chalk construction in light yellow-brown chalky mortar. Wall foundation 1248 is somewhat more problematic. The assessment report considered that it was probably added subsequently. It is unclear whether it formed an internal division, thereby creating an internal passage within Building B, or formed the south wall of the building, forming a passage/alley between Nos 10 and 12 Endless Street through the chequer to Rollestone Street. Furthermore, there is the possibility that foundation fragments aligned north–south, including 1077, formed internal sub-divisions within Building B. This theory is speculative but entirely plausible; other contemporary buildings of apparently similar cellular design and dimensions, where the length:breadth ratio equals 2:1, can be seen in the city. If this is so, the front part of Building B may have comprised an open hall equipped with a central, heavily scorched hearth (1087), built from re-used peg and glazed roof tiles. Additional, less heavily burnt structures, which were also built of re-used roof tiles, were also found within the building and may have related to subsequent modifications, possibly chimneys. Traces of probable, heavily truncated floor surfaces were also noted throughout the interior. This building, which may have formed a range within a more complex building, probably remained in use, with intermittent modifications in the 16th–17th century (Garland et al. 2021), until the major redevelopment of No. 10 Endless Street in 1740 (Chandler 2013), which itself preserved the line of the rear elevation as wall 111. This 18th-century building was built from bricks laid on a foundation of Chilmark limestone blocks, some of which were chamfered, suggesting that they were re-used. There was nothing to indicate the source of this material, but it is tempting to consider whether the blocks may have been obtained from the demolition of the weavers' guildhall, a building about which so little is known, but which may have included elements of stone construction. These components may themselves have been recycled from demolition of buildings at Old Sarum.

Building B was bounded to the north by superimposed layers of compacted chalky clay and silty clay 'brickearth', which were classified as occupation layers. The assessment report concluded that this area may have remained open throughout the life of the building, allowing access from Endless Street to the rear of the property.

The evaluation report suggested that buildings in the north-west corner of the chequer may have been built around a central courtyard, fronting onto Endless Street, as implied by Naish's survey of 1716. This survey included a supplementary range, which the evaluation defined, measuring approximately 7 m wide and aligned north–south. The building can best be correlated with Cotswold Archaeology's (2017) Building E in Area CA2 to include foundations (204/2156/2171), which measured approximately 0.48 m wide, with a central spine (206/2179) and cross-wall (209). The foundation on the west side (210; **Pl. 2.39**) lay beyond the limits of Cotswold Archaeology's excavation. Floors were of clay. The assessment report included Building E with post-medieval structures on Rollestone Street; however, its location, extending west from the spinal boundary of the chequer, suggests that it may be better linked to properties on the Endless Street frontage and therefore of much earlier date. Furthermore, this range does not appear on a deed of 1798 (WSA 1214/33), which suggests that Naish surveyed a structure that formed part of the medieval configuration.

Plate 2.39 Salisbury Bus Station: evaluation trench (WA2), showing Cotswold Archaeology Building E with foundations 210 and 209 (foreground) and 206 beyond, looking north-east

Development on Rollestone Street, in the east part of CA2, is more problematic, but there was nothing to indicate buildings comparable to Building B on Endless Street. The excavation assessment and summary reports concluded that the interior of the chequer primarily comprised yard surfaces with a series of poorly defined foundations that represented four buildings, C, D, E and F; all were given a 17th- or 18th-century construction date. Parts of Buildings E and F were exposed by the evaluation although this sampling project made it impossible to date the construction of individual buildings. Nevertheless, the apparent absence of bricks within the foundations suggested that they may be of medieval or late medieval date. Structures could also be correlated tentatively with Naish's survey, indicating their probable existence by that date.

The earliest structure recorded in CA2 comprised a circular kiln-type feature (2197), which predated the foundations of Building F. This structure, which was constructed of pitched roof tiles with an outer facing of squared limestone blocks, produced a small group of medieval artefacts, including two silver coins. Traces of iron working were found in the surrounding area, including a possible stoke-hole adjoining the north-east side of the kiln, although no metalworking debris was recovered from the primary fill of the kiln itself.

Similar medieval structures have been found in Salisbury, most pertinently at the junction of Milford Street and Gigant Street, where Currie and Rushton (2005) described a circular structure with a similar area of burning to the north-east. The traces of intense burning did not extend into the interior of the structure itself, suggesting that the two were unrelated and leading Currie and Rushton (*ibid.*, 227) to describe the structure as a possible dovecote. Butterworth (2005a, 240) included a similar 'substantial sub-circular structure' in descriptions of medieval deposits in New Street. These parallels suggest that the structure on Rollestone Street may be better classified as an oven and probably, as conjectured in the assessment report, earlier than the iron working.

Irrespective of whether the kiln/oven was of medieval date or not, no other demonstrably earlier, medieval, structures were found on the street frontage. Multiple superimposed medieval floor surfaces were also absent, suggesting that this part of the street may not have formed part of the 14th-century development in the city. Nevertheless, it seems likely that buildings had been erected on Rollestone Street before 1767 (Chandler 2013). The summary report acknowledged that buildings shown by Naish in 1716 indicated the likelihood that development occurred at an earlier date. Building F contained no bricks in the foundations but did include a hearth (2021) at the front of the building. This feature has been noted elsewhere in Salisbury after 1450, including No. 51 Brown Street (see above) and Anchor Brewery (Barber 2005). The foundations of Building F, if not the superstructure, may therefore define a late medieval or early post-medieval timber-framed building, allowing it to appear on Naish's map of 1716.

The argument for earlier buildings on the site is strengthened by the recovery of sherds of pottery and clay pipe fragments from the fill of a robber trench (401) (Wessex Archaeology 2014a), which indicated demolition in the 17th century.

Major redevelopment of the area may have created a vacant site, which was adopted for iron working and can be dated by the presence of coal, 18th-century pottery and clay tobacco pipe bowls from the foundations of hearths. This period may have been one of intense change within this part of the chequer, witnessing the redevelopment of No. 10 Endless Street in 1740, the construction of new properties at Nos 15 and 17 Rollestone Street in 1767, which may or may not have been Building F, and additional development at the corner of Rollestone Street and Salt Lane in 1784 (Chandler 2013). It is possible that evidence for this post-medieval reconstruction on Rollestone Street was truncated by the construction of the bus station, leaving only the lower earlier foundations.

Chapter 3
Finds

by Lorraine Mepham and Lorrain Higbee

Descriptions of major artefact assemblages, notably pottery and animal bone, were included by Hawkes (nd) and are summarised and revised here. Hawkes also included details of various supplementary finds assemblages including metal objects, glass, fired clay, ceramic building material (CBM), clay tobacco pipes and environmental evidence. Some categories, including glass – which was, apart from a small fragment of window glass from a medieval context, all of post-medieval or modern date – were quantified but not retained. These categories are also summarised below; more detailed study should be referred to the original archive.

Pottery
by Lorraine Mepham

Introduction

The pottery assemblage, recovered from nine of the 11 sites investigated between 1984 and 1990, comprises 11,048 sherds (226.442 kg). Apart from a single sherd of Saxon date, the assemblage is entirely of medieval or later date.

When this assemblage was first studied, it was the only collection of medieval and post-medieval pottery to have been recovered from Salisbury under controlled excavation conditions and presented the first opportunity to study a large assemblage from the city. Some effort was therefore expended in the process of creating a type series for fabrics and vessel forms, and in trying to set the assemblage in its local context in terms of known production sites and consumer sites in the area. In the meantime, several other major assemblages have been recovered from Salisbury, of which three have been published by Wessex Archaeology, from sites in Antelope, Trinity and Vanner's Chequers (Mepham 2000; 2005; 2016a), as well as other smaller assemblages. One kiln assemblage has also been published, from the only production site located within the city, recorded during a rescue excavation in Guilder Lane during construction of the ring road in 1973 (Algar and Saunders 2014). The dates of the individual Laverstock kilns, originally all placed in the 13th century (Musty *et al.* 1969) have been reassessed on typological grounds to extend into the early 14th century (Musty *et al.* 2001). This dating framework is again under review after recent re-examination (author's observation; D Brown and B Jervis, pers. comm.). Outside the city, other assemblages have been recovered from Wilton that illustrate the ceramic sequence as far back as the late Saxon period (eg, Mepham 2012) and the overall ceramic tradition of which the Laverstock wares formed a part has been reviewed (Mepham 2018). More detail on the major post-medieval supplier, the Verwood industry of east Dorset, has been published (Draper with Copland-Griffiths 2002), although excavated 17th–20th-century kilns still remain unpublished.

Given this updated background, it is not proposed to present here a detailed report on the medieval and post-medieval pottery recovered from the sites excavated between 1984 and 1990, nor have the original records been re-examined or updated, but the aim is to outline the broad trends and highlight areas of interest within the overall ceramic sequence for Salisbury. Illustrations from the 1984–90 excavations are enhanced here with additional vessels from other Wessex Archaeology sites in the city.

The Assemblage

Table 3.1 gives a breakdown of the medieval pottery assemblage from the 1984–90 excavations by ware type and by site, and a summary of post-medieval ware type totals is given in Table 3.2. The overwhelming predominance of the Laverstock industry on the city's ceramic market is obvious from Table 3.1 (see Mepham 2018, table 1 for data from other sites in Salisbury and the surrounding area) – other ware types are very sparsely represented and appear to relate largely to the industry based in the Warminster area, where documentary records refer to potters at Crockerton (Smith 1997). These Crockerton-type wares, often containing calcareous (chalk) inclusions and visibly micaceous, appear to have been more popular outside the city, and have been recorded from recent excavations close to Old Sarum (Mepham in prep.), where they were largely associated with 11th-/12th-century wares. In Salisbury they may therefore represent the last gasp of a regional industry that could not compete with the newly established Laverstock production centre.
One example from Nos 47–51 Brown Street may be from a tripod pitcher (Fig. 3.1, 1), which would fit with this early date range.

Laverstock fineware is less common than coarseware throughout the city, but the proportion, although it varies from site to site, is rarely less than 15% and can be as high as 36%. This is in contrast to rural sites in Salisbury's hinterland, such as Gomeldon, where it is 5%, and jugs are found more frequently in coarseware fabrics (Mepham 2018, table 1). The nature of that fineware, however, is of interest, as the highly decorated jugs that constitute the typical products of the Laverstock kilns were apparently not commonly used by the city's inhabitants – the slipped decoration here is less common and more restrained (Fig. 3.3, 20–28). Where then did the decorated wares go? The obvious answer is to Clarendon Palace, Laverstock's other main customer.

Detailed quantifications are not available for this site, but the published report certainly highlights a significant proportion of complex decorated jugs (James and Robinson 1988).

In terms of vessel forms, virtually the full range of the Laverstock output is represented in Salisbury. Some of the more specialised forms such as bottles, costrels, bunghole jars, candlesticks, dripping dishes and whistles did not occur on the sites excavated 1984–90 (see **Fig. 3.3, 31, 32**), although there was at least one lamp (**Fig. 3.3, 29**) from Nos 47–51 Brown Street and an aquamanile (**Fig. 3.3, 30**) from Rollestone Street. Jars, bowls/dishes and jugs (some with red painted decoration) are predominant, and there are also examples of a hybrid jar/dish form, the 'West Country' or inturned dish, as well as skillets (**Figs 3.1 and 3.2, 2–19**). Once again there is a contrast with the rural hinterland, where the range contracts and consists largely of jugs, jars, bowls/dishes and adaptations thereof that were geared towards food preparation, such as skillets and cauldrons. The only other form seen at Gomeldon was a single lamp (Mepham 2018, table 2).

Plate 3.1 Three of the most common medieval Laverstock pottery vessels found in Salisbury: jar, jug and skillet, from the collections of The Salisbury Museum

The evidence suggests that there is a distinction between medieval urban and rural material culture, and this is despite the fact that the rural population might have had equal access to urban markets. Following this model, the inhabitants of Salisbury chose luxury items (presumably not only pottery), relying on the local market, whereas the rural population were more likely to purchase household assets in order to generate surplus. They required pottery vessels for food preparation and storage (functional forms), while Salisbury's citizens also required tableware. The situation was undoubtedly more complex than this and could have been affected by, for example, economic factors (standard of living, purchasing power), the cost of an item and the choice available in the marketplace (Courtney 1997, 99). In contrast, a 2012 study of pottery consumption as an indicator of food culture in medieval Hampshire shows less of an urban/rural divide (Jervis 2012).

Ware	W64	W116	W129	W139	W192	W227	W246	W290	W345
V400	-	-	-	-	-	-	-	1/8	-
S-N calc	5/100	-	-	-	1/24	4/57	1/11	4/34	-
S-N flint	5/29	-	-	1/3	-	1/19	-	-	-
Crockerton	2/24	3/37	-	1/28	2/79	1/4	3/18	4/71	2/49
Lav fine	24/276	10/339	57/641	44/373	126/1260	217/3319	85/1280	116/609	13/154
Lav C a	18/173	1/4	3/42	4/39	2/52	-	3/200	5/29	-
Lav C b	76/675	57/513	75/1155	144/924	134/1440	178/3492	80/1791	362/2677	6/246
Lav C c	5/48	5/113	14/135	25/161	23/430	34/685	21/357	20/392	8/105
Surrey	-	-	1/2	16/55	3/19	5/52	8/66	15/107	8/136
Minety	-	-	-	-	-	3/58	-	-	-
Q410	-	-	-	-	2/61	-	1/5	-	4/71
Q411	-	-	-	-	-	2/144	-	1/7	-
Total	135/1325	76/1006	150/1975	235/1583	293/3365	445/7830	202/3728	527/3926	41/761

Table 3.1 Medieval pottery totals by site (number of sherds/weight in grammes)

Ware type	No. sherds	Wt (g)
Earthenwares		
Tudor Green	144	749
Cistercian-type ware	12	144
Early Verwood	215	4107
Redwares	215	8005
Border ware	6	40
Slipwares	173	1579
Verwood-type wares	4185	132,578
Early finewares		
Staffs-/Bristol-type yellow slipware	131	1149
Staffs-/Bristol-type mottled ware	23	284
Tin-glazed earthenware	232	3056
Stonewares		
Langerwehe stoneware	4	46
Raeren stoneware	15	553
Cologne/Frechen stoneware	170	3233
Westerwald stoneware	47	411
English stonewares	399	13,781
White salt-glaze	65	514
Fine red stoneware	6	86
Refined wares		
Refined whitewares	2457	27,694
Refined redwares	5	54
Creamware	234	1936
Pearlware	8	23
Agate ware	13	73
Basalt ware	5	24
Jackfield ware	5	187
Bone china	4	149
Porcelain	202	1162
Total	*8975*	*201,617*

Table 3.2 Overall totals of post-medieval wares

Towards the end of the medieval period (mid-/late 14th century onwards), the local products were supplemented by small quantities of whitewares from the Surrey/Hampshire border industry, in the form of Coarse Border ware (Pearce *et al.* 1985). No diagnostic sherds were found during the 1984–90 excavations, but subsequent fieldwork has yielded partially glazed jars, some of which were possibly tripod pipkins. The only other non-local type identified (apart from the Crockerton-type wares in the early part of the sequence) comprised three oolitic-tempered sherds from the Minety area of north Wiltshire. Wasters from Minety have been dated as 14th- or 15th-century (Musty 1973), but the industry had earlier origins going back at least to the 12th century (Vince 1983).

The post-medieval assemblage is dominated by products of the Verwood industry of east Dorset, but the transition from Laverstock to Verwood is not yet fully understood. This is largely due to the fact that both industries exploited similar pale-firing clays of the Reading Beds and London Clay outcrops. A 'transitional' ware, defined here as 'Early Verwood', but whose precise source is unknown, appeared alongside 'Tudor Green' ware (**Fig. 3.4, 43**) and Raeren stoneware in deposits excavated at New Canal, and was therefore dated as late 15th- to 16th-century. Vessel forms were limited to thin-walled and unglazed jars; some jugs have been found in more recent excavations (**Fig. 3.4, 33–4**).

The Verwood area kilns were certainly supplying the city from the 17th century; vessel forms from this period include pipkins, chafing dishes and bucket-handled jars (**Fig. 3.4, 35–7**). Later, the Verwood repertoire was dominated by jugs and large bowls and dishes for kitchen and dairy use; also seen here are a candlestick and a perfumery lid (**Fig. 3.4, 38–9**), the latter a 'novelty' introduction during a period of diversification in order to sustain the dwindling market for Verwood wares in the period after the First World War. Redwares, distinct from the pale-firing Verwood-type wares, are very scarce, and appear to have occurred mostly in the early post-medieval period, also supplying chafing dishes and pipkins. Some were in a slipware, green-glazed over an internal white slip, a type only very recently recognised as a 17th-century product of the Crockerton kilns (P Copland-Griffiths, pers. comm.); other slip-trailed and sgraffito wares may also be Crockerton products (**Fig. 3.4, 40–2**). Following the late medieval Surrey whitewares and 'Tudor Green' wares, the post-medieval products of the Surrey/Hampshire border industry found their way into the city from the 16th century; one of the earliest examples may be a puzzle jug, the spout from which was found in Vanner's Chequer (**Fig. 3.4, 44**).

Following the Raeren stonewares, Frechen and Westerwald stonewares were used from the 17th century, alongside tin-glazed earthenware and Staffordshire-/Bristol-type slipwares (**Fig. 3.4, 46**) and mottled wares. While the majority of the tin-glazed earthenwares were of British origin, probably from either London or Bristol, of particular interest is one earlier sherd, from a 15th-century Mature Valencian lustreware bowl, found at New Canal (**Fig. 3.4, 45**). English stonewares, including both Nottinghamshire and Staffordshire types (used primarily for straight-sided tankards), appeared from the beginning of the 18th century, augmented by white saltglaze from c. 1720. From this point on the ceramic repertoire expanded significantly, with the introduction of factory-produced refined wares (creamware, pearlware, whiteware) supplying a variety of new tableware forms.

The Ceramic Sequence

The establishment of a ceramic sequence for Salisbury has been problematic. The 1984–90 excavations yielded less than 1000 sherds from uncontaminated medieval contexts. There were no large pit groups and few of the sites produced good stratified sequences of pottery – the most substantial sequence derived from No. 39 Brown Street. The amount of diagnostic material was very small. More recent excavations in and around Salisbury have, however, helped to place these earlier results in some kind of chronological context.

Wares that fall early within the sequence include the coarser end of the Laverstock coarseware spectrum (fabrics E422A and to some extent E422B), the calcareous and flint-gritted wares found in Saxo-Norman vessel forms at Old Sarum and Wilton (fabrics C400, C402, F400, F401) and the micaceous Crockerton-type wares (fabrics C401, Q409). While close dating is not yet possible, it is likely that all of these apart from E422B had fallen out of use by the middle of the 13th century. There is some suggestion of a higher proportion of these earlier wares in the assemblage from Culver Street (although the total number of medieval sherds was very low), which could be linked to the putative pre-city settlement to the south-east around St Martin's Church.

Thereafter, Laverstock wares, both coarse and fine, dominated the city until the late medieval period. This in itself has limited the creation of a dated sequence as there appears to be little development in either wares or vessel forms during that period, and the existing chronological scheme based on the kiln products is under question. All that was suggested by the 1984–90 assemblages, based on the stratigraphic sequence from No. 39 Brown Street, was that the proportion of glazed finewares increased over time at the expense of the coarsewares, and that the existing handmade finewares were augmented by wheelthrown wares. The only means of identifying later medieval (14th-/15th-century) ceramic groups has been by the presence of the few chronologically distinctive forms such as bifid-rimmed jars, or the small quantities of Surrey whitewares.

Later 15th-/16th-century groups are characterised by 'Tudor Green' ware, Raeren stoneware and the transitional 'Early Verwood' ware. Thereafter, although the sequence is still dominated by utilitarian coarsewares, by now supplied by the Verwood area kilns but not often lending themselves to close dating, dating by association with other more chronologically distinctive wares is possible: German stonewares, tin-glazed earthenwares, Staffordshire-/Bristol-type slipwares and mottled wares, and then by the refined wares of the 18th century and later.

Conclusions

Study of the pottery assemblage from the 1984–90 excavations has enabled some comment to be made on the production and distribution of medieval and post-medieval pottery in south Wiltshire. In particular it provides a useful 'consumer' assemblage as a counterpart to the local production sites at Laverstock and in the Verwood area. Other fieldwork in and around Salisbury has supplied a wider chronological context, from the late Saxon period onwards, and highlights the stimulus on the local pottery industry of the new city's foundation. Laverstock supplied the inhabitants of Salisbury from the early 13th century to the almost complete exclusion of any products from elsewhere; the Verwood area kilns were similarly predominant from at least the 18th century, although also operating earlier.

The medieval assemblage, however, does have limitations as a chronological tool for the construction of a ceramic sequence, largely due to the absence of any deep stratigraphy in the city, or well-preserved and well-stratified groups of any significant size. Instead, there are other features that can illuminate aspects of daily life in Salisbury. The ubiquity of fine glazed wares across all sites, and particularly marked in the assemblages from Trinity Chequer, suggests that these were available to all levels of society in the city, although the more highly decorated Laverstock products seem to have gone elsewhere, perhaps to Clarendon Palace. In any case, pottery in itself is not a particularly good indicator of social status, being a relatively cheap commodity – even highly decorated wares could have been afforded by a wide range of the population. Metalwork and glass, both more readily recycled, are more useful in that respect. Contrasts noted with rural assemblages in the area, with a far lower proportion of glazed wares and a more limited repertoire of vessel forms, could be a result of consumer choice rather than prohibitive cost.

Interestingly, and somewhat frustratingly, there is virtually nothing here that reflects the extensive mercantile activity of the city during the medieval period and the close connections of the Salisbury merchants with the major port of Southampton, despite entries in the Southampton Port Books indicating that continental imports, including ceramic pots, were travelling inland to Salisbury. There is no trace, for example, of the basket of 'painted Genoa pots' taken to Salisbury on behalf of Andre de Pisa in 1439 (Brown 2002, 132). One single sherd gives a hint of this activity – part of a 15th-century Spanish lustreware bowl (**Fig. 3.4, 45**), found at New Canal, in a street known to have been occupied by wealthy merchants. A little later, the smattering of Raeren stoneware can be tentatively linked with consignments of cruses (beer mugs); several hundred were dispatched from Southampton to Salisbury in 1527 (*ibid.*, table 24).

The late medieval period remains somewhat shadowy in ceramic terms in Salisbury, as elsewhere: groups datable to between the later 14th and 16th centuries are scarce and are generally only recognisable by the appearance of non-local types such as Surrey whitewares, as the Laverstock industry shows little diagnostic development beyond the introduction of one or two new forms or modifications. Within the 1984–90 excavations, it was only at New Canal that a recognisable 15th-/16th-century horizon could be distinguished. Subsequently, a few more late medieval groups have been recognised in Vanner's Chequer. In production terms, a link between the medieval Laverstock and post-medieval Verwood industries has been identified. The source of this transitional 'early Verwood' ware is still uncertain, but it underlines the innately conservative nature of the Verwood industry, in which medieval manufacturing techniques survived even into the 20th century.

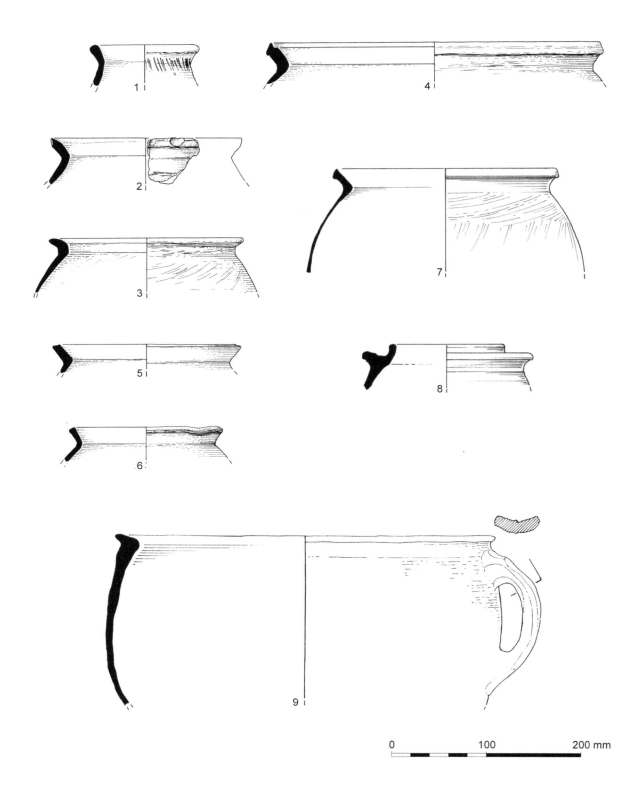

Figure 3.1 Medieval pottery (nos 1–9)

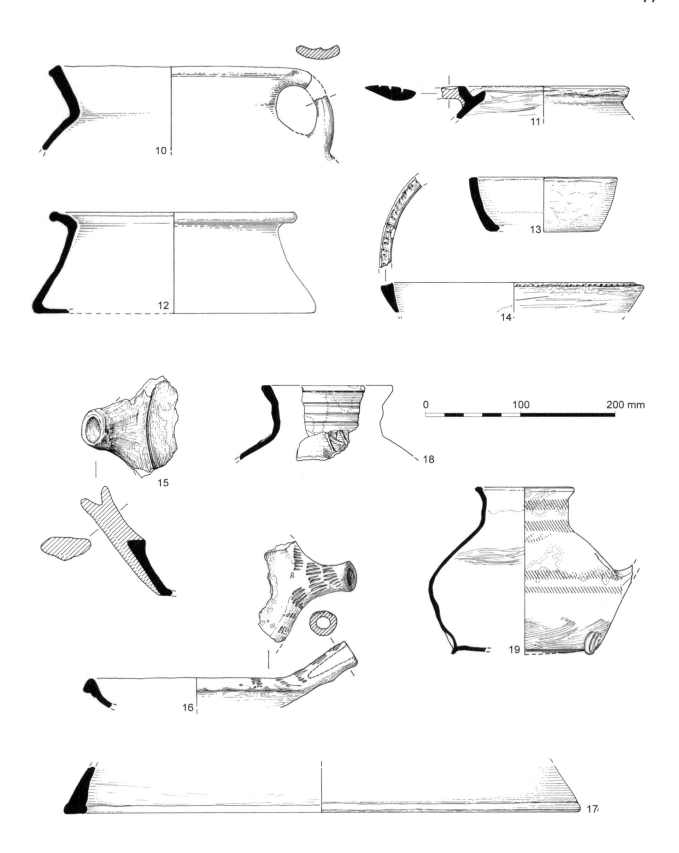

Figure 3.2 Medieval pottery (nos 10–19)

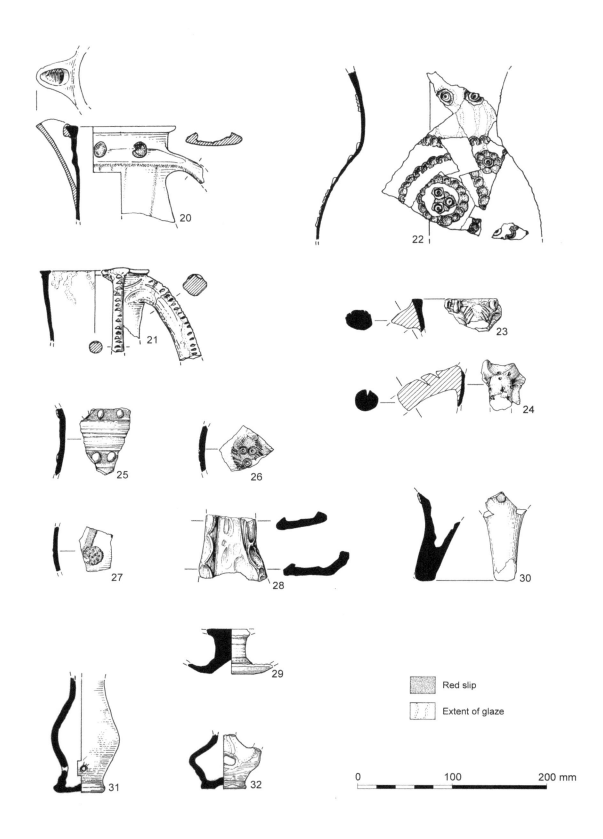

Figure 3.3 Medieval pottery (nos 20–32)

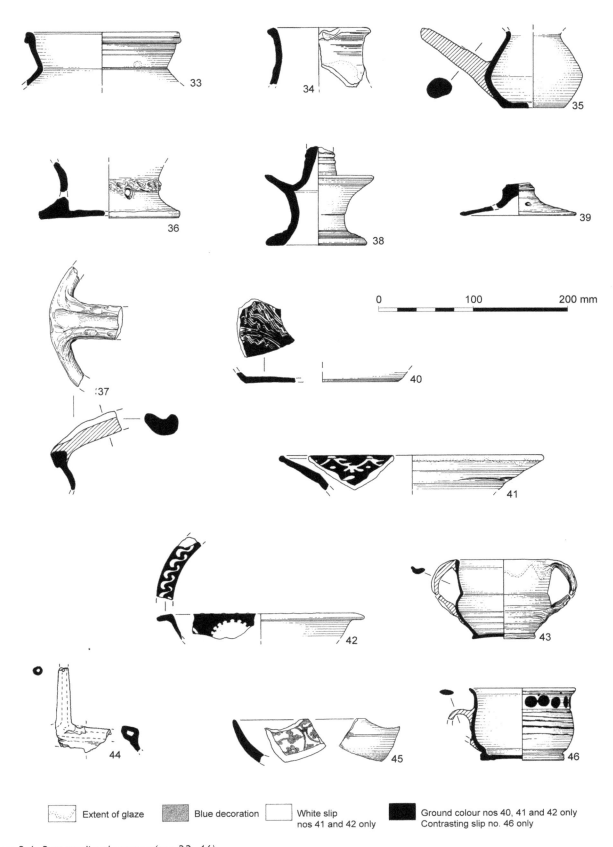

Figure 3.4 Post-medieval pottery (nos 33–46)

Extent of glaze   Blue decoration   White slip nos 41 and 42 only   Ground colour nos 40, 41 and 42 only Contrasting slip no. 46 only

List of illustrated pottery
Medieval (Figs 3.1–3.3)

1. ?Tripod pitcher rim; Crockerton-type calcareous-tempered ware; traces of curvilinear combed decoration. W227 (Nos 47–51 Brown Street), context 282

2. Jar rim; Laverstock-type coarseware; scratch-marked exterior; finger-impressed decoration on rim. W64 (Culver Street), context 52

3. Jar rim; Laverstock-type coarseware; scratch-marked exterior; sooted. W64 (Culver Street), context 43

4. Jar rim; Laverstock-type coarseware. W227 (Nos 47–51 Brown Street), context 767

5. Jar rim; Laverstock-type coarseware. W116 (St Ann Street), context 31

6. Jar rim; Laverstock-type coarseware; finely scratch-marked exterior, sooted; glazed interior. W192 (Gibbs Mew), context 116

7. Jar; Laverstock-type coarseware; scratch-marked. W5704 (Anchor Brewery), midden deposit 384

8. Narrow-mouthed jar with lid-seated rim; Laverstock-type coarseware. W5704 (Anchor Brewery), gully fill 193

9. Handled (possibly two-handled) jar; Laverstock-type coarseware; strap handle(s). W7924 (Ivy Street)

10. Handled (possibly two-handled) jar; Laverstock-type coarseware; strap handle(s). W5704 (Anchor Brewery), organic layer 555

11. Handled (possibly two-handled) jar with bifid rim; Laverstock-type coarseware; slashed strap handle(s); wiped exterior and interior; partially glazed on top of rim; slashed decoration on handle. W345 (New Canal), context 91

12. 'West Country' (inturned) dish; Laverstock-type coarseware. W5704 (Anchor Brewery), organic layer 555

13. Bowl profile; Laverstock-type coarseware; knife-trimmed exterior, partially glazed interior. W129B (Gigant Street Car Park), Trench B, context 576

14. Bowl or dish rim; Laverstock-type coarseware; scratch-marked exterior, partially glazed interior; stabbed decoration on top of rim. W227 (Nos 47–51 Brown Street), context 282

15. Skillet; Laverstock-type coarseware; finely scratch-marked exterior, sooted, partially glazed interior; applied strengthening strip beneath handle. W246 (Rollestone Street), context 440

16. Skillet with hollow cylindrical handle; Laverstock-type coarseware; discrete combing on top of handle and rim; partial internal glaze. W5704 (Anchor Brewery), midden deposit 384

17. ?Curfew rim; Laverstock-type coarseware. W192 (Gibbs Mew), context 116

18. Rim of jug/pitcher; Laverstock-type coarseware; partially glazed exterior, yellowish-green glaze; traces of red painted slip and applied strip decoration. W246 (Rollestone Street), context 440

19. Squat pear-shaped jug with discrete thumbed 'feet'; Laverstock-type coarseware; knife-trimmed around base; red painted decoration; partial glaze. W5704 (Anchor Brewery), midden deposit 384

20. Jug with bridge spout and strap handle; Laverstock fineware; applied slip pads around neck; glazed. W7924 (Ivy Street)

21. Jug with rod handle; Laverstock fineware; applied struts around rim; fingernail notches down handle and struts; glazed. W7924 (Ivy Street)

22. Jug body; Laverstock fineware; applied slip pellets in circles and rosette arrangements. W7924 (Ivy Street)

23. Rim and handle of glazed jug; Laverstock fineware; handmade; mottled apple-green glaze; applied slashed blobs on outside of rim; slashed decoration on handle. W192 (Gibbs Mew), context 10C

24. Handle of glazed jug; Laverstock fineware; handmade; mottled apple-green glaze; stabbed decoration on handle. W64 (Culver Street), unstratified

25. Neck sherd of glazed jug; Laverstock fineware; handmade; mottled yellowy-green glaze; horizontal grooving; horizontal applied slip strips, with rows of applied blobs. W129B (Gigant Street Car Park), Trench B, context 597

26. Body sherd from glazed jug; Laverstock fineware; handmade; mottled apple-green glaze; applied slip pad, with feathered decoration and ring-and-dot stamps. W129B (Gigant Street Car Park), Trench B, context 597

27. Body sherd of glazed jug; Laverstock fineware; ?wheel thrown; mottled yellowish glaze; applied slip strip and pad, with stamped 'prunt'. W129B (Gigant Street Car Park), Trench B, context 597

28. Handle of glazed jug; Laverstock fineware; handmade; mottled yellowish-green glaze; thumbed edges and ?finger impressions down centre of handle. W129B (Gigant Street Car Park), Trench B, context 597

29. Part of double-shelled lamp; Laverstock fineware; handmade; mottled apple-green glaze. W227 (Nos 47–51 Brown Street), context 721

30. Leg of glazed aquamanile; Laverstock fineware; handmade; yellowish glaze; applied slip blob at top of 'leg'. W246 (Rollestone Street), context 90

31. Small bottle; Laverstock-type fineware; post-firing perforation just above base. W5704 (Anchor Brewery), midden deposit 384

32. Whistle, missing rim, handle and spout; Laverstock fineware. W5704 (Anchor Brewery), midden deposit 384

Post-medieval (Fig. 3.4)

33. Rim of cooking pot or jar; early Verwood-type ware; wheel thrown. W227 (Nos 47–51 Brown Street), context 43

34. Jug rim; early Verwood. 85971 (Vanner's Chequer), pit 316

35. Pipkin; Verwood-type earthenware; glazed interior; sooted exterior. W345 (New Canal), context 25

36. Base of chafing dish; unglazed Verwood-type earthenware; wheel thrown. W290 (Belle Vue House), context 208

37. Bucket-handled vessel; unglazed Verwood-type earthenware; wheel thrown. W227 (Nos 47–51 Brown Street), context 585

38. Candlestick; glazed Verwood-type earthenware. W227 (Nos 47–51 Brown Street), context 43

39. Perfumery lid; unglazed Verwood-type earthenware. W129B (Gigant Street Car Park), Trench B, context 536

40. Base of slipware bowl or dish; glazed redware with sgraffito decoration. W116 (Nos 8–10 St Ann Street), context 41

41. Redware platter with trailed slip decoration. W139 (No. 39 Brown Street), context 65

42. Redware bowl with trailed slip decoration. W139 (No. 39 Brown Street), context 77

43. Two-handled cup; 'Tudor Green' ware; glazed interior and partial exterior. W345 (New Canal), context 378

44. Puzzle jug rim with upstanding pierced spout; early Border ware; green-glazed. 85971 (Vanner's Chequer), layer/pit 318

45. Hemispherical bowl; Mature Valencian lustreware; bryony foliage decoration. W345 (New Canal), context 305

46. Porringer; Staffordshire-type yellow slipware. W246 (Rollestone Street), context 1D

Ceramic Building Material (CBM)
by Lorraine Mepham

A total of 13,960 pieces (712,524 g) of CBM was assessed from nine excavated sites, of which 6,270 pieces were retained. Most of this comprised fragments of flat (peg) tile and brick. The peg tile does not necessarily lend itself to particularly close dating, but medieval levels across the city have consistently produced tile of a reasonably distinctive character, often fairly crudely formed in poorly wedged, iron-poor clays, firing pale salmon pink to pale orange-cream and often containing prominent iron oxides appearing as red-brown pellets. These tiles were often partially glazed (the glaze restricted to the lower one-third of the upper surface that would be visible after laying). It is assumed that the source(s) of these tiles must have been fairly local to the city; one such source is known at Alderbury in the 14th–15th centuries (Hare 1991, table 1). No peg tile production is known at Laverstock – medieval potters rarely produced these items – but what they did make was more elaborate roof furniture, seen here in the form of ridge tiles, frequently of crested form (Musty *et al.* 2001, cat no. 293). There are also a few fragments that could have belonged to chimney pots, finials or louvers (**Fig. 3.5, 1**); other examples were subsequently found at Anchor Brewery (**Fig. 3.5, 2–3**). The quantities and distribution of ceramic roof tiles across medieval Salisbury suggests that construction from the start used these instead of wooden shingles or thatch, which were by this time recognised as a fire risk.

There were also floor tiles, mainly undecorated and unglazed. Examples were recovered from all excavations, with larger assemblages from Nos 47–51 Brown Street and Rollestone Street. Two decorated examples from Nos 47–51 Brown Street (Nenk 2012) are, however, of interest. One is a segmented tile, bearing a heraldic fleur-de-lys design (**Fig. 3.5, 4**), of the type used in the great circular pavement at Clarendon Palace, which is assumed to have been laid in the chapel of King Henry III, built in the 1230s (Eames 1988, fig. 41, no. 6). Although this pavement was at first thought to be unique in England, it is now certain that there were other such arrangements at sites in Hampshire and Somerset (Eames 1991, 95). The origin of this example in Salisbury is uncertain, but as a single tile it was clearly not found *in situ*. The second is part of a triangular tile bearing repeating lattice motifs (**Fig. 3.5, 5**). This is a tile of the Wessex School, probably dating to the middle of the 13th century. Examples are known from Clarendon Palace, and also from Amesbury, Britford, and Wilton (*ibid.*, fig. 40, no. 164).

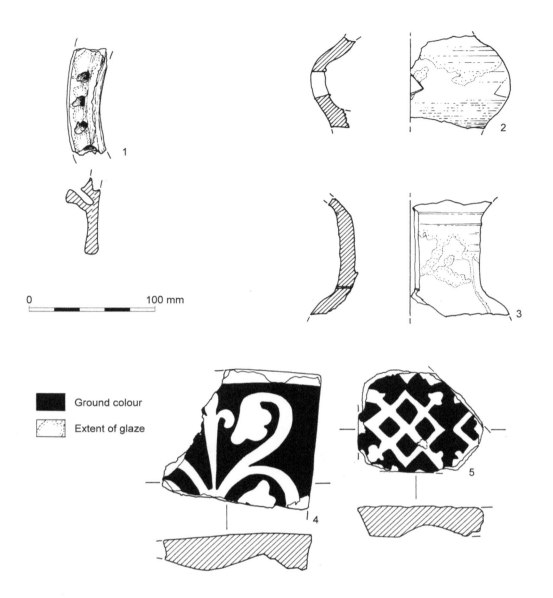

Figure 3.5 Ceramic building material (nos 1-5)

List of illustrated ceramic building material

1. Rim fragment with stabbed flange, possibly from a louvre, in pale-firing fabric, with partial apple-green glaze. W246 (Rollestone Street), context 254

2. Spherical element, possibly from finial. W5704 (Anchor Brewery), layer 289

3. Cylindrical element, possibly from finial, and possibly same object as no. 2. W5704 (Anchor Brewery), layer 289

4. Floor tile with heraldic design inlaid in white slip; glazed. W227 (Nos 47–51 Brown Street), context 340

5. Triangular floor tile, (split diagonally from square tile), chamfered, with repeated lattice design inlaid in white slip; glazed. W227 (Nos 47–51 Brown Street), context 618

Clay Mould Fragments
by Lorraine Mepham

A collection of fired clay fragments was recovered during excavations at Nos 47–51 Brown Street from a levelling deposit. This material, which was of a fine friable open-textured fabric, comprised a number of fragments derived from clay casting moulds for the manufacture of bells or smaller utensils, including cooking vessels (**Fig. 3.6, 1–3**). Bell foundries formed important components of the medieval economy in Salisbury and Winchester. The craft was well established in Salisbury from the late 14th to late 17th century, especially along the eastern side of the city, including production in Guilder Lane (Chandler 1983) and Culver Street (Algar and Saunders 2012). Products were distributed across south Wiltshire into the neighbouring counties of Dorset and Hampshire. Mould fragments from the production of tripod cauldrons that were found (Saunders and Algar 2017) in a well in Milford Street with pottery of late 14th- or 15th-century date confirm that metal casting was not restricted to bell manufacture.

Plate 3.2 Nineteenth-century crucibles, from Milford Hill House, Milford Hill. Scale: 0.1 m

Recovery of artefacts related to these activities can be unexpected. An archaeological watching brief in 2021 on land to the rear of Milford Hill House recovered fragments of three crucibles that contained residues from copper, bronze or brass working (**Pl. 3.2**). The fragments were found in a back-filled gravel pit and could be dated by associated pottery to the 19th century, probably the later part, when development on Milford Hill was expanding. The source of these crucibles remains uncertain, but a documentary search revealed two possible candidates that help to bring focus to the discoveries. A contemporary trade directory (Kelly 1875) documents a brass foundry, owned by Thomas Alexander, in Rollestone Street, possibly related to that connected to ironworking in Three Swans Chequer (Garland et al. 2021). Alternatively, a sale catalogue (DZSWS:SC.25.31) issued under order of the County Court of Wiltshire relates to the sale on 11 September 1903, by Walters and Rawlence, of the Friary Foundry Works. The premises were located on land approached from St Ann Street, in the area formerly occupied by the Franciscan friary. The business included a bell foundry, which maintained the tradition of bell casting in Salisbury from the medieval period.

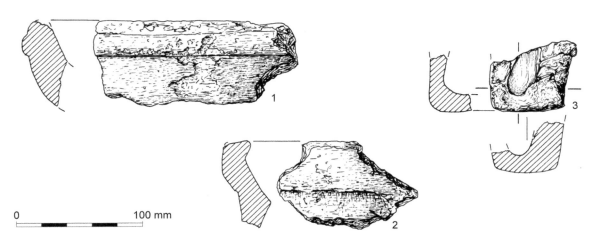

0   100 mm

Figure 3.6 Clay mould fragments (nos 1–3)

List of illustrated clay mould fragments

1. Flanged fragment from a clay mould; outer surface smoothed. External diameter at flange 340 mm. W227 (Nos 47–51 Brown Street), context 590

2. 'Rim' fragment from a clay mould; inner surface smoothed. Internal diameter at 'rim' 200 mm. W227 (Nos 47–51 Brown Street), context 591

3. Corner fragment, possibly from a clay mould for an aquamanile or ewer. W227 (Nos 47–51 Brown Street), context 590

Clay Tobacco Pipes and Pipeclay Objects
by Lorraine Mepham

Salisbury was a major pipe-making centre from at least the later part of 17th century. Prior to this, the Gauntlet family of Amesbury were supplying high-quality pipes with the characteristic 'gauntlet' heel mark from the mid-17th century, and other early pipe makers are recorded from Marlborough. The 1984–90 excavations produced a substantial collection of pipes within a date range of mid-17th to late 19th-century, which included Gauntlet pipes as well as others from makers from Marlborough and East Woodhay and West Wellow in Hampshire. The makers are listed in Appendix 1. All have been previously documented in the city (Atkinson 1970a; 1972; 1980). Pipes from Winchester Street/Rollestone Street (W246) were almost exclusively of 17th-century date, while those from the site in Trinity Chequer produced pipes mainly of the late 17th century and first half of the 18th century.

Of most interest is the collection of pipes from Trinity Chequer, predominantly from demolition and topsoil layers at Nos 47–51 Brown Street (W227) and which belong to the pipe maker Joel Sanger. The presence of overfired stem and bowl 'wasters' and pipe-making debris (including part of a 'muffle', used to provide protection for pipes during kiln firing; **Fig. 3.7, 1–2**) confirms that Sanger's workshop was close by, although he may have been sharing a kiln with another pipe maker (Chandler 1983, 119). Sanger was working c. 1710–40 (Atkinson 1972, 149), and there may have been up to half a dozen other pipe makers working in the city at that time.

By the middle of the 18th century, however, snuff-taking was replacing pipe-smoking as the fashionable way to take tobacco, and the pipe-making industry (**Pl. 3.3**) slowly declined. James Skeaines (or Skeaimes), who originally came from Newcastle-under-Lyme, was recorded as being a pipe maker in Salt Lane in 1848 when he married Mary Ann Morgan, widow of pipe maker William Morgan, one of a lineage of clay pipe makers in Salisbury. Skeaines established his own business, becoming a competitor with Mary Ann's former stepson, William James Morgan, son of her former husband by a previous marriage. The competition soured relations between the two households, which led to court proceedings (Lewcun pers. comm.).

Skeaines was the last documented pipe maker in Salisbury, appearing in trade directories until 1867 (Atkinson 1970a, 188; Mepham 2016b). After that, pipes came in from Southampton and Gosport, while decorated pipes were also supplied by manufacturers from London and even Paris. An incomplete pipe from Posener & Co of London features the legs of a figure resting on the pipe stem, while another pipe bowl is in the shape of a lady's bonnet with a purple painted ribbon. The latter pipe may have belonged to Gambier of Paris, as that company's products often featured painted decoration.

Other objects were also made of pipeclay. Fourteen wig curlers, an unusually large number for a single site, were recovered from Nos 47–51 Brown Street, and one from Winchester/Rollestone Street. Three sizes are represented. Only one complete curler was recovered (**Fig. 3.7, 3**), weighing 7 g. Larger curlers, probably weighing *c*. 22 g when complete, are the most common, and a single very thin curler, probably weighing only 2–3 g, was also found.

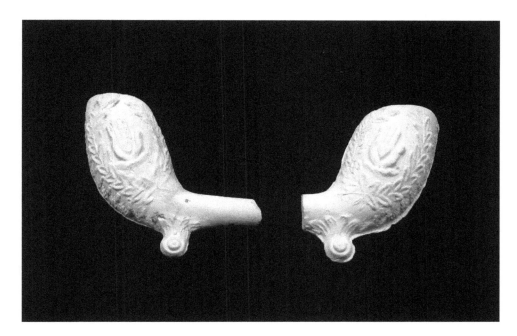

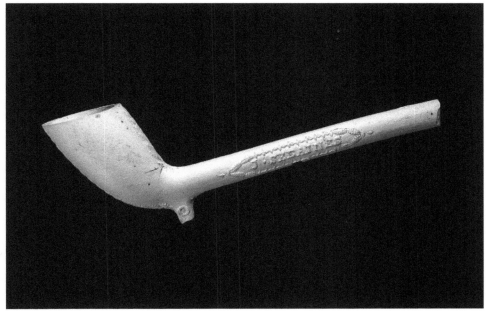

Plate 3.3 W J Morgan pipe with a glove within a wreath (Odd Fellows symbol) on sides of bowl, spur in the form of a stylised flower (top); and James Skeaines pipe, decorated seams (wheatears) with moulded open circles on the spur and J. SKEAINES/SALISBURY in decorative panels on side of stem (bottom)

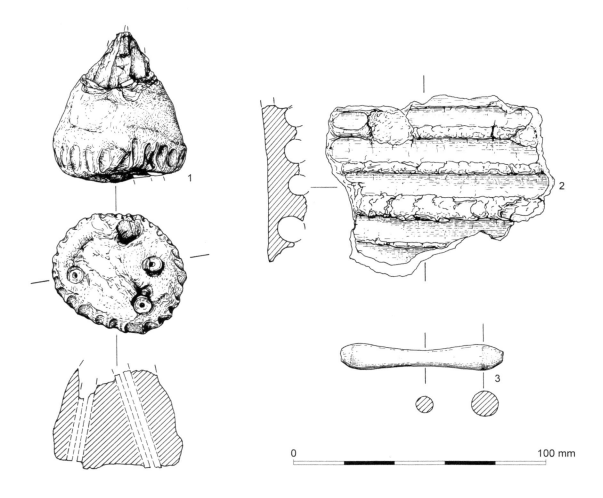

Figure 3.7 Pipe clay objects (nos 1–3)

List of illustrated pipeclay objects

1. Pipeclay object, possibly a muffle fragment. W227 (Nos 47–51 Brown Street), context 88, SF 20

2. Possible muffle fragment. W227 (Nos 47–51 Brown Street), context 88

3. Pipeclay wig-curler, complete. W227 (Nos 47–51 Brown Street), context 43

Metal Objects
by Lorraine Mepham

Hawkes considered only those objects from dated and stratified medieval contexts. The collection included a range of copper alloy costume fittings, predominantly pins, which accounted for approximately 33% of the copper alloy objects. These were supplemented by needles, brooch fragments (**Fig. 3.8, 1**) and belt and strap fittings (**Fig. 3.8, 2**). A miniature key from 39 Brown Street could have belonged to a casket or perhaps a book (LMMC 1940, 138–9, 144; **Fig. 3.8, 3**). A number of iron objects were also listed, including door fittings, keys, lock fragments and handles, and a single lead window came. Domestic implements and trade-related tools recovered included knife blades, of which two were found with inlaid cutler's marks (both from Brown Street; **Fig. 3.8, 4**), and a possible currier's knife related to leather working from Belle Vue House. Few of the objects were distinctly datable but generally spanned the period of the 13th to 15th centuries. The illustrated buckle pin, miniature key and strap-end or buckle plate with rocker-traced zig-zag decoration are all probably 13th-/14th-century. The report noted the absence of items related to the presence of pilgrims, despite the wealth of material found in the city drains and river (Spencer 1990), and concluded that the medieval metalwork assemblage was directly comparable in terms of composition with assemblages from other excavated medieval towns and cities including Christchurch (Hinton 1992), Colchester (Crummy 1988) and Exeter (Allan 1984).

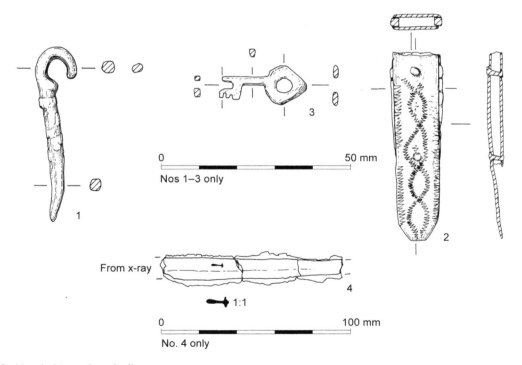

Figure 3.8 Metal objects (nos 1–4)

List of illustrated metal objects

1. Pin with moulding just below the hinge, typical of those from 13th- or 14th-century annular brooches. W139 (No. 39 Brown Street), context 1204, SF 14

2. A miniature key with lozenge-shaped bow, possibly from a casket or book. W139 (No. 39 Brown Street), context 1307, SF 43

3. A strap-end or buckle plate; two copper alloy rivets *in situ*; upper plate decorated with rocker-traced zig-zags around border and in interwoven waves down the centre. W290 (Belle Vue House), context 734, SF 10026

4. Fragmentary knife blade with 'T'-shaped cutler's mark. W129B (Trinity Chequer), context 583, SF 161

Animal Bone
by Lorrain Higbee

Introduction

The following account draws on an unpublished report (Hawkes nd) by K Reilly based on his and J Coy's analysis of the medieval and post-medieval animal bone assemblages from nine sites in the centre of Salisbury (**Table 3.3**). These provided a total of 7557 identified fragments of mostly hand-recovered bone but also some sieved material. The condition of the bone from all nine sites is consistently good, but the results of analysis are constrained by the broad chronological date range and small size of the datasets from many of the sites.

Chequer	Site	Code	Medieval	Late medieval/ early post medieval	Post medieval
Rolfe's	Culver Street	W64	147	-	26
South of White Hart	Nos 8–10 St Ann Street	W116	-	-	33
Trinity	Gigant Street Car Park	W129	1291	144	4014
Rolfe's	No. 39 Brown Street	W139			
Rolfe's	Nos 47–51 Brown Street	W227			
Rolfe's	Gibbs Mew, No. 68 Gigant Street	W192			
Three Swans	Winchester Street–Rollestone Street	W246	137	-	363
North of White Horse	Belle Vue House	W290	293	-	520
New Street	New Canal	W345	-	-	589
Total					7557

Table 3.3 Quantification of animal bone assemblages by site from excavations 1984–90

Results

Livestock

Most (71%) of the identified bones are from livestock (**Tables 3.4 and 3.5**). There is little overall difference in the relative abundance of livestock between periods. Cattle and sheep/goat bones are present in near equal amounts and account for approximately 40% each in both the medieval and post-medieval assemblages. There is, however, some variation in the relative abundance of livestock between sites (**Figs 3.9 and 3.10**).

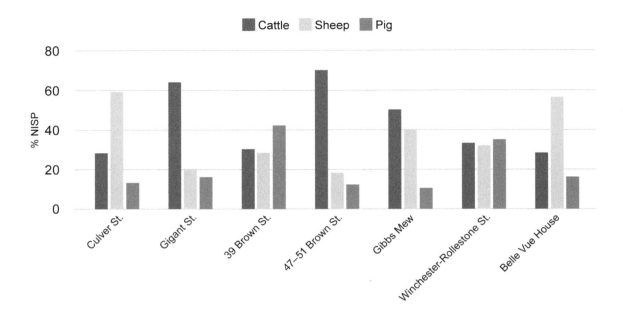

Figure 3.9 Relative importance of livestock from medieval deposits by site

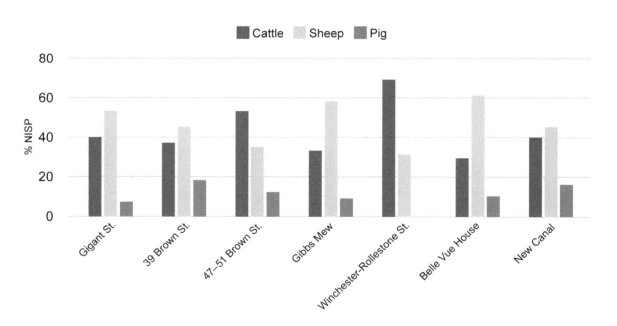

Figure 3.10 Relative importance of livestock from post-medieval deposits by site

Medieval deposits in Culver Street and Belle Vue House (both peripheral locations) have sheep/goat bone counts of over 50% NISP, while several of the assemblages from sites in Trinity Chequer (eg, Gigant Street, Gibbs Mew and Nos 47–51 Brown Street) have high cattle bone counts of 50% or more. The assemblage from Nos 47–51 Brown Street is, however, skewed by large dumps of industrial waste from tanning and horn-working. The small data sets from No. 39 Brown Street and Winchester/Rollestone Street should be treated with caution.

Post-medieval deposits show a more consistent pattern, with high sheep/goat bone counts recorded for almost all sites apart from Winchester/Rollestone Street and Nos 47–51 Brown Street, which have high cattle bone counts of between 53% and 69%, although once again the assemblage from Brown Street includes deposits of industrial waste that skew the dataset. The relative proportion of sheep/goat bones at the other sites is between 45% and 61% and no doubt reflects the ready availability of mutton. Sheep produced not only wool but also provided an invaluable source of manure; flocks folded on arable land provided vital nutrients to the traditional sheep-and-corn husbandry that was practised on the chalklands. Pig bone counts are consistently low at between 7% and 18%.

Plate 3.4 Sheep grazing on local downs would have been a familiar sight around medieval Salisbury

The assemblage includes few complete mandibles, so mortality profiles are based on the epiphyseal fusion of post-cranial elements. This information indicates that a significant proportion of cattle and sheep/goat were slaughtered between the ages of two and three years but most survived to maturity. Using O'Connor's (1982, 29) diagnostic index to sex sheep, it is evident that male wethers were selected for slaughter at a younger age than ewes, and that ewes were kept in greater numbers. This is consistent with sheep having been primarily raised and managed for wool production.

Similar information for cattle (Thomas 1988, 86) indicates that most were oxen or bulls, although much of this information comes from industrial deposits of horn cores and these are likely to have been selectively procured (see below). Most pigs were slaughtered as immature or juvenile animals. The Brown Street assemblage includes several bones from suckling pigs less than six months of age and this evidence suggests that pigs were probably being reared by individual households in the backyards of properties (Albarella 2006). Similar evidence has been recorded elsewhere in Salisbury (Higbee 2016).

Biometric data indicates that there was little or no change in the size or conformation of cattle between periods but a slight increase in the size of sheep/goat. These changes might be linked to improvements in animal husbandry brought about by the agricultural revolution, the effects of which have been noted at other sites in southern England (Albarella and Davis 1996, 42–57).

Dumps of cattle horn cores, and cattle and sheep/goat metapodials and phalanges, came from medieval and post-medieval deposits at Nos 47–51 Brown Street. This material is typical of the waste generated from horn-working, tanning and possibly the production of neatsfoot oil used by leather-dressers (MacGregor 1985, 119; Serjeantson 1989, 139; Harman 1996, 89). Particularly large dumps came from four post-medieval pits towards the rear of No. 51 Brown Street, and are likely to represent waste from craft related activity connected to an individual or family, possibly John Leminge, a skinner, who occupied the premises after 1628. The distal ends of cattle metapodials were also used in the construction of a 13th–14th-century floor surface (616) at this site. Industrial deposits have been recorded from other sites in Trinity Chequer (Hamilton-Dyer 2000, 48) and from Vanner's and Griffin Chequers on the periphery of the medieval city (Higbee 2016).

Analysis of the horn cores indicates a range of sizes, but the larger specimens from male castrates are more abundant, particularly in the post-medieval assemblage. The city's craft guilds are likely to have had control over the supply network in carcass by-products and it is likely that related industries clustered together as has been found in other urban areas (Yeomans 2005; 2007). Further details relating to the large horn core assemblage are available in K Reilly's archive report.

Species	Rolfe's	Trinity	Three Swans	White Horse	Total
cattle	33	626	38	73	770
sheep/goat	70	242	36	145	493
pig	16	169	40	43	268
horse	-	2	-	-	2
fallow deer	-	3	4	-	7
roe deer	-	1	-	-	1
dog	1	1	-	-	2
cat	-	2	-	1	3
rabbit/hare	4	14	3	8	29
rat	-	10	-	-	10
chicken	16	68	11	17	112
goose	5	30	5	2	42
duck	-	5	-	-	5
crow	-	2	-	-	2
dove	1	4	-	-	5
pheasant	-	1	-	-	1
swan	-	1	-	-	1
thrush	-	2	-	-	2
woodcock	-	1	-	-	1
conger eel	-	25	-	3	28
flatfish	-	1	-	-	1
gurnard	-	3	-	1	4
haddock	-	4	-	-	4
hake	-	1	-	-	1
herring	-	59	-	-	59
ling	-	1	-	-	1
salmon	-	5	-	-	5
scad	-	3	-	-	3
sea bream	-	2	-	-	2
wrasse	-	3	-	-	3
amphibian	1	-	-	-	1
Total identified	147	1291	137	293	1868

Table 3.4 Number of identified animal bones (or NISP) from medieval deposits by Chequer

Species	Trinity*	Rolfe's	White Hart	Trinity	Three Swans	White Horse	New Canal	Total
cattle	25	5	4	1293	251	143	207	1928
sheep/goat	7	7	11	1262	112	296	233	1928
pig	76	6	2	408	-	48	82	622
horse	-	-	-	5	-	1	-	6
red/fallow deer	2	-	-	4	-	-	8	14
roe deer	-	-	-	1	-	-	-	1
dog	-	-	-	-	-	3	3	6
cat	2	-	-	11	-	-	5	18
rabbit/hare	15	1	2	108	-	6	7	139
rat/mouse	-	4	-	14	-	-	-	18
chicken	14	3	7	209	-	16	31	280
goose	1	-	-	17	-	2	2	22
duck	1	-	1	4	-	-	1	7
dove	-	-	-	4	-	2	-	6
heron	-	-	-	-	-	-	1	1
raven	-	-	-	-	-	-	1	1
snipe	-	-	-	2	-	-	-	2
starling	-	-	-	2	-	-	-	2
swan	-	-	-	1	-	-	-	1
thrush	-	-	-	2	-	-	-	2
turkey	-	-	-	1	-	-	-	1
woodcock	-	-	-	1	-	1	-	2
bass	-	-	-	2	-	-	-	2
cod	-	-	2	12	-	2	6	22
conger eel	-	-	-	23	-	-	-	23
eel	-	-	-	177	-	-	-	177
flatfish	-	-	-	20	-	-	-	20
gurnard	-	-	1	13	-	-	-	14
haddock	-	-	-	6	-	-	-	6
hake	-	-	1	6	-	-	-	7
herring	-	-	-	362	-	-	-	362
ling	1	-	-	3	-	-	2	6
mackerel	-	-	1	14	-	-	-	15
pollock	-	-	1	-	-	-	-	1
ray	-	-	-	4	-	-	-	4
salmon	-	-	-	6	-	-	-	6
scad	-	-	-	11	-	-	-	11
sea bream	-	-	-	3	-	-	-	3
wrasse	-	-	-	3	-	-	-	3
Total identified	144	26	33	4014	363	363	589	5689

Table 3.5 Number of identified animal bones (by NISP) from late medieval to early post-medieval* (Trinity Chequer) and post-medieval deposits in all Chequers

Other mammals

Bones from a small range of other mammals were also found; these account for approximately 3.5% NISP of the medieval and post-medieval assemblages. The most significant are those that were occasionally eaten, including red, roe and fallow deer, with hare and rabbit, the last a species that could be obtained from managed warrens (Hamilton-Dyer 2005). The availability of venison was restricted but certain cuts were gifted to those directly involved in the hunt (Sykes 2007) and this might explain the presence of deer bones from the Trinity, Three Swans and New Street assemblages, and indeed some indication of the socio-economic status of some of the inhabitants of these areas. The other mammals include domesticates such as horse, dog and cat, and commensal species such as rodents.

Birds

Bird bones account for 11.4% and 4.7% NISP of the medieval and post-medieval assemblages respectively. Chicken bones dominate and account for between 66% and 85% NISP. Most were adult hens kept primarily for their eggs. Goose bones are also common from medieval deposits and account for 24% NISP. These species clearly formed part of the domestic household. Chandler (1983, 166) notes that instructions were issued in 1418 that 'pigs, geese and chickens' should not be allowed to roam freely beyond the boundaries of the home. A range of other species are present, including game birds such as pheasant, woodcock, snipe and wild duck, commensals such as crow and raven, and small garden birds such as thrush and starling. Bones from a few unusual and highly prized birds were also recovered. These include swan from medieval and post-medieval deposits at Gigant Street, heron from post-medieval deposits at New Canal and turkey from a post-medieval deposit in Three Swans Chequer.

Fish

Most of the fish bones came from sites in Trinity Chequer, where deposits were routinely sieved to improve the recovery of small bones. Fish bones account for between 6.8% and 11.9% NISP of the medieval and post-medieval assemblages respectively. Most are marine species but there are also some migratory species (eel and salmon) that could have been caught more locally.

Herring bones are common and account for over 50% NISP in both periods. Conger eel is also relatively common (at 22%) in the medieval assemblages from sites in Trinity Chequer and Belle Vue House, and eel (26%) in the post-medieval assemblage from 39 Brown Street. A diverse range of other fish was available in the city, particularly during the post-medieval period. The most common types are gurnard, scad, mackerel and flatfish.

Conclusions

Salisbury's meat market was well supplied with cattle and sheep/goat from the rural hinterland. The cattle came from herds kept for secondary products and traction, and the sheep/goat from flocks primarily managed for wool and manure. Pigs were raised in the city, most probably in backyard areas by individual households, and are ideally suited to this type of husbandry, offering a relatively low-cost means of producing meat since they can be fed on kitchen scraps. They are equally suited to foraging in the streets (Albarella 2006, 79), although this was not permitted in Salisbury, where households were instructed to confine their stock within the boundaries of the home (Chandler 1983, 166).

The cattle market, which may have included other livestock, was held at Barnards Cross in the south-east corner of the city and close to Trinity Chequer. Butchers were ordered in the 15th century to slaughter their beasts in the open space behind Butcher Row, possibly to allow blood and other effluent to drain into the Town Ditch/New Canal (Crittall 1962, 86).

In addition to beef, mutton and pork, some game (venison, hare and rabbit) was also eaten but most variety came in the form of poultry and fish. Domestic poultry, particularly chickens, were kept by individual households, most probably for their eggs, with meat a secondary consideration. Swan, heron and turkey were also recorded. These birds would have been expensive to purchase (Albarella and Thomas 2002; Poole 2010) and indicate the presence of wealthy residents in Trinity, New Street and Three Swans Chequers.

Most of the fish bones recovered from Salisbury are from marine species and these are likely to have come through the port of Southampton (Hamilton-Dyer 2000, 50), although Leland commented that fish caught as far away as the River Tamar was also sold at Salisbury market (Leland, cited in Crittall 1962). Much of this commodity probably arrived in Salisbury as preserved salted codfish, pickled herring or even smoked conger eel. Conger eels were regarded as a highly prized delicacy in the medieval period and the relatively high number of bones from sites in Trinity Chequer and Belle Vue House (although this is peripheral with no clear evidence of residential use) provide a further indication that these areas were home to some wealthy residents. Hamilton-Dyer (2005) has noted the considerable demand for and supply of eels from Southampton in the 15th century to many of the towns and cities of southern England as recorded in Brokage Books of the period (Stevens and Olding 1985).

Industrial processes such as tanning and horn-working appear on the present evidence to have been concentrated in Trinity Chequer and out towards the periphery of the city (Higbee 2016). Horn-working may have been closely linked to the cutlery industry, for which Salisbury gained a reputation (Chandler 1983). These industries may have provided some of the wealth enjoyed by those living in Trinity Chequer during the medieval and post-medieval periods, allowing access to some of the luxury food stuffs recovered from these excavations.

The apparent lack of municipal waste disposal practices led to the accumulation of midden material and industrial waste within the chequers (Barber 2005, 206). The animal bones from meals eaten in the many households around the city provide information about the diets of the residents and in some instances an indication of their socio-economic status. Industrial processes, including those involving carcass by-products, were carried out close to residential areas and must have added significantly to the noisome smells within the city.

Chapter 4
Discussion

by Phil Harding, Lorraine Mepham and Lorrain Higbee

Introduction

The history of Salisbury has been admirably and vividly described by Chandler (1983), who approached the story from a documentary perspective. The study ably complemented the description given by the RCHME (1980), which reconstructed the medieval city using results of an architectural survey of extant buildings, supplemented by data from documentary sources (**Fig. 4.1**). A more concise, but nevertheless well-conducted, survey of the city buildings has also been undertaken by Orbach *et al.* (2021). These surveys have recognised that many buildings were of multi-period construction, but the results nevertheless have confirmed the distribution and survival of medieval timber-framed buildings, most notably in the central part of the city; 14 examples of such buildings, dated to the 14th century, remain extant. Many of these structures were redeveloped and ultimately replaced in brick from the 18th century, when this material became more readily available. Other medieval timber-framed buildings have been disguised behind claddings of mathematical tiles, which outwardly resemble bricks, but which are a feature of some buildings in the city. The survey contains details of many medieval buildings that survived from the medieval period, but which were regrettably demolished in the 1960s. The archaeology of standing buildings has developed immeasurably since the survey was undertaken and is now recognised as a discipline of archaeology that can be incorporated more readily into results from excavations. These embryonic studies were undertaken before the onset of systematic excavations in the city; indeed the RCHME (*ibid.*, xliv) conceded that this approach provided the only realistic hope of being able to reconstruct original ground plans of lost buildings with evidence of associated outbuildings. The narrative can now be supplemented by results of excavations that begin to illustrate Salisbury's story from the archaeological perspective. However, this narrative would be incomplete without reference to the record of human communities who occupied the locality long before the city was founded. The traces of their existence are recorded in data held in the Wiltshire and Swindon Historic Environment Record (HER), which contains a comprehensive catalogue of archaeological sites, monuments and finds that relate to the county.

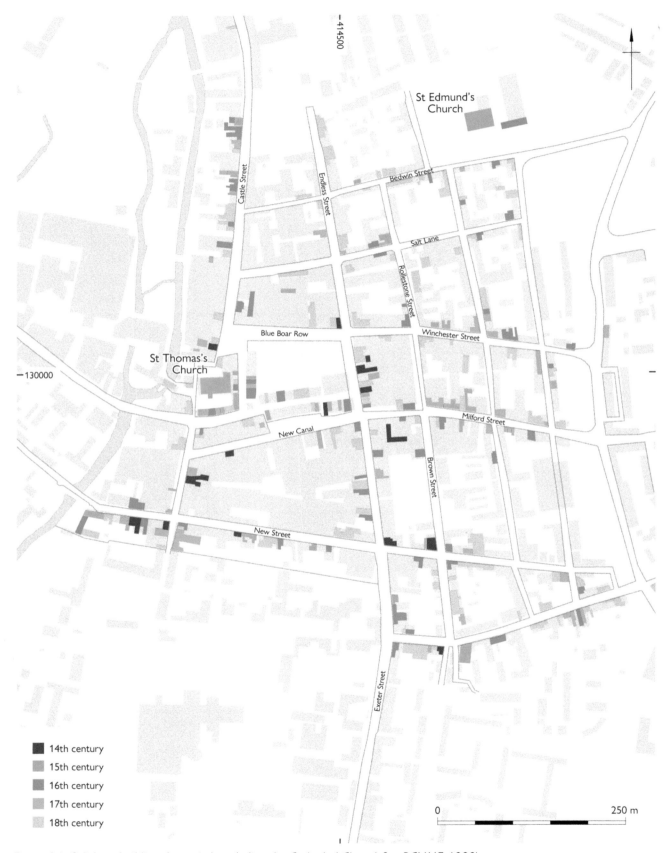

Figure 4.1 Salisbury buildings by period, excluding the Cathedral Close (after RCHME 1980)

The foundations of the excavation dataset for Salisbury were laid by investigations undertaken by the Salisbury Museum Archaeology Rescue Group (SMARG) during construction of Salisbury's Inner Ring Road in the 1960s and early 1970s. Additional, more systematic, excavations were carried out between 1984 and 1990, the completion of which is contained in this report and is long overdue. These pioneering projects constituted the first systematic attempts (Cave-Penney 2005) to recover archaeological data relating to the development of the city of Salisbury. Sadly, they were undertaken within a structure and at a time before developer-funded archaeological work became part of the planning process and when the need for funding to complete post-excavation analysis was less rigorously pursued. Hawkes (nd) assessed the results of the 1984–90 work, which was primarily concentrated in the Trinity Chequer, and considered that they were restricted in quality, quantity and extent. He stated that they failed to provide a sufficiently representative sample with which to reconstruct the range and character of domestic buildings in the city. In addition, he noted, at a site-specific level, the scarcity of diagnostic artefacts, which restricted the reconstruction of reliable chronologies. Finally, he considered that the absence of any investigations of courtyard buildings and the lack of work within 'prime locations' (*ibid.*, 5), most notably High Street and Market Place, provided a poorly balanced view of the medieval city. This somewhat unduly negative assessment was only partially true and failed to fully address the available information, including any related documentary material that existed. Despite the limitations, these excavations document work that might otherwise not have been undertaken; they deserve recognition. Standards of excavation in the intervening period have improved and, although work on 'prime locations' remains desirable, the quantity of excavated data has increased (Algar and Saunders 2012; 2014; Barber 2005; Butterworth 2005a; 2005b; 2005c; Cotswold Archaeology 2017; Currie and Rushton 2005; Garland *et al.* 2021; Harding 2016; Rawlings 2000; Saunders and Algar 2015; 2017). These excavations, some of which have been accompanied by detailed documentary research (Chandler 2013; 2015; 2016), have been of limited extent. Small-scale projects remain the norm, but these have been supplemented by more expansive excavations (Garland *et al.* 2021; Harding 2016) where trench locations and extent have been determined by the position of new buildings. Nevertheless, a large-scale area excavation remains to be commissioned within the city. The completion of these projects has created a vast database, which also includes grey literature reports, that allows the body of unpublished material to be placed in context. The collective results can also incorporate distributions of extant medieval buildings to create a combined view with which to reconstruct the development of the city.

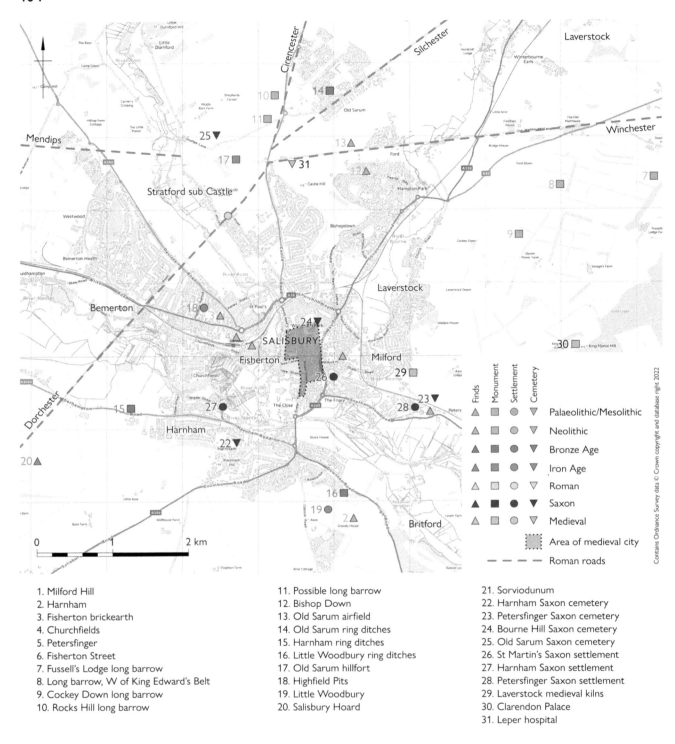

Figure 4.2 Selected sites in the surrounding landscape

1. Milford Hill
2. Harnham
3. Fisherton brickearth
4. Churchfields
5. Petersfinger
6. Fisherton Street
7. Fussell's Lodge long barrow
8. Long barrow, W of King Edward's Belt
9. Cockey Down long barrow
10. Rocks Hill long barrow

11. Possible long barrow
12. Bishop Down
13. Old Sarum airfield
14. Old Sarum ring ditches
15. Harnham ring ditches
16. Little Woodbury ring ditches
17. Old Sarum hillfort
18. Highfield Pits
19. Little Woodbury
20. Salisbury Hoard

21. Sorviodunum
22. Harnham Saxon cemetery
23. Petersfinger Saxon cemetery
24. Bourne Hill Saxon cemetery
25. Old Sarum Saxon cemetery
26. St Martin's Saxon settlement
27. Harnham Saxon settlement
28. Petersfinger Saxon settlement
29. Laverstock medieval kilns
30. Clarendon Palace
31. Leper hospital

The Blank Canvas

The Salisbury landscape remains dominated by five rivers, which have drawn people to the area for thousands of years. The Rivers Wylye and Nadder meet at Wilton before flowing to join the Rivers Avon and Bourne at Salisbury, with the River Ebble joining further downstream (**Fig. 1.1**). Traces of the earliest human presence, pre-dating the foundation of the medieval city, are dotted across the valley slopes at Bemerton, Fisherton and Milford Hill (Wessex Archaeology 1992b) adjoining the segment of the River Avon floodplain that was adopted to accommodate the city of Salisbury. Many of these discoveries were made in the 19th century and have remained poorly understood until systematic archaeological methods have become available to clarify them. The provenance of Lower and Middle Palaeolithic (900,000–40,000 years ago) hand axes, collected by H P Blackmore on Milford Hill during the construction of Victorian villas, remained unresolved until 1995. Excavations (Harding and Bridgland 1998), which produced a hand axe, on the top of Milford Hill (**Fig. 4.2, 1**) at the Godolphin School (**Pl. 4.1**, **left**), showed that the implements were contained within deposits that had been laid down by the River Avon. The study has been supplemented by additional investigations in the immediate area, including work in the grounds of the former Youth Hostel (Wessex Archaeology 2018b), which have now produced detailed sections of the terrace deposits (**Pl. 4.1**, **right**).

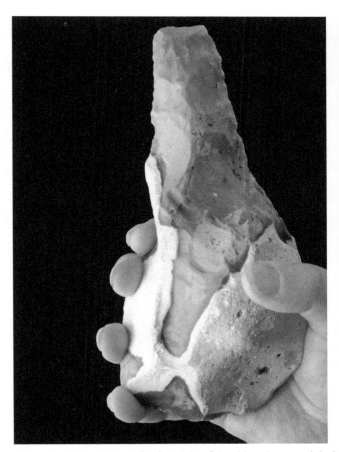

Plate 4.1 Milford Hill: (left) Godolphin School hand axe and (right) section at the Youth Hostel/Milford Hill House showing the bedded river gravel deposits

The date these hand axes were made and deposited remains uncertain; however, they have been linked (Harding and Bridgland 1998) within the River Avon terrace sequence to discoveries at Harnham (**Fig 4.2, 2**; Bates *et al.* 2014), where dating is more precise. Excavations uncovered undisturbed manufacturing debris from the production of hand axes, together with environmental evidence that was dated by a variety of techniques to approximately 250,000 years ago (Egberts *et al.* 2020).

Human presence in the Salisbury area remained intermittent, leaving few traces and fluctuating according to the advance or retreat of successive ice sheets as glacial and interglacial periods alternated. Interest resurfaces at Fisherton (**Fig. 4.2, 3**), where remarkable preservation of animal remains, including a diverse range of mammals (Stevens 1870) including mammoth, reindeer, lion and hyaena, have been found with bird bones, eggshell and molluscs. These discoveries were made during extraction of sandy silt for brick manufacture in the 19th century. The importance of the site was increased by the discovery of a distinctive type of flint hand axe, a bout coupé, a type that has been associated with Neanderthal groups living approximately 50,000 years ago. The date of the Fisherton 'brickearth' has been debated extensively, but two samples have been dated using Optically Stimulated Luminescence (OSL) techniques, which establish the time when quartz sediment was last exposed to light. The results provided dates of 47±8 Ka BP (GL13001) and 56±9 Ka BP (GL13002) (TVAS 2014b), coinciding with a time, dated by deep sea cores, when there was a transition from a cold to warm climatic period approximately 50,000 years ago.

The final phases of the last glaciation, approximately 10,000–12,000 years ago, brought people back to the area at the end of the final episode of cold conditions. Evidence of these incursions, associated with the Late and Final Upper Palaeolithic periods in Europe, is extremely rare, being represented in the River Avon valley by worked flint assemblages at Nea Farm, Somerley, Hampshire (Barton *et al.* 2009) and Hengistbury Head, Dorset (Barton 1992). A previously poorly documented collection of similar material from Churchfields (**Fig. 4.2, 4**; Harding and Barton 2021) on the west side of the city can now be added to this corpus. The assemblage, which was apparently found in 1860, is remarkable for the fact that it includes artefacts that can be fitted back together (**Pl. 4.2**), demonstrating that the site was previously undisturbed. The collection is of added interest by the inclusion of a blade, apparently made of Greensand chert, a raw material that is readily available in the Vale of Wardour, approximately 8 km to the west of Salisbury. The blade, which measures 116 mm long, can now be linked with a similar blade, also of Greensand chert, 104 mm long and also thought to be Upper Palaeolithic, from West Amesbury (Pettitt with Chan 2020). These isolated occurrences help to extend the movement of people along the valley network from the Salisbury area at a time when evidence of human presence is scarce.

Plate 4.2 Churchfields: Upper Palaeolithic refitting flint blades, dorsal and ventral views

The importance of the collection from Churchfields has been enhanced by the discovery of material of potentially similar date found during a routine archaeological evaluation at Petersfinger (**Fig. 4.2, 5**; Wessex Archaeology 2019b). It is not certain precisely how these two discoveries relate to one another in time, but they have added significantly to the distribution of sites that pre-date the Mesolithic period (9000–4000 BC), within the River Avon valley. They clearly demonstrate the importance of serendipity in the discovery of these small clusters of isolated material. The collective results have shown that low terraces bordering the flood plain, which at Churchfields and Petersfinger are both at confluence points in the river system, may have been selected preferentially as locations for occupation. Excavations within Salisbury have also indicated continued human activity into the Mesolithic period; flint knapping waste has been identified in the area now occupied by Fisherton Street (**Fig. 4.2, 6**; Wessex Archaeology 2007a). This small sample joins material collected from Downton (Higgs 1959) and, more recently, from Amesbury (Jacques *et al.* 2018; Leivers and Moore 2008), highlighting the potential of the River Avon valley and its tributaries to contain material of this period.

The arrival of more settled communities soon after 4000 BC, bringing funerary monuments (Ashbee 1966) and traces of more formalised settlement into the archaeological record, is well represented in the area, the most easily recognised features being the long barrow burial mounds. The Wiltshire and Swindon Historic Environment Record (HER) lists five confirmed or suspected long barrows immediately north and east of Salisbury, of which all have been flattened by prolonged ploughing (**Fig. 4.2, 7–11; Pl. 4.3**).

Plate 4.3 Possible Early Neolithic long barrow (Gill 2021) immediately north of Old Sarum. Originally identified from aerial photographs, the monument may be seen as two parallel lines of darker green, aligned obliquely to the tractor 'tram-lines', separated by an area of more chalky soil, possibly remains of the mound

Studies of the valley sediments at Amesbury (French *et al.* 2012) indicate that some parts of the river valley itself were markedly different in the third millennium BC to those of the modern flood plain. The valley bottoms and flood plains were probably colonised by alder and hazel carr with sedges, while the upper slopes comprised mixed woodland and open grassland, which eventually dominated the surrounding area.

The rate at which archaeological discoveries have been made has increased rapidly in recent years, especially across the chalk uplands. New monuments have been recognised from both aerial surveys and archaeological fieldwork as new housing developments have taken place beyond the expanding city boundaries (Headland Archaeology 2019a; 2019b; Powell *et al.* 2005; Powell 2015; Wessex Archaeology 2014e). This is amply demonstrated by the distribution of Bronze Age round barrows, of which the Victoria County History listed 17 examples (Grinsell 1957) in the area defined in **Figure 4.2**. These monuments were primarily extant but included a number that had been ploughed flat and survived as 'ring ditches'. The HER for the same area now catalogues 53 ring ditches, mostly new additions, that have been identified following prolonged study of aerial photographs, geophysical surveys and archaeological evaluations; 16 of these were concentrated in the flood plain of the River Nadder immediately west of Harnham (**Fig. 4.2, 15**; Headland Archaeology 2019a; 2019b). Most of these new discoveries remain undated, although their distribution, across the chalk downs and overlooking the river valleys, make it likely that some, at least, represent traces of long-lost Bronze Age burial mounds.

The picture of rural settlement is one of continuity within an evolving agricultural landscape, spreading from foundations in the Neolithic period before the adoption of more formal field systems in the Middle and Late Bronze Age, which persisted to the Romano-British period. Evidence of prehistoric activity has increased most noticeably in the area around Bishopdown (**Fig. 4.2, 12**; Wessex Archaeology 2014e), on slopes overlooking the River Bourne valley, where an Early Neolithic burial, Middle Neolithic pits and Middle Bronze Age burials (**Pl. 4.4**) have been uncovered. The later prehistoric evidence suggests occupation of the site continued into the Early Iron Age. These discoveries have extended to the fringes of Old Sarum Airfield (**Fig. 4.2, 13**; Wessex Archaeology 2015), where a Middle Neolithic pit containing a large assemblage of Fengate ware pottery and worked flint was also found, and further north-west (**Fig. 4.2, 14**), where Early Bronze Age ring ditches, former burial mounds flattened by ploughing, were excavated (**Pl. 4.5**; Wessex Archaeology 2006b). Similar levels of prehistoric activity have also become apparent on the lower valley sides and the flood plain of the River Nadder, immediately west of Harnham, where Bronze Age ring ditches and Iron Age enclosures have also been reported (**Fig. 4.2, 15**; Headland Archaeology 2019a; 2019b). Evidence of burial use extending from the Bronze Age into the Iron Age has also been confirmed near Little Woodbury (**Fig. 4.2, 16**; Powell 2015) where Bronze Age ring ditches and Iron Age burials were found on the same site.

Plate 4.4 Bishopdown: Bronze Age crouched inhumation burial

Plate 4.5 Old Sarum: intercutting Bronze Age ring ditches

These broad studies have not only helped understanding of landscape development but also allowed access to the people themselves. This is possible not only through analysis of funerary practices (Powell 2015) but also with increasing use of ever-improving scientific techniques, most notably isotope analysis, which can provide evidence of where incoming populations originated (Fitzpatrick 2011). Increased artefact assemblages from refuse pits (Powell *et al.* 2005) allow greater access to evidence of industry, economy and trade.

Plate 4.6 Old Sarum hillfort with remains of the Norman castle (centre) and cathedral (right) within the Iron Age ramparts

Many monuments in the landscape remain as upstanding earthworks, most familiarly Neolithic and Bronze Age burial mounds and the impressive Iron Age ramparts of Old Sarum (**Fig. 4.2, 17; Pl. 4.6**). This site was subsequently adopted as an Anglo-Saxon mint before providing defences for the castle, which was constructed following the Norman Conquest, and constitutes a significant component in the story of Salisbury. Archaeological investigations at this important monument have been limited, being restricted to revealing the principal buildings of the castle and the foundations of the old cathedral by W H St J Hope between 1909 and 1915 (Hawley 1912; 1913; 1915; Hope 1910; 1911; 1914; 1916). Excavations also took place subsequently in the eastern suburbs (Stone and Charlton 1935) and at the eastern gateway (Rahtz and Musty 1960; Musty and Rahtz 1964). Interest in the area resurfaced in 2014 when a project was launched by the Universities of Southampton and Swansea to undertake geophysical surveys (Langlands et al. 2018; Strutt et al. 2014) within the castle and the surrounding landscape, with supplementary trenching in the fields outside the ramparts towards Stratford sub Castle. This project highlighted the density of medieval buildings within the ramparts and extramural settlement along the approach roads. A series of relatively small-scale excavations have evaluated these geophysical results outside the west gate extending down to the River Avon flood plain (Langlands and Strutt in prep.). This concentrated archaeological fieldwork has made it possible to focus attention away from the high-status occupants at Old Sarum onto other elements of the population, both religious and secular. The evidence spans the period before, during and after the use of Old Sarum as a cathedral city and its transfer from the old to new city.

Iron Age settlement has been an established part of the archaeological story on the fringes of the valley immediately overlooking the city for many years. Iron Age features were discovered in the mid-1860s when Salisbury was expanding beyond its medieval boundaries. These discoveries included traces of an extensive Iron Age enclosure in the area between Highfield Road and Devizes Road on the ridge overlooking the confluence of the Rivers Avon and Nadder (**Fig. 4.2, 18**). The site was enclosed by a V-shaped ditch, 4.40 m across and approximately 1.90 m deep, with pits, known as the 'Highfield Pits' (Stevens 1934), which were thought, erroneously, to have been prehistoric dwellings. Human remains were also found. Opportunities to confirm these findings, establishing the extent of the settlement and increasing the quantity of Middle Iron Age domestic refuse, have been provided only when properties in this area have been redeveloped (Wessex Archaeology 2000; 2014d).

The most crucial contribution to Iron Age studies from the Salisbury area arose from excavations at Little Woodbury (**Fig. 4.2, 19**; Bersu 1940), an enclosure where Iron Age round houses were recognised in Britain for the first time. Subsequently, excavations (Powell 2015) in advance of housebuilding have found traces of contemporary agricultural activity in the surrounding area, including a boundary ditch with fence lines and pit digging, possibly related to chalk quarrying. Most significantly, nine Iron Age inhumation burials were also found.

Perhaps the most unusual find of Iron Age date in the immediate area was the discovery of the Salisbury Hoard on the outskirts of Harnham (**Fig. 4.2, 20**). This find (Stead 1998), which was discovered illegally using a metal detector, contained approximately 600 pieces of Bronze Age and Iron Age bronze metalwork, making it one of the largest collections of this type and date to be found in Britain. The collection, which included objects that had been manufactured over a period spanning 2000 years, had finally been buried in a pit in about 200 BC. It contained socketed axes, spear heads, daggers and gouges, as well as a number of miniature shields and cauldrons, objects of exceptional rarity. Supplementary excavations after the discovery established that the hoard was buried within an area of Iron Age settlement, which provided invaluable context for the discovery.

The local Iron Age lifestyle flourished into the Romano-British period, when occupation based around the river crossing in the valley below Old Sarum was established at Stratford sub Castle (**Fig. 4.2, 21**). Excavations at this settlement, Sorviodunum, have been limited, due primarily to the fact that much of the Romano-British settlement underlies the modern residential area; however, small excavations in 1965 (Algar 1970, 208) revealed traces of timber-framed buildings fronting onto the Portway Roman road with pottery dating from the 1st to 4th century AD. This Romano-British community lived in the shadow of Old Sarum, which served as a hub for the local road network with links to towns at Cirencester, Silchester, Winchester and Dorchester, with other connections to the Mendips, an important source of lead. These routes can still be traced in the landscape; however, few opportunities have been found to confirm their survival or construction by excavation. Traces of the Portway, leading north from Old Sarum, have been confirmed (Wessex Archaeology 2007b) by archaeological evaluation at the Old Sarum Airfield. Parts of the raised carriageway, the 'agger', survived, showing that it was constructed of flint and chalk with gravel capping and was defined by flanking ditches 23 m apart.

Post-Roman activity in the area was centred on populations that persisted at Old Sarum but also developed in the Anglo-Saxon burgh and nunnery at Wilton (De'Athe 2012). Traces of contemporary activity within the area of the future medieval city are rare; excavations from the period 1984–90 and subsequent work have recovered only faint traces. Two sherds of Early–Middle Anglo-Saxon pottery, which may have derived from the common field *Myrifield*, were found during redevelopment work in the Old George Mall (Butterworth 2005a). More predictably, a residual sherd of pottery was recovered from Culver Street (W64), and redeposited material, including a loom weight fragment and pottery dating from the 10th–12th century, was found to the rear of Damascus and Emmaus Houses (Reynolds and Manning 2013). These discoveries were made in the south-east fringes of the city and were probably derived from the adjacent, documented Anglo-Saxon settlement centred around St Martin's Church

(**Fig. 4.2, 26**). Furthermore, Anglo-Saxon settlement is likely to have existed in the form of hamlets, manors or farms elsewhere along the fringes of the flood plain. This included occupation at the crossing point of the River Bourne at Milford, from which it has been conjectured (Langlands 2014) that similar activity, including the presence of a minster, may have occurred at the bridging point of the River Avon around the Bishop's Mill and the future site of St Thomas's Church. Anglo-Saxon cemeteries have been found on Bourne Hill (**Fig. 4.2, 24**; Wessex Archaeology 2003), Petersfinger (**Fig. 4.2, 23**; Leeds and Shortt 1954; Saunders and Algar 2020) and Harnham (**Fig. 4.2, 22**; Akerman 1854), with another further down the Avon valley at Charlton Plantation (Davies 1984). Two other graves, of late 5th- or early 6th-century date, were found north of Old Sarum (**Fig. 4.2, 25**; Eagles *et al.* 2014) with the likelihood that they were related to an associated settlement in the River Avon valley. Confirmed traces of associated contemporary settlement have been located at Petersfinger (**Fig. 4.2, 28**; AC Archaeology 2009) and Harnham (**Fig. 4.2, 27**; Wessex Archaeology 2006a). Settlement at Fisherton can also be included through evidence contained in Saxon charters.

Early Development

The underlying story involving the removal of the cathedral and associated settlement from Old Sarum to the present location as a planned city is well known. The project provided preferential treatment for the new cathedral. This building was located within a massive Close (**Pl. 4.7**) that occupied 33 hectares (83 acres) and constituted 32% of the land allocated for the new city (RCHME 1993).

Plate 4.7 Showing the extent of the Close, bordered by the River Avon (bottom) and with the cathedral dominant

The adoption of a 'green field' site for the construction of this new settlement, dating back only 800 years, contrasts markedly with other major medieval cities, including York, Winchester or Exeter, which can trace their origins for at least 2000 years to the Roman period or beyond. However, as Chandler (1983, 17) has stressed, Salisbury was not alone and accompanied a succession of new towns at Devizes, Downton, Hindon and Stockbridge, which were established and became economically viable in the early 13th century. The reduced timeframe since the foundation of the city, together with the fact that many later medieval timber-framed buildings remain extant, means that deep stratigraphy is frequently not well represented in Salisbury. Furthermore, excavations have frequently noted that stratigraphic boundaries are often poorly defined, making precise dating by pottery difficult to achieve. Mepham and Underwood (nd) lamented that nine sites excavated before 1990 produced fewer than 1000 sherds from well-stratified contexts. This situation has improved with additional excavations, although as Mepham has emphasised (see Chapter 3), the availability of good reference collections remains woefully inadequate. Despite these caveats the limited information provided by the artefacts does illuminate the story the surviving deposits can tell.

Chandler (1983), using work by K H Rogers (1969) and the RCHME (1980), conjectured two phases of development within the city proceeding from initial construction in an area south of New Canal and centred on New Street (**Fig. 4.3**). He considered that these areas were influenced by existing field and road boundaries within *Myrifield*. Daniell (in prep.) has conjectured that this embryonic settlement was defined by land contained within the Town Ditch and the Close Ditch, which itself enclosed the Close. Demand for property within the city apparently outstripped supply and expansion became necessary, a response indicated by subsequent and more carefully planned development in chequers north of Market Place and east of the Endless Street–Catherine Street line. The speed of development within the new city was apparently matched by a reciprocal reduction in occupation in extramural areas at Old Sarum. Excavations (Langlands and Strutt in prep.) outside the west gate and within the area of the probable canons' close have noted the scarcity of pottery dating to between the 14th and 16th century, suggesting that these former occupants had relocated to the new city by the late 13th century.

Chandler utilised documentary sources to place these rapid developments within the early part of the 13th century, a timespan that is hard to detect archaeologically. Structural and documentary evidence (RCHME 1980) confirms occupation was well established along High Street and the east side of Market Place, with an additional spread along Milford Street by the 14th century.

Figure 4.3 Aerial view of Salisbury from the south, showing extent of the medieval city with its distinctive chequer layout. The curving dual carriageway follows the approximate line of the city rampart

Beyond the limits of the city centre the picture is less clear and very little opportunity has arisen to test the detail archaeologically. Chandler (1983), citing documentary evidence, considered that extensive development was present along Fisherton Street by the 13th century. Speed's map clearly shows an unbroken row of buildings along the north side of the street by 1611, a view that is confirmed by Naish's survey of 1716, which similarly indicates that buildings, some with back ranges or courtyards, were well established along both sides of Fisherton Street by the early 18th century (**Fig. 4.7**, below). Very little of this evidence remains extant. Survey by the RCHME (1980) recorded isolated properties from the 16th century lining the street. These sources indicate that the arterial routes were undoubtedly developed at an early stage, although settlement otherwise remained within the limits of the planned city. The accuracy of Naish's survey was partially tested by a small trial excavation undertaken by Wessex Archaeology at Nos 30–36 Fisherton Street (Clarke and Baker 2020; Wessex Archaeology 2019a). The trench confirmed that the street frontage within the precinct of the Dominican friary, an area shown by Naish as undeveloped, remained in that condition until the early 18th century when make-up layers were introduced in preparation for the construction of a brick house. Trial excavations on the flood plain (Wessex Archaeology 1996a; 1996; 2005) have failed to locate traces of medieval occupation on the wider extramural fringes.

Development along the southern fringes of the city may also have been intermittent, although the archaeological evidence does little to clarify the issue. Speed's survey shows the south side of St Ann Street as undeveloped land, a fact contradicted by Naish together with extant buildings (RCHME 1980), most notably towards the west end of the street, which include examples dating from the 14th century. It is possible that development in the street was influenced by a number of factors, including the proximity of the Franciscan friary precinct, the cattle market at Barnard's Cross in the south-east corner of the city, and Bugmore, on the marshy fringes of the River Avon flood plain.

Expanded Layout

The expanded medieval city was based on a chequered grid system. Streets were laid out around a spacious marketplace, which became a focal point in the economy and administration of the city. Initially an open area, the market was subjected to infilling by temporary structures, which extant buildings indicate had become permanent by the 15th or 16th centuries. Most chequers were rectangular and were sub-divided into individual tenements along a north–south central axis. Individual tenements, measuring 7 x 3 perches (approximately 35 x 15 m) (Chandler 1983), were aligned east–west from the central axis. This pattern has been exposed most clearly in excavations at the former bus station (Chapter 2, **Figs 2.10–11**). Blair *et al.* (2020) have shown that this unit of measurement, the perch, was used throughout the Anglo-Saxon period, when it was used by monastic institutions and expanded to include planned nucleated villages and field systems. The 'long' perch (5.5 m) was apparently adopted as a standard measurement in Wessex in preference to the 'short' perch (4.57 m), which prevailed in eastern and central parts of Britain. They concluded that traces of systematic planning disappeared after the 11th century; however, the practical application of a gridded settlement in Salisbury may owe much to skills established by ecclesiastical communities. These influences may also be fossilised in the layout of the Close. Individual plots, as surveyed, varied in size according to the status of the occupant, and some properties, like tenements in the city, were amalgamated or sub-divided (RCHME 1993) throughout the medieval period. However, properties, most notably along the west side of the Close, retain boundaries which suggest that, following the pattern in the city, they were laid out with frontages approximately 7 perches (35 m) wide. Many of the extant buildings in the Close, especially on the west and north sides, retain remnants of their medieval core, which is now often encased in subsequent masonry and brickwork. This has restricted any opportunities to examine the foundations of these impressive structures, although small-scale excavations, including work by Musty (1963) and Wessex Archaeology (1994), have taken place on the east side of the Close in the area now occupied by Bishop Wordsworth's School. These excavations, with others undertaken subsequently that add little to the results, make this the most intensively examined part of the Close. Medieval wall foundations and rammed chalk floors have been revealed although no complete building plans have been compiled. Other excavations in this part of the Close have exposed the foundations of a 14th-century hall that formed part of the Vicar's Hall, close to the St Ann's Gate (Wessex Archaeology 2021). These small-scale projects have revealed the robust nature of foundations associated with stone and flint buildings within the Close, in contrast to those constructed to support the timber-framed structures that filled the city (**Pls 4.8 and 4.9**).

Plate 4.8 Wall foundations of the 14th-century Vicar's Hall. Typical of many high-status canons' houses in the Cathedral Close

Plate 4.9 Wall foundations of typical domestic dwellings in medieval Salisbury, as seen in Vanner's Chequer (Harding 2016). Scales: 1 m and 0.2 m

Hawkes (nd) noted that Trinity Chequer initially contained 27 standard tenements but, drawing on results of archaeological work at Nos 47–51 Brown Street (W227), where buildings were constructed with 5 m-wide frontages, considered that these had undoubtedly been sub-divided by the 14th century. Barber (2005) noted sub-divisions of a similar size at the Anchor Brewery site on Gigant Street, and also in Trinity Chequer, but postulated that they had been incorporated into the original building programme. The 'backlands' of No. 17 Rollestone Street may have been similarly sub-divided, although it is unclear when this may have occurred or whether it resulted in similar changes to street frontage properties. Chandler (1983, 50) cited documentary sources that show that tenement sub-divisions were relatively commonplace by 1455.

It is possible that this practice also moved in the opposite direction and that individual properties, as originally surveyed, were subsequently amalgamated, possibly to accommodate large properties for the wealthy. Chandler (2013) noted that Richard Gage, an alderman and cloth merchant, bequeathed land in Endless Street to the Weavers' Guild in a will of 1433. Chandler conjectured that this site, in the area of the former bus station, may have been given to create a hall for the guild. This body had been in existence from at least 1412 but became especially prominent in the 15th century, by which time it may have required a larger parcel of land. Excavations on the site of the former bus station (see Chapter 2, Salisbury Bus Station; Cotswold Archaeology 2017; Garland et al. 2021; Wessex Archaeology 2014a) failed to identify foundations that could be correlated with those of the Weavers' Guildhall. A lease of 1695 (Chandler 2013) describes the hall as comprising 'a court with a hall, two parlours next the street, the parlour within the hall, the buttery in the hall, the kitchen, the two larders within the kitchen, the malting floor on the south side of the court, the boiling room next to the cistern, the use of the pump, backside court and house of office'. It is unclear from this description whether the building was confined to the north-west corner of the chequer – No. 12 Endless Street – or was more expansive and occupied Nos 12 and 10, or that it intruded into properties facing onto Rollestone Street. Similarly, it is impossible to know whether, as conjectured in the review of Salisbury Bus Station in Chapter 2, the building may have included limestone ashlars, which may have provided foundation material for the 18th-century building that probably replaced the medieval buildings. Similar ashlar plinths are included in the mid-/late 18th-century properties further to the north at Nos 54 and 56 Endless Street.

The details depicting the growth of settlement within individual chequers and tenements, including these possible sub-divisions, are difficult to elucidate archaeologically. Hawkes (nd) suggested that the evidence favoured a model of piecemeal and episodic development, a characteristic recognised by Rawlings (2000) in Ivy Street where a tenement apparently remained undeveloped for some considerable time. Barber (2005), in contrast, using data derived from excavations at Anchor Brewery in Gigant Street (Pl. 4.10), favoured a systematic rolling programme of expansion from a central part of the city.

He acknowledged that evidence was slight but noted that pottery from Ivy Street contained earlier vessel forms than those from the Anchor Brewery, suggesting that Antelope Chequer was developed at an earlier date than Trinity Chequer. He supported his argument by also noting that buildings in Gigant Street were constructed using a consistent building design, albeit similar to many others in the city, but nevertheless suggesting that these properties had formed part of a single development.

Plate 4.10 Anchor Brewery site, Gigant Street: view to south-east, showing foundations of Period 3 (c. 1350–1450) Building 1 (foreground) and 2 (centre) with poorly preserved Buildings 4 and 5 beyond

In the event it is likely that elements of both schemes were adopted. The concept of outward expansion from the city centre and along principal arterial routes nevertheless appears most probable, as can be seen by the distribution of extant medieval buildings in the city. These remnants show the oldest and least modified structures concentrated around Market Place and High Street, with early buildings extending from this central cluster, along Castle Street and Winchester Street. Archaeological excavations have confirmed that medieval development continued rapidly across the city, although some extremities (Harding 2016) apparently remained vacant until at least the 15th or 16th century.

Medieval planning within each chequer was inextricably linked to the initial survey of tenements and construction of the systematic network of water channels within the city. Tenement boundaries and the enclosed plots underpinned much of the settlement and t hey were infilled with a range of buildings that were repaired, renewed, divided or amalgamated through time. These modifications often resulted from changes in ownership, forms of construction, or materials.

The initial concept of a new city undoubtedly included proposals for at least one place of worship. Tatton-Brown (1997) has argued that records of a wooden chapel, in which mass was celebrated on Trinity Sunday 1219, probably refer to a building that was erected close to the site of the new cathedral. Additional sources note a chapel, dedicated to St Thomas and probably on the site of the extant church, in 1238. Subsequent documentary sources (Rich-Jones and Dunn Macray, 1891) confirm that a building, by then listed as a church, was established by 1246. Details of this building and its appearance have been hotly debated (Haskins 1909; RCHME 1980; Tatton-Brown 1997), most notably regarding whether it was cruciform, with no clear consensus. No archaeological excavations have taken place to clarify the origins of the church or to test the possibility of earlier activity on the site (Langlands 2014). However, a geophysical survey (Wessex Archaeology 2020), undertaken during a period of renovation within the nave of the present church, which dates from 1400, provided an opportunity to undertake the first underground survey inside the building. The results failed to detect traces of any earlier stone foundations related to a smaller nave beneath the current one, but did identify a series of six anomalies at the west end of the building (**Fig. 4.4**).

These anomalies, which were interpreted as post pads for a timber structure, were spaced approximately 4 m apart and measured c. 1.5 m across. They were aligned symmetrically within the present nave and the mid-point of the nave between the opposing doorways. The anomalies became clearly visible in the vertical axis approximately 0.85 m below the present ground surface and remained visible in the plots for a further 0.30 m, providing a base level approximately 1.10 m below the present nave floor. The precise function and date of this structure and its relationship to the current building remain unknown. The possibility that it represents traces of an earlier timber church can be argued, but remains conjectural until the unlikely scenario permits excavations to take place to resolve the construction and date of the pads. The project did detect traces of a former river channel that had long silted-up. This palaeochannel is likely to have created unstable conditions that, combined with inadequate foundations, may have accounted for the documented collapse of the east end of the chancel in 1447. Similar engineering defects on the River Itchen flood plain have been attributed to the collapse of the tower of Winchester Cathedral in 1107 and for subsidence of its east end, which, by 1905, urgently needed underpinning.

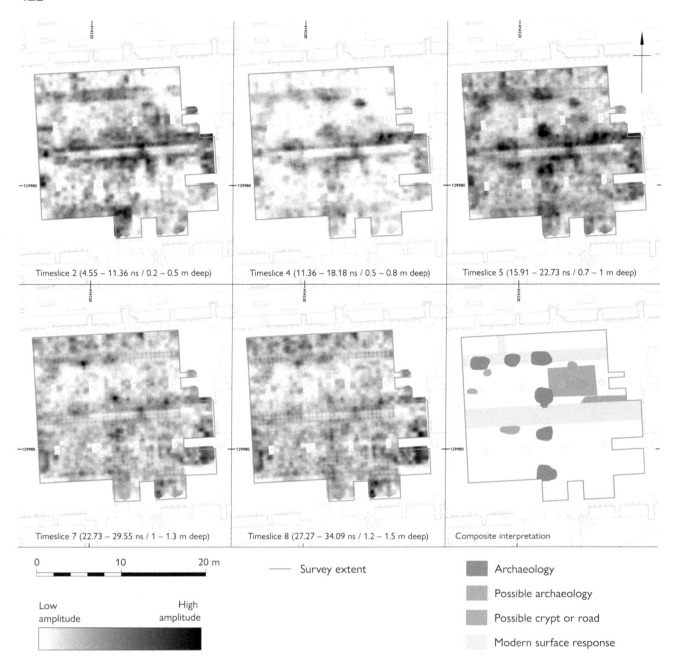

Timeslice 2 (4.55 – 11.36 ns / 0.2 – 0.5 m deep)

Timeslice 4 (11.36 – 18.18 ns / 0.5 – 0.8 m deep)

Timeslice 5 (15.91 – 22.73 ns / 0.7 – 1 m deep)

Timeslice 7 (22.73 – 29.55 ns / 1 – 1.3 m deep)

Timeslice 8 (27.27 – 34.09 ns / 1.2 – 1.5 m deep)

Composite interpretation

0   10   20 m

—— Survey extent

Low amplitude   High amplitude

Archaeology

Possible archaeology

Possible crypt or road

Modern surface response

Figure 4.4 St Thomas's Church: results of ground penetrating radar survey showing raw data and interpretation of results

The survey failed to detect a comparable row of post pads parallel to the south side of the nave, although it is possible that they were located immediately south of the survey grid. Similarly, there is nothing to indicate whether they were all contained within the nave or extended into St Thomas's Square to the west or beneath the tower to the south. As a result, the new data added nothing to resolve the hotly debated issue of whether the bell tower was originally a free-standing structure or not. Most importantly, the total absence of surviving foundations has refuted the existence of an earlier stone nave beneath the present nave. Such a stone building is likely to have been much smaller or located elsewhere, possibly beneath the present chancel. The conclusion must be that the present nave was constructed on a virgin site or alternatively replaced a completely wooden structure.

The extensive grid of artificial watercourses that characterised the medieval city (**Fig. 4.5**) was fed by water diverted from the Mill Leat of the Bishop's Mill and River Avon. The construction of this urban drainage system undoubtedly utilised knowledge that was derived from established water management projects at mills, monasteries (Bonde and Maines 2012) and fish farms (Harding 2008). The system represented a major achievement of civil engineering, which required labour to construct and maintain in working order and included sluices to manage the water flow. The likely participation of the Church in this project in Salisbury is endorsed by the fact that part of the Town Ditch system was apparently routed through the precinct of the Franciscan friary, possibly serving the reredorter of the friary. Daniell (in prep.), in discussing the origins of the channel system, has acknowledged this undoubted skill-base but also argued that local expertise may have existed that was capable of designing the scheme. Furthermore, he argues that the project may have utilised an existing system of water meadows, predetermining the layout of the Close and city, to avoid interrupting the flow vital to the success of the scheme. The RCHME (1993, 38) similarly concluded that the Close Ditch featured in the earliest layout of the city, and is possibly contemporary with the establishment of tenements for canons' residences that were laid out before 1200.

The RCHME (1980) plotted two forms of channel: a grid comprising 4620 m of surface watercourses, which followed the street lines of the residential chequers, and a network of deep-water channels and drainage ditches with a combined length of 5160 m, which were primarily located across the flood plain beyond the southern parts of the city. The former also included channels that were thought might represent later additions to the system (*ibid.*, xxxiv). These channels were mapped through Gore's Chequer and Cross Keys Chequer and were, by implication, projected through Three Swans Chequer. However, excavations at the site of the former bus station (Garland *et al.* 2021; Wessex Archaeology 2014a) failed to detect any trace of this channel on the projected line.

Figure 4.5 Watercourses: city plan showing system of surface watercourses and deep watercourses, supplied from Mill Leat and River Avon, also showing principal bridging points depicted by Speed and Naish

Plate 4.11 Modern water channel in Churchill Gardens, of probable similar dimensions, construction and appearance to the medieval Town and Close Ditches

The deep-water channels included the Town Ditch, which ran along New Canal and marked the southern limit of Market Place, and the Close Ditch, which defined the northern and eastern limits of the Cathedral Close, effectively creating a moated enclave. Both ditches were supplied with water from the outfall of the Bishop's Mill. Excavations of this important part of the city's history have been limited, principally due to the lack of opportunity and the high water table. Small sections have been cut through two unlined ditches, either one of which may represent Hussey's Ditch, one of the surface watercourses, during archaeological evaluations at Belle Vue House on Endless Street (W290;

Fig. 4.5, 1; Wessex Archaeology 2017a); neither section proved definitive. These unimpressive candidates aside, no examples of the surface watercourses have been recorded, despite the large number of modern services that have been placed beneath the city streets. An engraving of Minster Street by W H Bartlett published in *Picturesque Antiquities of the English Cities* by John Britton in 1829 (reproduced in Chandler 1983, pl. 18) indicates that these courses were located towards the edge of the carriageway, were probably over one metre wide and were stone lined. The character of the Town Ditch and Close Ditch are similarly obscure. The former has been recorded in an incomplete section at No. 47 Brown Street (W227; **Fig. 4.5, 3**) where it measured 1.4 m wide and was also stone lined, while one side of the latter was revealed in a trench at Church House, Crane Street (**Fig. 4.5, 2**; Cambrian Archaeological Projects 2001). This excavation showed that the ditch was over 1.4 m deep and was constructed of Chilmark stone. Some indication of the appearance and impressive size of these channels can be appreciated from a segment (**Pl. 4.11**) that now forms part of the Churchill Gardens recreational park. This segment, which is of comparable dimensions to the Town Ditch and Close Ditch as seen in archaeological excavations, was slightly re-aligned in the late 20th century. It is shown on the 1880–1 1:500 Town Map, suggesting that it can be extrapolated to join the system of watercourses depicted by Naish that once flowed across the River Avon flood plain at Bugmore before flowing back into the River Avon.

Plate 4.12 Salisbury city defences in Bourne Hill Gardens

Defences

The limits of the new city were largely defined and protected by the natural boundaries created by the River Avon on the south and west sides with the spur of Milford Hill to the east. The northern approach was less well defined. However, as early as 1227 Henry III (1216–72) granted the bishop rights to enclose the city with a defensive bank and ditch (RCHME 1980). This work is believed to have been completed on the northern and eastern sides of the city. Plans to strengthen the defences with a stone wall, possibly to emulate the imposing feature surrounding the Close, apparently never materialised. Traces of the bank, 4–5 m high, remain in Bourne Hill Gardens (**Pl. 4.12**), while the line can be traced further south along the aptly named Rampart Road. Entrance to the city was controlled on the north and east by stone gatehouses erected on Castle Street and Winchester Street.

Despite the importance of the works and uncertainties about their completion, very little work has been undertaken to study these important remains from an archaeological perspective. The most detailed study remains that undertaken by SMARG during the construction of the Inner Ring Road (Saunders and Algar 2015), which followed the line of the defences for much of its course. This watching brief was restricted to observing sections at four locations where pedestrian underpasses were constructed and also in a cutting designed to provide access to a multi-storey car park. The sections exposed in this cutting established that the defensive bank sealed traces of 13th-century occupation, thereby suggesting a relatively rapid expansion from the centre of the city and indicating a potential start date for construction of the defences towards the second half of the century. The bank measured approximately 8–10 m wide and comprised layers of orange gravel.

The character of the ditch was established in sections created by the construction of a pedestrian underpass at the east end of St Ann Street. These exposures indicate it probably averaged 12 m wide with a V-shaped profile and an estimated depth of 4 m, a consideration that may have been determined by the level of the water table.

More recent research has focused attention on locating the 'lost' section of the defences on the north side of the city. A series of trial trenches (Wessex Archaeology 2004) excavated in College Street Car Park, with two additional trenches in the area of the former swimming pool, approximately 35 m north of the surviving bank, failed to find any firm evidence for the course of the medieval defences in this area. Archaeological evaluations at Belle Vue House (Wessex Archaeology 1992a; 2017a), immediately east of the site of the former Castle Street gatehouse, have similarly failed to detect any traces of the bank or ditch, supporting speculation that the defences may never have been completed.

Trinity Chequer

The work undertaken between 1984 and 1990 pioneered area excavations to reconstruct the development of medieval Salisbury. The greatest concentration of archaeological investigations took place within Trinity Chequer, where a range of tenements containing footprints of both complete and partial buildings (**Table 4.1**) were sampled. Further excavations in the chequer were undertaken in 2000 (Barber 2005) and 2002 (Currie and Rushton 2005). Archaeological preservation in the chequer was variable but sufficiently intact to reconstruct aspects of life and modifications to the chequer's development, character and appearance, in comparison with other chequers. The combined results have helped to illustrate how Salisbury and its occupants connected with outlying areas economically, socially and religiously. These projects, as well as those undertaken subsequently, focused on sites related to domestic, commercial and light industrial use; however, the medieval city was sufficiently small to ensure that urban populations lived in close proximity to a range of other institutions including religious foundations and hospitals. These establishments and the people that staffed them undoubtedly had an impact on the lives of all residents.

The basal deposits across the entire chequer featured sterile buried soils reminiscent of those that have been recorded wherever excavations have taken place in Salisbury, confirming the 'green field' nature of the site. Primary occupation was often preceded by deposition of variable dumps containing crushed chalk, gravel and clay with bands of organic matter, which provided foundation layers (Barber 2005) to stabilise the flood plain.

Site	Complete tenement	Partial tenement
Gigant Street		
Anchor Brewery site (Barber 2005)	4	2
No.36 Milford Street/No.34 Gigant Street (Currie and Rushton 2005)	-	2
Gigant Street Car Park (W129D)	-	1
Gibbs Mew, No.68 Gigant Street (W192)	-	1
Brown Street		
Gigant Street Car Park (W129A) and Nos 47-51 Brown Street (W227)	2	2
Gigant Street Car Park (W129B)	-	1
No.39 Brown Street(W139)	1	-
Total	7	9

Table 4.1 Approximate number of individual buildings within Trinity Chequer documented in archaeological excavations

Comparable layers of charcoal, clay and gravel were found immediately above the gravel in Brown Street and on Endless Street (Cotswold Archaeology 2017; Wessex Archaeology 2014a). The surface of these deposits was often marked by disconnected scatters of pits, postholes, stakeholes and gullies, possibly evidence of temporary construction gangs. Similar evidence of primary occupation has been documented (Cotswold Archaeology 2017; Harding 2016) intermittently elsewhere on street frontages across the city.

Archaeological data within the chequer to confirm and map the expansion from the city centre in the 13th century is sparse; however, small windows of opportunity provide rudimentary illumination. Pottery from excavations in Antelope Chequer (Mepham 2000) was characterised by Type 1 jars, forms that dated from the 11th to 13th century, suggesting that development had commenced there by the mid-13th century. In contrast, excavations at the Anchor Brewery site (Barber 2005) on the eastern margins of Trinity Chequer contained well-stratified groups of pottery including jars of Type 4, with handled jars and skillets – forms that were developed at Laverstock from the mid-13th century (**Fig. 4.2, 29**; Musty et al. 1969). These specific examples in adjoining chequers represent a modest period, possibly spanning only decades, from the foundation of the city apparently diffusing outwards into Trinity Chequer. Primary development on the Brown Street frontage of Trinity Chequer was less detailed and provided no more than a date within the 13th or 14th century, based on comparable building design, wall alignments and pottery. Closely datable artefacts remain rare; however, a silver penny of Edward I (1272–1307) or Edward II (1307–27), from an early phase of floor refurbishment in a building at No. 39 Brown Street, indicates that this tenement had probably been developed by the first half of the 14th century.

Medieval Settlement

Buildings in the city undoubtedly varied in size and design according to the location and status of individual tenements within each chequer and the wealth of respective developers. Chandler (1983) has discussed variations in design and alignment of a number of extant properties in Salisbury. He stressed that these buildings are generally those of high-status occupants and may not represent the type of houses owned by the less well-off. Homes of the latter have been better represented by results of subsequent archaeological excavations, thereby helping to redress the balance between rich and poor in the record of Salisbury's residents.

Study of medieval urban building design is not new and was first addressed in a survey undertaken by Ralph Treswell in London between 1607 and 1614 (Schofield 1987; 1995). The buildings included in that survey undoubtedly reflected those that had remained largely unaltered since the medieval period. The classification has been adopted here to classify medieval urban house plans in the city in preference to the system adopted by RCHME (1980, lxiv), which has been used successfully to classify buildings in rural areas. Treswell identified four distinct types of house plan, varying in extent and complexity. The scheme commenced with houses of Type 1, which may have comprised no more than a single room on the ground floor. Type 2 houses comprised medium and small two-storey houses with a shop and warehouse on the ground floor, accommodation on the first floor and a detached kitchen to the rear, although this arrangement was by no means standardised. Larger, well-appointed buildings of Type 3 filled much of the tenement with between three to six rooms on the ground floor while the most expansive, Type 4, were constructed around a courtyard of varying dimensions, often with a hall to the rear. This elementary typology was adopted by Schofield and Vince (2003, fig. 3.5) when discussing medieval buildings in Britain. They confirmed that similar building types can be found across many parts of Britain, including Salisbury, where buildings of Types 2 and 3 were well represented. Extant examples of these building types can now be supplemented by additional discoveries of Types 1, 2 and 4 as a result of excavations in Salisbury, although no Type 3 houses have been added to the corpus (**Fig. 4.6**).

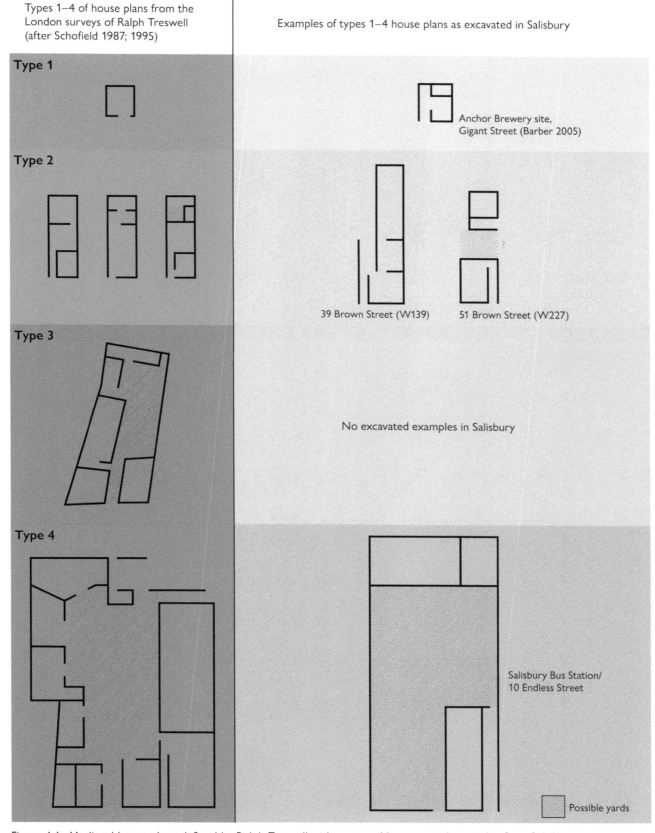

Types 1–4 of house plans from the London surveys of Ralph Treswell (after Schofield 1987; 1995)

Examples of types 1–4 house plans as excavated in Salisbury

Type 1

Anchor Brewery site, Gigant Street (Barber 2005)

Type 2

39 Brown Street (W139)   51 Brown Street (W227)

Type 3

No excavated examples in Salisbury

Type 4

Salisbury Bus Station/ 10 Endless Street

Possible yards

Figure 4.6 Medieval house plans defined by Ralph Treswell with comparable excavated examples from Salisbury

Plate 4.13 Medieval courtyard buildings: The Red Lion Hotel, Antelope Chequer, 14th century

Plate 4.14 Medieval courtyard buildings: Windover House, St Ann Street, 15th/16th century

Plate 4.15 Medieval courtyard buildings: The Pheasant Inn, Gore's Chequer, 15th century

The most impressive buildings were those occupied by potentially wealthy owners, many of the merchant class, of courtyard (Type 4) design. Examples include the Red Lion Hotel in Milford Street (**Fig. 4.7, 1; Pl. 4.13**), where the expanded central yard was approached through a formal gateway. Other examples were arranged around a more restrained open area, as in Windover House, St Ann Street (**Fig. 4.7, 2; Pl. 4.14**; RCHME 1980, 125). Elsewhere, the courtyards have been infilled or reduced in area, but have been documented, as at Nos 47–49 New Canal (*ibid.*, 100) (**Fig. 4.7, 3**) and the hall of John Halle (*ibid.*, 103), also on New Canal in New Street chequer (**Fig. 4.7, 4**), a property that occupied a corner tenement extending to Catherine Street. Additional extant buildings with courtyards of varying sizes comprised both residential properties and hostelries and include the former Vine Inn (*ibid.*, 61) in the Cheese Market (**Fig. 4.7, 5**), the former Chough Hotel (*ibid.*, 132) on Castle Street (**Fig. 4.7, 6**), the Queen's Arms Inn (*ibid.*, 111) on Ivy Street (**Fig. 4.7, 7**) and The Pheasant Inn (*ibid.*, 145) on Rollestone Street (**Fig. 4.7, 8; Pl. 4.15**). This list can be expanded to include examples that have been demolished or documented, including Balle's Place on Winchester Street (**Fig. 4.7, 9**; *ibid.*, 136; Bonney 1964) and a large property known as *Glastyngburiecorner*, on the corner of Milford Street and Gigant Street in Trinity Chequer (**Fig. 4.7, 10**; Currie and Rushton 2005). Foundations of another probable example, near the junction of Endless Street and Salt Lane (**Fig. 4.7, 11**), were revealed by excavation at the site of the former bus station at Nos 8–10 Endless Street (see Chapter 2, Salisbury Bus Station; Cotswold Archaeology 2017; Garland *et al.* 2021; Wessex Archaeology 2014a). Documentary records (Chandler 2013) of this building complex, on land that was owned for much of the medieval period by the powerful Weaver's Guild, specifically make reference to 'courts' in the itinerary of facilities. Many of these affluent residential properties were situated at important locations; others functioned, at one time or another, as hostelries, while others served as commercial premises, including guildhalls. Many of these buildings can seemingly be detected in Naish's survey of 1716, a survey that is not without its flaws, but that nevertheless depicts, in a stylised fashion, contrasting elements of medieval architecture in the city.

A recurring pattern (**Fig. 4.7**) of the survey apparently shows more expansive buildings with courtyards or cross ranges to the rear, implying examples of Treswell's Type 3 and 4 houses. They apparently occupied large parts of the tenement, as the well-preserved, extant 14th-century example at No. 9 Queen Street shows (RCHME 1980, 82–4). Extant buildings in Queen Street, together with the excavated foundations at No. 10 Endless Street (see Chapter 2, Salisbury Bus Station), indicate that these prestigious properties were probably aligned perpendicular to the street frontage. They were designed on a sufficiently large scale and incorporated upper storeys, possibly adjoining an open central hall.

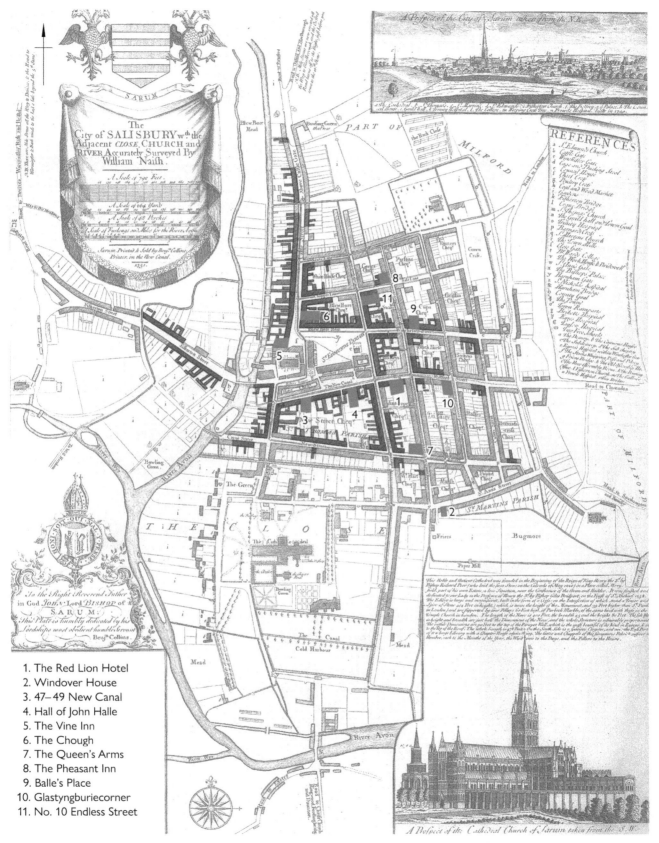

1. The Red Lion Hotel
2. Windover House
3. 47–49 New Canal
4. Hall of John Halle
5. The Vine Inn
6. The Chough
7. The Queen's Arms
8. The Pheasant Inn
9. Balle's Place
10. Glastyngburiecorner
11. No. 10 Endless Street

Figure 4.7 William Naish's map of 1716 showing distribution of buildings with courtyards and/or complex service ranges

Other trappings of affluence can be seen in the highly desirable corner plot, *Glastyngburiecorner*, at Nos 36 Milford Street/34 Gigant Street. This tenement extended from the corner of the chequer to the Town Ditch (RCHME 1980). The scale of the property that occupied it was confirmed by excavation (Currie and Rushton 2005). The pace of development accelerated from an initial, ill-defined phase represented by a circular structure, resembling an oven/kiln of similar diameter found subsequently at Rollestone Street (Garland *et al.* 2021). Currie and Rushton (2005, 257) conjectured that the example in Milford Street represented a dovecote serving a house that fronted onto the street. This phase was followed by a period of industrial use, as represented by a series of hearths. The site was redeveloped after 1350 as a grand, stone-built structure, which was approached through a gateway on Gigant Street. This arrangement, whereby a side street was used to provide access to a courtyard of a major building, was repeated elsewhere in the city (RCHME 1980). The survey noted several instances where large properties on Milford Street were accessed from the rear through Pennyfarthing Street.

These buildings occupied strategic locations in the central part of the city – along the major access routes, frontages of chequers centred on Market Place, and corner tenements. In contrast, Naish shows buildings on the reverse side of these favoured locations, along New Street Chequer, Cross Keys Chequer and Three Swans Chequer, extending into the outlying chequers, including Trinity Chequer, as continuous linear terraces. These buildings appear to be more closely represented by Treswell's Type 1 and 2 houses, as has been shown by numerous excavated examples.

Excavations on the south side of New Street Chequer (Butterworth 2005a) produced nothing to indicate high-status occupants. Buildings here were constructed on the pattern defined by Treswell's Type 2 houses, structures which have recurred across many parts of the city – in New Street (Butterworth 2005a), Gigant Street (Barber 2005) and Brown Street (see Chapter 2). The excavations have shown that these less affluent dwellings, which probably constituted the norm for all other residents, frequently included a hearth on the ground floor, a feature that was accompanied by refuse of a domestic nature and suggestive of use as a parlour.

Although these buildings conform closely with Treswell's Type 2 buildings, it is possible that they developed and expanded from simpler beginnings comprising no more than a single room on the ground floor, reminiscent of Treswell's Type 1 house. Collective excavations in Trinity Chequer (see Chapter 2; Barber 2005; Butterworth 2005b; Currie and Rushton 2005) have indicated that many of the initial buildings within the chequer apparently conformed to a single design and were of comparable size and construction to those on New Street. Barber (2005) considered that buildings at the Anchor Brewery site on Gigant Street, immediately south of *Glastyngburiecorner*, were initially rudimentary, comprising one room, and postulated that foundations of Phase 2 (1250–1350) buildings may have been laid directly on levelling deposits. He suggested that these buildings may have been 'entirely of clay and timber construction' (*ibid.*, 173) or founded on cill beams leaving little or no clear trace in the ground, and were only formalised subsequently by flint plinth foundations. The pattern was apparently repeated elsewhere in Trinity Chequer where Butterworth (2005b) described mid-/late 13th-century buildings at the Elim Chapel site, which were of beam slot and post construction and were only replaced subsequently by foundations of mortared flints. This sequence cannot be confirmed on Brown Street (see Chapter 2, W129 and W139), where, as elsewhere in Salisbury, it was difficult to identify closely dated episodes of development within the general 13th–14th-century time frame. However, Trench W129A contained a shallow U-profiled gully, which may have been a beam slot. This feature mirrored the alignment adopted by the rear elevations of later buildings and was subsequently replaced by a mortared wall foundation. The use of horizontal timber beams, which were anchored in slots, has been documented in early medieval buildings at both Winchester, Hampshire (Biddle 1967) and Newbury, Berkshire (Vince *et al.* 1997) where dwarf wall foundations were not adopted until the late 13th century.

The degree by which timber foundations may have preceded mortared foundations in the earliest medieval buildings in Salisbury remains largely unconfirmed. Some support may be gained from the fact that the earliest centres of worship in the city comprised timber chapels. It is unclear whether these structures were entirely wooden or timber-framed, and whether built with earth-fast posts or founded on timber cill beams or dwarf flint walls. Limited excavations, beyond the city limits (Langlands and Strutt in prep.), on two 13th-century building platforms forming part of the secular settlement at Stratford sub Castle, have also failed to locate traces of wall foundations. Langlands and Strutt considered that these rural structures were probably similar to those at Gomeldon and attributed the absence of foundations to truncation by agriculture, although timber beam construction may be equally plausible.

Improved foundations characterise many timber-framed medieval buildings in Britain after 1300 (Schofield and Vince 2003) making the ground plan and distribution of structures clearer. Most components, which include flint, clay, chalk and timber, could all be sourced locally, and have been represented both on excavations and in extant medieval buildings in the city (**Pl. 4.16**).

Plate 4.16 Old George Mall, New Street: flint and chalk wall foundations of 13th–14th-century date

Flints with weathered cortex, the natural outside rind of the flint, suggest that most were picked from fields, while others with orange staining may have been dug from local gravel pits. Medieval quarry pits have been identified within the city limits (Harding 2016) to exploit deposits of silty clay 'brickearth' for daub. Clay from a different geological age, London Clay of the Tertiary period (48–56 million years ago) supplied material for ceramic roof tiles, which were employed from the foundation of the city to reduce the risk of fire. These priorities were acknowledged in an ordinance of 1431 banning the use of thatch (RCHME 1980, xliv). Production was maintained at Alderbury from the mid-14th century until the late 15th century. These products were predominantly plain but were occasionally glazed on the lower edge, providing a decorative feature to the city's appearance. Brunskill (1994) noted that the preferred angle of roof pitch for clay roof tiles was 45°, a feature that can still be observed in many timber-framed buildings in the city. Further detail relating to the appearance of roofs in Salisbury can be gained from the recovery of valley- and hip-tile fragments from excavations in Trinity Chequer (Every 2005), which establish the presence of buildings with projecting roofs or hipped gables within the chequer. Roof lines were embellished with glazed ridge tiles manufactured from clay at Laverstock (Musty *et al.* 1969), which frequently included a knife-cut cockscomb crest (**Pl. 4.17**). Other additions may have featured louvers, chimneys with ornate pots or decorative zoomorphic finials. This final form of roof furniture is rarely found on excavations, although an example, possibly made at Laverstock and featuring a stylised cow, was found on the former Albany and Greyhound Hotel at Fordingbridge, Hampshire (Loader 2003).

Plate 4.17 The Medieval Hall, Cathedral Close: cockscomb ridge tiles would once have been a familiar feature of the city skyline, as would louvers before the gradual introduction of chimneys

More elaborate finials, louvers and, subsequently, chimney pots were also manufactured at Laverstock. Decorated floor tiles were also produced locally at Clarendon, where complex floor designs were installed in the palace c. 1237–45. These sumptuous pavements, using tiles from the Clarendon kilns, were also installed at the cathedral, including the floor of the Muniment Room, dating from about 1260, above the vestry (RCHME 1999, 168). Many of the high-status floors remained intact but were sadly replaced during work by Wyatt in the late 18th century. Discarded tiles, which may have been related to this destruction or previous activity, were found during excavations at the cathedral (Wessex Archaeology 2009). However, these desirable products, which may have been made using local labour employed by 'alien craftsmen' from overseas (James and Gerrard 2007, 79) were unaffordable to urban residents.

Chalk also provided a versatile, readily available building material and has been documented in excavations across the city. It was employed in foundations and cess pits, where it was used in block form, or in outbuildings and tenement boundaries, where it may have been used in cob construction. The extent to which cob may have featured in larger buildings, where timber framing with wattle and daub infill was prevalent, is unclear. Its use may have been more common in outlying areas where increased space allowed construction of buildings with thicker walls. Nevertheless, cob featured in the area into the 19th century, most notably at Milford Hill House, where observations during an archaeological watching brief confirmed details of the construction. Milford Hill House was built as a residence for a wealthy banker, Charles Everett, soon after 1830 (Durman 2007), when brick construction was the norm.

Chalk was unobtainable within the city limits, although quarries, with access to chalk that could be shaped, undoubtedly featured in the local landscape. It is unclear whether exploitation proceeded on a truly industrial scale or as needs arose; indeed, it is tempting to consider that a chalk pit on the site, which was subsequently incorporated into the ornamental gardens, may have supplied chalk for the construction of the house.

Squared Greensand blocks have been documented in foundations across the city (**Pl. 4.18**), where they have been interpreted as supports for timber framing. This material was available from outcrops along the fringes of the Vale of Wardour, approximately 12 km to the west.

Most domestic buildings within Trinity Chequer that were not of high status comprised a floor area measuring approximately 30 m², extending approximately 6 m back from the street frontage. This measurement most closely resembles a perch, which as noted above apparently functioned as the preferred unit of land measurement in the city. Excavated foundations across Salisbury (Barber 2005; Butterworth 2005a; Hawkes nd), together with extant timber-framed 15th- and 16th-century buildings, including properties at No. 32 Milford Street, the New Inn, New Street and No. 63 Castle Street, confirm that it was also adopted as a standard measurement of building width.

Plate 4.18 Greensand block supporting vertical member of timber-framed building

Plate 4.19 Building width, possibly based on a perch, as seen in No. 63 Castle Street, early 16th century

In many instances, subsequent structural modifications or rebuilds apparently retained the footprint of an earlier building, as can be seen in the street frontage of the Red Lion Hotel, where a 19th-century range (RCHME 1980) also measures approximately 6 m wide. Standardised linear measurements occur throughout the city (**Pl. 4.19**) and in the cathedral, where detailed survey (Kidson 1993) indicates that the nave and aisles were constructed using a grid with spacings 19 ft 6 in (5.94 m) apart, close to the measurements that were employed in domestic buildings in the city. Kidson discussed in considerable detail the issue of unit length and whether the architects might have employed the standard English foot (0.3048 m) or retained the classical Roman foot (0.2972 m) in their calculations. Irrespective of which measurement was involved, the observations indicate that some consistent approaches to design undoubtedly prevailed in the construction of both ecclesiastical and urban properties.

Elements of structural engineering were well known to medieval architects. Brunskill (1994) has emphasised the fundamental importance of squares, or conjoining squares to create rectangles, in the cellular construction of timber-framed buildings. Service ranges provided not only additional space but also contributed increased stability by reducing outward thrust along wall lines. These fundamental principles can be recognised in the cellular construction of extant medieval buildings in Salisbury and reinforce the important role that architects played in their erection. The rectangular ground plan, where length equals twice the width, is also replicated in both extant properties and excavated examples. It occurs in buildings that are aligned both perpendicular and parallel to the street frontage and is clearly demonstrated along Fish Row and Butcher Row, as in Nos 7–9 Fish Row (RCHME 1980, monument 71; **Pl. 4.20**) and No. 33 Butcher Row (**Pl. 4.21**), which date from the 14th and 15th centuries. Buildings of comparable dimensions and likely appearance have been revealed in excavations at No. 10 Endless Street (Chapter 2, Salisbury Bus Station) where a rectangular range, Cotswold Archaeology's Building B, was aligned perpendicular to the street frontage and measured approximately 15 m long and 7 m wide. This building alignment mirrors that in Queen Street, where No. 9 Queen Street is representative. It conjectures a street scene characterised by buildings of two or more storeys – as Garland *et al.* (2021) suggested for No. 10 Endless Street, arguably incorporating a hall and central hearth – extending along these adjacent street frontages and forming a characteristic feature around the economic hub of the city.

Areas beyond this central cluster, as represented by excavations at Anchor Brewery, Brown Street and New Street, arguably follow the pattern depicted by Naish where terraces were aligned parallel to the street frontage. These properties, reflecting less affluent accommodation, may have initially comprised conjoining cellular structures comprising a single room – Treswell's Type 1 house construction (Schofield and Vince 2003, fig. 3.5), with an internal partition to create a through-passage to the 'backlands'. This pattern was most clearly demonstrated at the Anchor Brewery (Barber 2005), where each room was equipped with a central fireplace, implying that they were individual units. Further internal screen sub-divisions at the rear of the principal living accommodation created possible sleeping quarters.

Plate 4.20 Medieval buildings with length=twice width with gable facing the street: Wheatsheaf Inn, Nos 7–9 Fish Row, 14th century

Barber (*ibid.*) adopted the concept proposed by Hawkes (nd) that these initial buildings were also of single-storey construction but considered that living space may have been increased by the installation of raised sleeping platforms. These recurring features, supplemented by small pottery assemblages, suggested that the development at the Anchor Brewery site represented a single phase of work. Similar construction and design can be postulated for properties on Brown Street; however, building design on this side of the chequer may have become more ambitious. Excavations at Nos 39, 51 and 65 Brown Street (Chapter 2, W139 and W129) have all produced evidence suggesting that these properties may have been enlarged with the addition of a service range at the rear at some point, probably in the 15th century. These extensions created dwellings of Treswell's Type 2, which may have typified many of the houses shown by Naish in the outlying chequers. The absence of such evidence from the Anchor Brewery may stem from the selected areas of excavation, which did not extend beyond the street frontage ranges. The additional accommodation provided by service ranges increased the available floor space and may have encouraged the construction of jettied upper storeys, although it is evident from extant buildings in the city that two-storey structures were already relatively common by the 14th century. Schofield (1991) has observed that jettied buildings were present in London by 1246, after which the fashion may have spread out to other parts of the country. This suggests that buildings in Salisbury may initially have been of single-storey construction for only a short period of time before being redeveloped with upper floors. Elsewhere, jettied construction may have been adopted in the earliest buildings in the city, with additional storeys added as Salisbury enjoyed increasing medieval prosperity.

Plate 4.21 Medieval buildings with length=twice width with gable facing the street: No. 33 Butcher Row, similar design and dimensions, probably 15th or 16th century

144

Plate 4.22 Three conjoining medieval cottages (now the New Inn), late 15th/early 16th century, New Street

Plate 4.23 Three cottages of similar design and 15th-century date, St John's Street

Extant buildings (**Pls 4.22 and 4.23**) also demonstrate that reconstructing building design from foundations can be complex. The ground plan of the 15th-century New Inn, New Street (RCHME 1980, 79), mirrors precisely the dimensions and layout of the excavated buildings at the Anchor Brewery on Gigant Street and Nos 39 and 47–51 Brown Street (**Fig. 4.8**). These buildings, aligned parallel to the street frontage, may therefore have shared similar characteristics in the superstructure. The survey of the New Inn confirmed the existence of three conjoined medieval cottages, each with a single cellular room and through-passage (**Fig. 4.9**). Ranges shown to the rear of the cottages were dated to the 18th century, although it is possible that these extensions were constructed on earlier foundations. Significantly, evidence contained in the roof structure indicated that, at some point in their use, the upper parts of two of the cells on the street frontage were originally combined within a more expansive first floor hall, while retaining a through passage below (**Fig. 4.10**). This creates a possibility that a similar more expansive reconstruction may also be applied to properties in Brown Street and Gigant Street (**Figs 4.9–4.10**). Furthermore, the survival of medieval roof trusses in these upstanding buildings not only provides data allowing reconstruction of the superstructure but also makes it possible to envisage the approximate height of the medieval roof line. This may also have been variable within a general skyline, incorporating some continuous ridge lines interspersed with projecting gables or featuring elements of both designs. This data provides tantalising alternatives by which buildings in Trinity Chequer can be reconstructed. It suggests that although buildings may have occupied a standard foundation footprint, some may have been much larger or smaller than the archaeological evidence might indicate before they were sub-divided or amalgamated. Other structural variations have also been noted within the city; Rawlings (2000) recorded a building that included a rear extension in its original medieval design, on the west side of Brown Street, in Antelope Chequer.

Buildings of comparable construction and dimensions have also been documented at Winchester and Norwich, cities where populations were already firmly established by the 13th century. A row of houses in St Pancras Lane, Winchester, erected in the 13th century, measured approximately 5 m square, each one constructed on cill beams with cob walls with an internal screen passage. Biddle (1967, 264) considered that this development constituted well-conceived accommodation for 'low-class workers'. In Norwich (Atkin 1985), a number of rectangular domestic buildings, measuring c. 7 m by 4 m, were built along the street front in the early 13th century. These buildings were constructed with clay walls and incorporated tenement boundaries and outbuildings.

Figure 4.8 Ground plans of Nos 47–51 Brown Street, Anchor Brewery, Gigant Street and New Inn, raw data

Figure 4.9 Ground plans of Nos 47–51 Brown Street, Anchor Brewery, Gigant Street and New Inn, interpreted as individual cottages

Figure 4.10 Ground plans of Nos 47–51 Brown Street, Anchor Brewery, Gigant Street and New Inn, interpreted as paired units to include an open hall and adjoining chamber

Medieval buildings of this type, with similar standards of living accommodation, are now sufficiently well documented in Salisbury and probably followed an established pattern, albeit at a reduced level of affluence, that could also be recognised in the surrounding countryside. Excavations at the deserted medieval village at Gomeldon, approximately 7 km north of Salisbury (Musty and Algar 1986) revealed a number of 12th- and 13th–14th-century long houses, broadly contemporary with the foundation of the new city (**Pl. 4.24**).

The village was subsequently deserted, making it impossible to continue comparisons with later styles of building in Salisbury. The long houses were of single-storey construction and contained restricted living accommodation, covering 14–17 m², with an adjoining byre. They incorporated flint foundations/ walls that were not laid within a foundation trench but placed directly on the foundation layer, in a fashion reminiscent of primary foundations in Gigant Street (Barber 2005). Musty and Algar (1986) considered that the walls of the long houses were constructed entirely of unmortared flint, unlike structures in Salisbury, which were apparently timber-framed on mortared flint foundations. It is equally possible that some buildings were constructed of cob, which may have provided a readily available source of building material in rural areas. Byres were obsolete in the city, but cross passages featured in both city and country, allowing access through the interior of the building. Some hearths at Gomeldon were placed near a wall, while others were located, like those in Salisbury, in the centre of the room. Musty and Algar noted that Building 2 at the village was of cruck construction, a form of framing for which only limited evidence survives in Salisbury, but which may have been more prevalent; the RCHME (1980) survey noted examples in a 15th-century building in Winchester Street, 16th-century cottages in Fisherton Street and also in Bemerton. Building 3 at Gomeldon was accompanied by an external cess pit approximately 1 m², a structure type that is also well represented in the city.

Plate 4.24 Gomeldon deserted medieval village showing surviving earthworks and area of Musty and Algar's (1986) building 6b, seen in the foreground as a rectangular area of brown vegetation with building 6a beyond, similarly visible as differential vegetation

Prosperity

Medieval Salisbury was probably approaching full development by the 15th century when it became a 'boom' city (Chandler 1983) and weaving dominated its economy. Many of the extant buildings in the city date from this period of success (**Fig. 4.1**), which witnessed the reconstruction of St Thomas's Church – all this development largely funded by wealthy merchants. Buildings of 15th-century construction, many of three storeys with additional attics, maintain a distribution centred on the economic hub of the city (RCHME 1980), with a row of buildings around St Thomas's Church and others occupying and infilling Market Place. A number of courtyard houses, including John Halle's house on New Canal, together with large inns, apparently confirm construction or expansion in the 15th century. Halle's residence was constructed of flint and ashlar, making it distinctive within the pattern of timber-framed buildings. Currie and Rushton (2005) noted the association of William Teynturer, a successful late 14th-century merchant, with property at the junction of Milford Street and Gigant Street. Pottery assemblages, linking excavated sites to this phase of 15th-century prosperity, are generally scarce in Salisbury (Mepham 2016a). Building foundations are consequently difficult to link with this period of economic success; however, Barber (2005) considered that buildings fronting onto Gigant Street had been rebuilt with flint foundations, on their original footprint, in the period spanning 1350–1450. These significant episodes of rebuilding may reflect activity that affected properties across the city. Limited modifications undoubtedly also took place to exterior facades and interior fittings, according to occupants, fashion or wealth. Barber (2005) drew comparisons between the ground area of excavated medieval 'cottages' in Gigant Street with extant two-storey 15th-century buildings on Guilder Lane (**Pl. 4.25**) to reconstruct the above-ground appearance of medieval Salisbury. Buildings of this appearance were undoubtedly common across the city by this time. Excavations have also suggested that major structural alterations took place on Brown Street, most notably at No. 39 Brown Street, where the property was apparently rebuilt in the 15th century (Chapter 2, W139, **Fig. 2.2**).

The archaeological record confirms this level of continuity into the 15th or 16th centuries when structures were gradually rebuilt, and it is likely that this persisted into the 18th century when brick construction became more fashionable. Some properties retain traces of a later medieval timber-framed core (RCHME 1980), camouflaged beneath subsequent facades, to the present day, as in Nos 51–5 Winchester Street, where buildings of apparent 19th-century date conceal a structure with a 15th-century cruck truss (*ibid.*, 141) or No. 91 Castle Street, where an 18th-century facade masks a building with 15th century origins (*ibid.*, 152). Episodes of infilling or redevelopment have also been seen in the results of excavations, as at Gigant Street (Currie and Rushton 2005). These episodes of redevelopment were not restricted to the 'boom' years of the 15th century. They created spaces that may have remained open for short or extended periods of time before properties were rebuilt; post-medieval pits containing horn cores were found within the footprint of the building at No. 51 Brown Street (Chapter 2, W227; **Pl. 2.32**), suggesting that this tenement may have been open and awaiting redevelopment. Other evidence of a hiatus in occupation may be represented at Nos 15–17 Rollestone Street, where buildings are shown by Naish in 1716 on this street frontage. Documentary records note buildings at the address being erected on open land in 1767, although Chandler (2013) conceded that it was unclear whether these buildings represented the first use of the land or replaced previous structures. The summary report of the excavation (Garland *et al.* 2021) found the results were inconclusive; however, it has been argued above that buildings were present on large parts of Rollestone Street before the late 18th century. Other apparently open spaces remained as courtyards, as documented for John Halle's residence in New Canal.

Rebuilding of structures is unlikely to have been systematic, making it difficult, if not impossible, to identify distinct, clear phases applying to all parts of the city. Urban expansion is more evident in Vanner's Chequer, where some tenements on these city fringes remained undeveloped until the 15th–16th centuries. This development, which included construction on Salt Lane, may also have included work on the house of Thomas Freeman, which was standing in 1455. Harding (2016) speculated that this expansion into previously unoccupied tenements may have been stimulated by an increase in the population, which itself may have resulted from improved prosperity.

Plate 4.25 Fifteenth-century weavers' cottages on Guilder Lane, Swayne's Chequer

Significant changes have been identified in the internal layout of buildings, most notably changes linked to the relocation of fireplaces against walls, which resulted in the introduction of chimneys and facilitated the installation of upper floors. These modifications, which have been noted in several parts of the city, include a number of instances (Barber 2005; Harding 2016; Chapter 2, W227) where the fireplace was relocated to the angle between the street frontage and the screen passage. This arrangement created a situation where the chimney stack was located close to the eaves of the roof, as is illustrated by William Twopeny at 'The Barracks' in Brown Street (RCHME 1980, pl. 9), an impressive stone-fronted 15th-century house that was largely demolished in the 19th century. It now remains only as a wall fragment, containing a blocked three-light window, near the entrance to the White Hart Hotel car park. The accompanying text (*ibid.*, xliv) noted that the location of hearths frequently followed this pattern in Devon but considered that it was unusual in Salisbury; however, results of excavations across the city suggest that that this was by no means an irregular occurrence, most notably at the Anchor Brewery (Barber 2005), where three, and possibly four, conjoining houses in period 4, dating from 1450, were built or rebuilt with hearths on the street frontage. The repeating ground plan and design of these buildings suggest that they were developed or redeveloped from a consistent plan and were contemporary. Similar chimney arrangements have also been noted at No. 51 Brown Street and also in Salt Lane (Harding 2016) and are still visible in the modern city (**Pls 4.26 and 4.27**). The repeating pattern at the Anchor Brewery provides some potential indication of the appearance of this part of Gigant Street in the later part of the 15th century. Furthermore, the design and ground plan of these buildings is remarkably similar to that of the planned street of Vicar's Walk, Wells, Somerset (Walker 1836; Hollinrake Archaeology 2011) where opposing terraces of two-storey houses, with a hearth in the front wall, were originally constructed from 1348. These buildings closely replicate those of Treswell's Type 1 houses and were designed to accommodate individual members of the clergy. The Vicar's Walk was remodelled when the chimneys were raised and crowned, after the death of Bishop Beckington in 1465, although whether the redevelopments within two closely related dioceses were linked remains entirely speculative.

Service ranges, which occur in extant buildings dating from the 15th–16th century, have been identified across the city, including No. 91 Castle Street (RCHME 1980, monument 441), which was constructed in the 15th century. A similar range at No. 39 Brown Street was demolished in 1965 (RCHME 1980, 112), the foundations of which were excavated as part of W139 (see Chapter 2). Elsewhere, Rawlings (2000) noted a modest extension, containing a chalk-lined cess pit, which was attached to a medieval building on Brown Street. Foundations of a larger range were noted in excavations at Nos 39 and 51 Brown Street (Chapter 2, W227) and in Salt Lane (Harding 2016). Service ranges were not universal; none were identified on properties at Anchor Brewery (Barber 2005). These jettied extensions, of two-storey construction, created a deeper total building footprint, comprising between two or three

Plate 4.26 Showing chimney on the street frontage: example in the Close

Plate 4.27 Showing chimney on the street frontage: examples off St Ann Street

rooms on each floor, sometimes with a small open yard to one side. This model most closely corresponds to town houses of Treswell's Type 2 (Schofield 1987; 1995; Schofield and Vince 2003, fig. 3.5), which appeared in London from the 14th century and are moderately well represented in Salisbury as extant buildings. Archaeological fieldwork has now confirmed that similar houses were prevalent across most parts of the city. These modifications collectively created greater variations in the appearance of the ridge and roof line, the construction of gables facing the street frontage and the installation of dormer windows.

The excavations at No. 39 Brown Street have also hinted that some apparent service ranges, which formed an integral part of buildings on the street frontage, may, in fact, have been detached building ranges providing additional residential space in the tenement 'backlands'. This possibility can be argued elsewhere in the city, most notably along Castle Street, where Naish depicted numerous ranges aligned perpendicular to the street frontage. Examples of these timber-framed dwellings were included in the RCHME survey (1980), including Nos 2 and 3 Ivy Place (ibid., 151), of 17th-century date, and a warehouse and cottages to the rear of No. 87 Castle Street (ibid., 152) which were erected in the 16th century, broadly contemporary with the range at No. 39 Brown Street. It is unclear how extensive this gradual expansion, detected by excavation and survey, may have been replicated across other parts of the city from the 16th–17th century to supplement the available residential space for an expanding population. Nevertheless, it may have led ultimately to more tenements being infilled by buildings that were arrayed around courtyards in the 18th and 19th centuries, creating accommodation for poorer residents. Thynne's Court, on St John's Street, can arguably be identified on Naish's survey of 1716, and may have been constructed by that date. It comprised nine cottages, which, by 1871, were arranged around a 'cramped and airless courtyard' (Chandler 1983, 245). Similar infilling occurred in Finches Court, Winchester Street (ibid., pl. 13) in the 18th century and at Fulford Place, Castle Street (ibid., pl. 12) which, by the start of the 20th century, had joined a list of premises that were considered 'unfit for habitation' (ibid., 63) or had been condemned.

Later Developments

A major change in building construction was initiated by the use of bricks. This material may have been used in the area as early as the 15th century, when a kitchen range was added to the complex at Clarendon Palace (James and Robinson 1988, 116), but this did not immediately extend to the city itself. Significant changes occurred from the late 16th century, accelerated in the 18th century and continued into the 19th century when bricks became more readily available and fashionable. The transformation, which impacted on the appearance of the city and its skyline, appears to have been gradual initially. The use of brick was restricted to projects within the Close, including early-17th-century additions to the King's House (RCHME 1993) and to projects for wealthy owners, as Cradock House (**Pl. 4.28**) demonstrates. This impressive building was erected in 1619 for Mathew Bee, a former mayor of the city.

Survey by the RCHME (1980) of buildings beyond the Close indicates that adoption of brick was slow, listing only three buildings featuring late-17th-century construction. Archaeological excavations have added limited evidence for the early use of bricks in the city; a hearth and wall foundation, containing 'Tudor' bricks, was found in Salt Lane (Harding 2016) (**Pl. 4.29**) with 17th-/18th-century pottery and 17th-century clay pipe fragments in an associated levelling layer, suggesting use of this material in less affluent premises.

Plate 4.28 Cradock House, 1619, representing early use of bricks in Salisbury

Plate 4.29 Salt Lane: 17th-/18th-century use of brick in (top) hearth construction and (bottom) wall foundation

Bricks may have been used sparingly, initially to create door pillars or chimney stacks; however, their use increased more rapidly in the 18th century when new structures were erected, as in the redevelopment of No. 10 Endless Street in *c.* 1740 (see Chapter 2, Salisbury Bus Station). Other buildings were extensively rebuilt or remodelled to varying degrees, most notably to enhance street frontage ranges. Examples can be seen not only at the excavated site at No. 39 Brown Street but also in extant buildings at Nos 91 and 93 Castle Street, where adjoining structures, which may have formed a single medieval building, retain many features of 15th-century construction behind 18th-century facades. Timber-framed panels were also infilled with brick. The increased status that may have been attached to bricks was elsewhere resolved by cladding timber-framed buildings with mathematical tiles (**Pl. 4.30**), a technique that created the effect of brickwork, without the expense.

Plate 4.30 Windover House, St Ann Street: mathematical tiles of the 19th century, showing (top) facade, (left) construction and (right) junction with brick construction

These modifications remodelled not only the outward appearance and internal layout of the buildings but also the fixtures and fittings, including the installation of casement windows and subsequently sash windows. These periods and their associated structures were primarily represented in the excavated areas by brick foundations, which often correlated with First Edition Ordnance Survey mapping.

It is unclear to what extent bricks were introduced from a local source. Brickmaking may have been established at Fisherton in the late 17th century (Wright 2017) and two kilns were listed for the period 1714–18. However, the availability of local raw material does not appear to have accelerated the use of bricks in the city. The Guildhall was rebuilt in 1795 using Fisherton 'grey' bricks, although more extensive exploitation of the 'brickearth' did not proceed until the 19th century, when production proliferated. Wright (*ibid.*) concluded that no reliable techniques were available by which locally manufactured bricks could be identified from those imported from further afield; nevertheless, he confirmed that production peaked in the second half of the 19th century. Very few archaeological excavations have investigated brick production, possibly arising from a lack of academic interest and opportunity. Trial trenching within the former brick fields have identified rectangular, backfilled quarry pits, up to 0.6 m deep and 1.5 m wide (**Pl. 4.31**) Each pit was separated from its neighbour by a narrow baulk and some were backfilled with brick wasters.

Plate 4.31 Highbury Avenue, Fisherton brick fields: former 'brickearth' extraction pits exposed in the side of a trench

Wright (2017) noted that similar extraction pits have been observed at Whaddon, 8 km south-east of Salisbury, where deposits of London Clay were exploited, and in Southampton. Kiln structures have similarly been examined only rarely in Salisbury; a kiln flue remains visible near Skew Bridge Road, Bemerton (*ibid.*) while excavated examples comprise traces of a two-flue, updraft kiln, which was found at the site of the former Old Manor Hospital. Both stoke holes were blocked by over-fired bricks (Wright pers. comm.).

'Backlands'

Archaeological excavations within the city have, unsurprisingly, focused attention on street frontage locations and often overlooked the potential of the 'backlands'. However, increased construction infill of the chequers, as a result of redevelopment for residential use, has increased opportunities to examine these areas (**Fig. 4.11**). They are traditionally viewed as having formed sparsely developed open areas with yards, gardens, small-scale stock pens and workshops that were infilled by the late 19th century. Marsh Chequer is now considered to be one of the few examples that retains characteristics of a more open medieval chequer. This image was reflected in surveys by Speed in 1611 and in a more detailed survey by Naish in 1716, who showed largely undeveloped areas behind regular, stylised street frontage terraces. This survey also depicted several high-status medieval buildings that extended into the 'backlands', disrupting the symmetry of the street frontage. These buildings included the Trinity Hospital in Trinity Chequer, Thomas Freeman's residence in Vanner's Chequer, and buildings confirmed by excavation (Wessex Archaeology 2014a) at the former bus station in Three Swans Chequer. In contrast, the Red Lion Hotel, a major courtyard structure in Antelope Chequer, was surprisingly omitted by Naish. The survey also showed that parts of the city, including a block of land that extended through Gore Chequer from Endless Street to Rollestone Street, remained undeveloped. These details have seemingly been confirmed by evaluation of deposits on the Rollestone Street frontage (Wessex Archaeology 2017b), where a large open area containing no medieval foundations was enclosed by an early-17th-century boundary wall. Similar undeveloped breaks in the terraces were confirmed by Rawlings (2000) on Ivy Street, and apparently also at Goddard's Garage (W196) on St Edmund's Church Street in Three Cups Chequer (Wessex Archaeology 1987), where excavations detected an interruption in the terrace at a point shown by Naish.

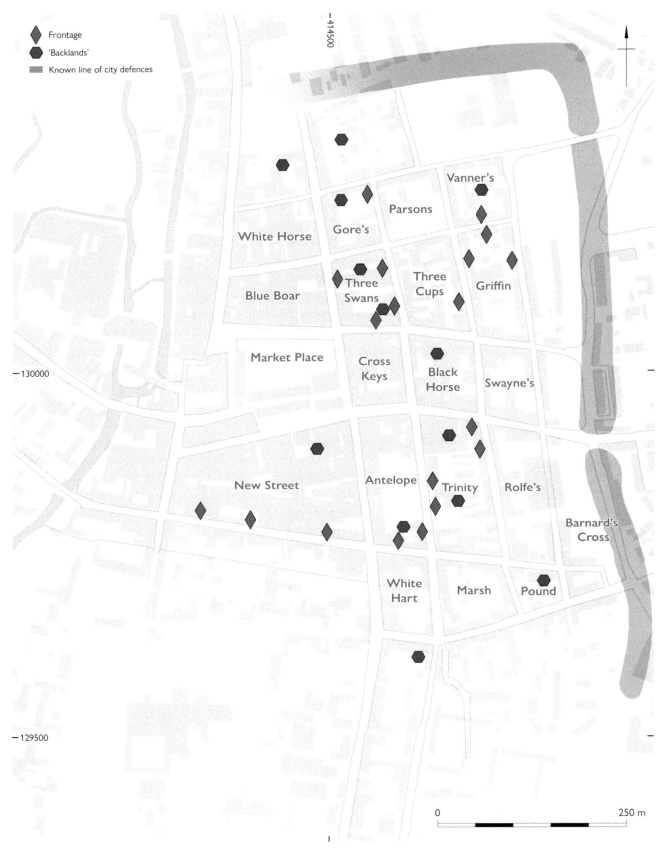

Figure 4.11 Distribution of trenches examining street frontage locations and those in the 'backlands'

The results of these excavations into the 'backlands', which contributed to the economy of the city, now make it possible to reconstruct their appearance in more detail. Some of these projects (Harding 2016; TVAS 2014a) have seemingly confirmed the scarcity of buildings; however, Butterworth (2005b) contradicted the evidence by locating traces of a well-built structure, which may have been part of a courtyard property, of mid-/late 13th-century date, within the Trinity Chequer 'backlands'. The excavations at Nos 49 and 51 Brown Street (see above) have also confirmed that use of the 'backlands', especially in the later medieval and post-medieval periods, was more extensive than previously thought. Service ranges, cobbled yards, wells, latrines, pits and ancillary structures, extending to the Town Ditch, were relatively common. The discovery of outbuildings in both Vanner's Chequer and Trinity Chequer, each with a hearth located in the corner of the building, suggests that these structures may have performed significant functions within the household, including detached kitchens and workshops, and were not mere 'garden sheds'. Similar patterns of buildings within the chequer have now been recognised at the site of the former bus station (see Chapter 2; Cotswold Archaeology 2017; Garland et al. 2021; Wessex Archaeology 2014a). The range, density and impermanence of these buildings, the dating and use of which often remains conjectural, undoubtedly varied between individual chequers, tenements and owners, but nevertheless inject a more vibrant use of the 'backlands' than may have been envisaged previously.

The high-status premises within the walled Cathedral Close, which provided homes initially for the clergy and subsequently for the wealthy, also contained equivalent 'backlands'. Opportunities to examine these highly desirable plots have been limited, but test pits have been dug at the front and rear of the King's House, now Salisbury Museum (Wessex Archaeology 2016; 2017c; 2018a). These small examinations made it possible to trace foundations of late medieval and post-medieval buildings and ranges, which documented marked changes to the appearance of the Close but also confirmed a predictable contrast between open areas at the front of the building and those at the rear. The former comprised relatively sterile surfaced courtyards, producing only limited quantities of roof tile in the make-up layers, while the latter, which were maintained as gardens, contained collections of clay tobacco pipe, animal bone and pottery.

Water Supply, Cess Pits and Refuse Disposal

The medieval city was founded on the flood plain of the River Avon, a source which theoretically provided a constant supply of fresh drinking water, but which brought with it an ever-present threat of flooding. In addition, the urban population created quantities of domestic and human waste, the recovery of which, from pits and cess pits across the city (**Fig. 4.12**) has added immeasurably to understanding the lives of the inhabitants.

Water channelled through the watercourses (**Fig. 4.5**) was exploited for domestic use, although the system also functioned to flush waste products into the main river, making the water insanitary for drinking.

The proximity of the water table made it possible to supplement the water supply from chalk-lined wells, which have been encountered in many excavations (**Pls 4.32 and 4.33**) across Salisbury (Cotswold Archaeology 2017; Harding 2016; Saunders and Algar 2017; Wessex Archaeology 2013). Most were located conveniently behind the main residential range (**Fig. 4.12**) where they could be accessed by adjoining households. When revealed, they are typically 0.8 m in diameter and lined with chalk blocks near the surface, although bricks became more common in later examples. Despite their frequency, only one example (Saunders and Algar 2017), in Milford Street, has been fully excavated. The results demonstrated that these features contain a wealth of untapped information, emphasising that further examples should be examined provided safe methods of working are implemented. Their ubiquitous construction renders them difficult to date; however, construction probably commenced in the medieval period (*ibid.*) after which they were used and replaced (Harding 2016) continuously. Despite the filtering properties of chalk, which may have made water sourced from wells more attractive, supplies from wells were invariably tainted by fluids seeping from adjacent cesspits (Chandler 1983), which are also well represented in the city's archaeological record. Public health was therefore a constant issue before the installation of a municipal water supply in the 1850s.

Conditions in medieval and later Salisbury were clearly insanitary, as can be confirmed by repeated accounts of disease throughout the city. The identification of cess pits is largely indisputable; most are distinguished by deposits of mineralised excreta at the base, which contain well-preserved plant and food remains. Cess pits were often located to the rear of the tenement (**Fig. 4.12**), keeping insanitary smells away from the street frontage, although this pattern is not consistent. Butterworth (2005a) recorded chalk-lined cisterns, which may have included cesspits, containing 13th-century pottery, immediately behind the street frontage while others, including intercutting examples, were located towards the rear of the property.

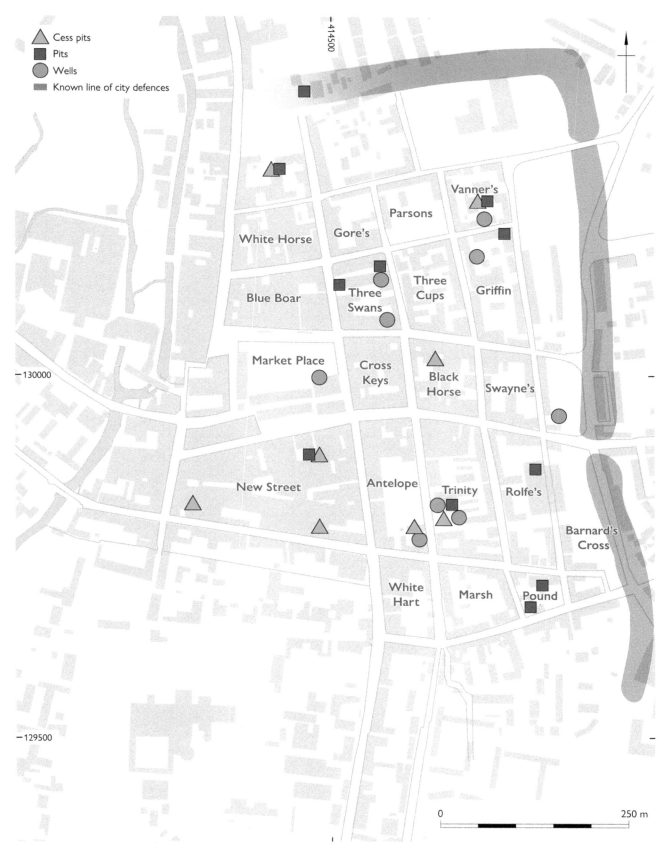

Figure 4.12 Distribution of excavated cess pits, pits and wells in Salisbury

Plate 4.32 Chalk-lined wells at ATS site, St Edmund's Church Street

Plate 4.33 Chalk-lined wells in Salt Lane

Plate 4.34 Medieval chalk-lined cesspit at Bedwin Street

Plate 4.35 Medieval chalk-lined cesspits at Nos 7–11 Brown Street

These features were predominantly chalk-lined (**Pls 4.34–4.35**), although an unlined example, within a small service range at a property in Brown Street (Rawlings 2000), was later replaced by a more substantial chalk-lined structure. It seems reasonable to suppose that cess pits were protected from the elements by a timber superstructure, although no archaeological evidence has been recorded to confirm this. Living conditions in Salisbury were probably no worse than many experienced by medieval urban communities. Barnwell and Palmer (2019) undertook a detailed study of working-class communities, centred primarily on urban populations of the 18th and 19th centuries. Similar standards of hygiene and odours had probably remained largely unchanged since the medieval period and similarly prevailed in Salisbury. Cess pits required emptying, a process that was not undertaken routinely. The resulting nightsoil was extracted and used as fertiliser. This process may have involved transport through the house, a prospect that may have been necessary in Salisbury, where access to the rear of the tenement was frequently via a through-passage.

Human waste is also likely to have been deposited directly into any of Salisbury's water courses, especially where a channel flowed to the rear of any tenement, theoretically allowing material to be flushed ultimately into the River Avon. The RCHME (1993, 168) noted the presence of stone latrine chutes in the Close Wall that emptied into the Close Ditch, confirming its use as an open sewer. This option may well have also proved attractive in chequers such as Trinity Chequer, where the Town Ditch ran through the central axis of the chequer, at the rear of tenements fronting on Brown Street and Gigant Street. No corresponding privies have been recorded for the Town Ditch, although it undoubtedly served a similar function and may have reduced the need for chalk-lined cess pits in tenements that were adjacent to the Town Ditch.

Domestic and industrial refuse was routinely tipped into the water channels, as can be confirmed by the large quantities of metalwork that were collected in the 19th century and that now form the Drainage Collection (Saunders 2009) in Salisbury Museum. This distinctive component represents probably only a fraction of the material that was undoubtedly discarded in the watercourses. More wide-ranging collections of refuse have been recovered as a result of systematic excavations of archaeological layers. Some of the stratigraphic detail and preservation of the artefact assemblages from these projects has been blurred by more recent disturbance, obscuring the amount of detail that can be extracted, especially where they relate to the process of refuse disposal. Wherever levels of detail have been sufficient to document daily life, the recurring trend has illustrated medieval residents living in what may now be considered 'squalid' conditions (Barber 2005, 206). Households demonstrated a distinct lack of controlled waste disposal, with refuse routinely discarded on middens. The summary report for No. 51 Brown Street echoed these sentiments, describing 'occupation or midden debris' (Wessex Archaeology 1992a, 21) in the early phases of occupation. These descriptions noted that floor surfaces of 13th- and 14th-century date were frequently covered with trampled debris. This feature of medieval domesticity persisted until the 15th and 16th century, when quantities of comparable and easily dated material on floors were reduced. This observation was especially evident both in Brown Street and at the Anchor Brewery (Barber 2005), where it was attributed to the introduction of wooden floors, which could be swept and cleaned more easily.

The use of pits for refuse disposal has been discussed wherever excavations have been undertaken in Salisbury. Hawkes (nd) referenced the shortfall of domestic waste in the archaeological record and the apparent scarcity of pits within the city for refuse disposal, citing the high water table or city statutes by way of explanation. Seeking alternative explanations, he argued that some form of systematic refuse collection strategy may have been in operation. Nevertheless, pits were found in the excavations between 1984 and 1990, including at Belle Vue House, a site that Hawkes considered may have been sufficiently peripheral to provide an exception to the rule. Pits were also found in this campaign of excavation at Culver Street, which produced pottery dating from the earliest phases of the city, and at Brown Street and New Canal. Finds assemblages, including 13th- and 14th-century pottery, animal bone and metalwork were often only found in restricted quantities, suggesting that these pits may have served an alternative function.

Plate 4.36 Salt Lane,
Vanner's Chequer: refuse pits
below medieval floor levels

Subsequent excavations across many parts of the city have now increased the number of pits, their character, location and date (**Fig. 4.12**). The increase in data has shown that, despite remaining relatively scarce, pits occur more frequently than previously thought. They have now been found not only on the lower slopes of Milford Hill at Emmaus House (Reynolds and Manning 2013), Belle Vue House, Culver Street and Vanner's Chequer (Harding 2016), where they arguably avoid the high-water level, but also in increasing numbers from sites on the flood plain, including New Canal, Brown Street and Endless Street (TVAS 2014a).

Pits containing 13th- and 14th-century material have been found in all parts of the city, including concentrations along the street frontage, pre-dating the earliest buildings, as at Vanner's Chequer (Harding 2016) (**Pl. 4.36**) and the former bus station (see Chapter 2; Cotswold Archaeology 2017). In contrast, pits were conspicuously absent from the central part of the bus station site (Garland *et al.* 2021), possibly due to the fact that these areas had been maintained as yards. However, pits have also been reported where excavations have ventured into backland areas of the city, where deep soil deposits have accumulated. These features have included examples with 13th- and 14th-century pottery, but elsewhere have contained assemblages of 15th- and 16th-century date, as at Vanner's Chequer (Harding 2016) and New Canal (see Chapter 2), locations where domestic refuse may have been attached to high-status residences. Other pits in Vanner's Chequer were more expansive (**Pl. 4.37**), over 1 m deep, and produced only small quantities of medieval pottery. Harding (2016) argued that these features could be explained more satisfactorily as quarry pits, which were dug to exploit the 'brickearth' to provide source material for wall and floor daub.

Plate 4.37 Vanner's Chequer: 'brickearth' quarry pits

Elsewhere, pits in No. 51 Brown Street were filled with horn cores, with another at ATS site in St Edmund's Church Street, which contained skulls, implying that they were related to craft-specific activity (**Pl. 4.38**). These features demonstrate that pits throughout the life of the city have served a range of functions, many unrelated directly to refuse disposal.

The use of pits for disposal of domestic refuse in Salisbury may have fluctuated according to fashion, household status, population size or health and period. It is possible, indeed likely, that some of the shallower pits were subsequently re-worked into cultivated soils forming the 'backlands'. Much of the refuse was undoubtedly organic, providing potential green manure to maintain soil condition in the 'backlands' or possibly moved to arable land surrounding the city. Further domestic waste may have been recycled as fodder for pigs, which were probably maintained and fattened by individual households in the 'backlands', as Higbee (2016) has demonstrated in Brown Street and elsewhere in Salisbury.

Plate 4.38 Craft-related pit fills: dumped horse skulls at ATS site St Edmund's Church Street, Griffin Chequer

Beyond the Boundaries

Archaeological excavations have been concentrated predominantly within residential parts of medieval Salisbury. However, the city is most widely known for its cathedral, the construction of which encouraged the foundation of the accompanying urban quarter. Apart from its undeniable religious function, the cathedral also contributed to the economy of the city, attracting and dispatching pilgrims across the country and beyond. Artefacts associated with pilgrimage have been found in exceptional numbers in Salisbury (Spencer 1990). They confirm that residents participated in this ebb and flow, undertaking journeys of up to three weeks' duration, visiting shrines at Dover or in East Anglia, and less frequently the continent. Many of the badges that have been recovered are unprovenanced, although large numbers were found in the River Avon or associated watercourses. Spencer (*ibid.*, 11) considered that this process may have perpetuated traditions and superstitions originating from prehistoric deposition of objects in rivers. The scarcity of pilgrim mementos from terrestrial deposits has been confirmed by the limited number of examples from excavations in the city. A single broken example, showing the head of St Thomas Becket, was found in a pit at No. 47 Endless Street with 15th-century pottery (TVAS 2014a). Spencer (1990, 20) noted that badges of this design were inherently weak at the junction of the head and neck and frequently snapped at this point. Badges featuring the bust of Becket were produced in large numbers following his martyrdom, of which at least 15 examples are known from Salisbury (*ibid.*, 20), including one other specimen from a drainage ditch in Endless Street. It is to be expected that souvenirs of Salisbury's own saint, St Osmund, would have been commissioned by the cathedral locally. The process of canonisation was a prolonged one and Osmund's sainthood was not granted until 1457, making it unlikely that souvenirs would have appeared before that date; nevertheless, several stone moulds for making dress accessories, similar to those used for casting pilgrim badges, and faulty castings and scrap metal have been recovered from the River Avon to support this hypothesis.

Salisbury also garnered other institutions with strong religious connections, including St Edmund's College, a foundation with dual duties combining both ecclesiastical and parish work; St Nicholas's Hospital, offering care for the sick, poor and travellers; De Vaux College, a pioneering university foundation teaching theology and arts; and Dominican (Richards 2020) and Franciscan friaries. These establishments were all located on the periphery of the city and were demolished after the Dissolution; only St Nicholas's Hospital, located north of Harnham Bridge, retains large parts of its medieval core, while De Vaux, immediately west of St Nicholas's Hospital, also contains fragments of medieval construction. In addition, many towns and cities in medieval England included hospitals for the care of those suffering from leprosy. Salisbury maintained at least two such institutions dedicated to St John the Baptist and St Anthony at Old Sarum (**Fig. 4.2, 31**) and another at East Harnham (Chandler 1983).

Despite their undoubted importance and robust stone build, traces of these former establishments and their ground plan have remained hidden. This vacuum has been partially filled by rediscovery of foundations related to St Edmund's College (Chaffey and Fitzpatrick 2015), in the north-east corner of the city. The archaeological findings, derived from a series of small evaluation trenches and archaeological watching briefs, identified two ranges, each approximately 5.8 m across, with cellars underlying the south range. These ranges were probably constructed around a quadrangular cloister garth approximately 15 m across. Fragments of door and window mouldings manufactured from dressed Chilmark stone provided additional architectural detail of the superstructure. A gatehouse may have faced onto Bedwin Street with land surrounding the college maintained as an open area with gardens. Archaeological excavations have also located probable traces of the hospital of St John the Baptist and St Anthony, which served as a refuge for those afflicted by leprosy. The precise location of this institution, which, like similar establishments, was situated on the outskirts of the city, remained unknown until traces of a ditched enclosure were revealed unexpectedly during installation of a water main. The enclosure surrounded a building that was constructed of chalk and faced with flint, and was accompanied by a cemetery containing at least 30 graves (Powell 2006). The site was located approximately 500 m along the line of the Roman road leading from the east gate to Old Sarum castle. Documents record the existence of the hospital by 1231, although details of its decline are less certain. Powell (*ibid.*) noted that the archaeological fieldwork, which was restricted to exposing the outline of the building and graves, failed to produce any late medieval material, suggesting that the hospital may have been largely inactive by then.

Archaeological projects have also located possible traces of other structures that once adorned the city streets. Observations during alterations to Market Place (Wessex Archaeology 2014c) located a series of stone foundations in the north-east corner of the square. The foundations, which were located approximately 1.5 m from the existing ground surface, survived to a height of between 0.5 m and 0.75 m and were built of neatly jointed blocks of Chilmark limestone. They could be traced for approximately 7 m from east to west before they disappeared beyond the limits of the trenching. Two explanations for these foundations can be suggested, including the possibility that they represent a long-lost remnant of the Old Council House, about which so little is known. This building was erected for secular administration and was originally built at the west end of Market Place. It was subsequently rebuilt at the east end of Market Place in the early 1580s, near the present war memorial. There is no precise footprint of the building, which was probably built on stone or flint foundations. Eighteenth-century illustrations (Benson and Hatcher 1843, 533) show it with a timber frame of three stories, open colonnades at the sides and a central turret. It was seriously damaged by fire in 1780, after which it was agreed to amalgamate the Bishop's Guildhall and the Council House in a single guildhall, which still forms the principal civic building in the city. Alternatively, it has been suggested (Wessex Archaeology 2014c) that the foundations may have formed part of a bridge abutment spanning the water channel at the junction of Winchester Street and Queen Street. Similar strategically placed crossing points are shown (**Fig. 4.5**) in surveys by Speed in 1611 and by Naish in 1716 including one at this junction, although these foundations are arguably too distant from the street intersection to be convincing. Nevertheless, access points, which can be easily overlooked, undoubtedly provided an essential component of the formal communications network within the city and deserve to be recognised. They were undoubtedly supplemented by other precarious crossing points of the type shown in the engraving by W H Bartlett published by John Britton in 1829 (see Chandler 1983, pl. 18).

Salisbury Residents

But what of the Salisbury residents themselves? Chandler (1983, fig. 5) painted a picture of a population that was difficult to predict for much of the medieval period, but which may have risen to approximately 4000–5000 by 1400, rising to 7000–8000 by 1455 – a level it maintained for much of its history. This figure is likely to represent permanent residents, although the total may well have been supplemented on a daily basis, much as it remains to the present day, by travellers, pilgrims and elements from the surrounding rural community. The medieval city was populated by a range of entrepreneurs as well as practical creative craftspeople, who may have traded from shops within their homes or from on-street stalls, with supplementary elements of the community living in poverty. The social status of these diverse residents and their occupations may be reflected in the archaeological record by more expansive building designs and the composition of artefact assemblages. Chandler (*ibid.*) has examined a large quantity of documentary evidence relating to Salisbury, its residents and their related occupations. Some of these initial residents may have relocated from Old Sarum; others were incomers, attracted by the new city. Chandler (*ibid.*, 39) noted that immigration has featured extensively throughout the story of Salisbury, initially from locations within a radius of 20 miles of the city but increasingly from further afield in later periods. These incoming groups often filled gaps created by population decline following periods of plague.

Linking individuals to excavated tenements is a challenging prospect, but the data does exist in the form of the Salisbury Domesday books (Hobbs and Chandler 2012). These documents, written in Latin, recorded all property transactions, including details of buyers and sellers, locations and neighbouring properties in the city between 1317 and 1479. Similar studies in Winchester (Keene 1985), Bristol (Leech 1997) and Exeter (Rippon and Holbrook 2021b) have made it possible to link people with places in a way that should also be possible for Salisbury (Chandler pers. comm.). Linking archaeological discoveries with specific named medieval Salisbury residents has been attempted in a small number of instances. High-status properties are inevitably better represented by documents linking them to owners and professions; Currie and Rushton (2005) used mid-14th-century records to relate Edward, son of Philip Glastynbury, in the sale of premises at the corner of Nos 36 Milford Street/34 Gigant Street to William Teynturer. Similar research has also highlighted the potential relationship of people to places at No. 10 Endless Street (Chandler 2021), where medieval building foundations may be linked to a series of named individuals, including Alice Sime, who occupied the tenement in 1421 (Chandler 2013), with later occupants including Francis Dove, Francis Mercer and Samuel Case (Chandler 2021). These men, two of whom served as mayor of Salisbury, occupied the medieval premises in the late 17th and early 18th centuries, before major redevelopment in 1740. Complementary research of documents relating to Nos 47–51 Brown Street (summarised above), has provided a glimpse of the diverse, less affluent individuals who may have occupied the tenements identified by subsequent excavations. Some of these have been named, including Sebode the cutler, John Leminge, skinner, Thomas Spencer, feltmaker, and Joel Sanger, clay pipe maker, while others are known only by their occupations: carpenters, wire drawers and bakers.

These disclosures confirm that residents of Salisbury lived a range of lifestyles, representing a variety of statuses. Life was more physically demanding for those with more practical lifestyles. These former residents lie in the graveyards of churches or religious orders that are located within the city boundaries. Opportunities for study are rare; no large excavation of a medieval cemetery has been undertaken in the city of the type that has taken place in York, where over 1000 burials were excavated at the church of St Helen-on-the Walls (Dawes and Magilton 1980). Inhumation burials have, nevertheless, been exposed and recorded, representing physical remains, containing evidence of diet and lifestyle, of past Salisbury residents. Most of these remains, invariably discovered during routine renovation at the city's churches, have not been exhumed or were reburied soon after they were lifted.

Discoveries cover a range of social classes, including those who were sufficiently wealthy and eligible to be interred at Salisbury Cathedral. Two inhumation burials were found during excavations (Wessex Archaeology 2009) within the Beauchamp Chantry Chapel, including one that may have been of Bishop Beauchamp's older brother William, Lord St Amand, who served as sheriff of Wiltshire in 1436, 1442 and 1447 and died in 1457 (**Pl. 4.39**).

Plate 4.39 Burial in Beauchamp Chapel, Salisbury Cathedral, possibly that of William, Lord St Amand

Five incomplete burials, all apparently of adult males, had been disturbed by the construction of the 15th-century chapel. They showed only slight evidence of physical stress, suggesting that they were not of the labouring classes. The excavation was restricted to the footprint of the chapel, but nevertheless the results provided fascinating hints that burials may have been clustered by aspect, age or sex (Daniell 1997, 99; Gilchrist and Sloane 2005, 70), this area to the south-east of the cathedral being largely occupied by adult males. Other former residents lie in the lay cemetery surrounding the cathedral, an area that remains untouched archaeologically.

Archaeological investigations have also recovered human remains, which appear to represent less affluent residents, at the site of the former Dominican friary in Fisherton Street, which was dissolved in 1538 (Wessex Archaeology 2019a). Parts of at least six individuals, aligned west–east, were recovered, from which it was possible to estimate that two males were of comparable height – approximately 1.71 m – to the medieval period average (Roberts and Cox 2003), with another slightly taller at 1.77–1.80 m. These individuals, in contrast to those from the cathedral, apparently led a more physically demanding lifestyle accompanied by age-related degeneration of the joints and spine. The bones may also have documented people living in insanitary conditions; two skulls showed surface damage of the type that results from localised scalp irritation and infection, possibly related to lice infestation, a condition that may not have been uncommon.

In contrast, documentary sources reveal that some relatively affluent members of the community elected to be buried at the friary. This preference for the well-off to be buried in mendicant churches, rather than the local parish church, became a common practice from the early 13th century and persisted in later medieval towns and cities across the country. 'It seems that the churches of the provincial friars filled with lay tombs, memorials and chantries with an intensity comparable to their city counterparts' (Clark 2019, 298). Haskins (1909) described how George Meriot requested burial in the friary in 1410 while, at the same time, providing benefactions to St Thomas's Church for repair to St Stephen's Chapel. Similarly, Elias Home, in 1348, Robert Strode and John Denburg, in 1361, and Sir Roger Beauchamp, in 1406, all opted for burial within the Dominican friary (Pugh and Crittall 1956a). The friary enjoyed considerable royal sponsorship throughout the 13th century (ibid., 331). This was marked by materials from Clarendon Park for construction purposes as well as personal visits from the monarch.

Plate 4.40 Details of the Doom painting, St Thomas's Church, with (left) those welcomed to heaven and (right) those fated for hell

These discoveries and observations have been formed from only a small number of burials but may provide some indication of life in medieval Salisbury. Research from larger samples collected from cemetery excavations in Cambridge (Dittmar *et al.* 2021) has demonstrated that daily life for urban medieval populations was frequently accompanied by risk. The samples, representing a range of population composition, were taken from a parish cemetery, a hospital and Augustinian friary. The survey showed that fractures – resulting from accidents from daily manual work or, not infrequently, violence – were common. Fractures were especially frequent in males who were buried in the parish burial ground, which suggested that the poorer elements of society were, unsurprisingly, at greatest risk of injury.

Medieval populations are also depicted pictorially on the famous Doom painting that adorns the chancel arch of St Thomas's Church in the city. This illustration (**Pl. 4.40, left**), showing the rewards awaiting those who had lived God-fearing lives, with access to heaven, are shown on the north side of the arch. They are countered (**Pl. 4.40, right**) by sinners, on the south side, who are being herded into the jaws of hell. These people include a bishop and a wealthy figure of society who is shown clutching two bags containing ill-gotten financial gains. This painting, which was extensively repainted by the Victorians, originally dates from 1470, when Salisbury was at its most prosperous.

It represents all humankind and it is tempting to believe that the painter, like many medieval woodworkers and stone masons with an appropriate sense of humour, may have been influenced by specific Salisbury residents of whom they had personal knowledge.

Representative members of the Salisbury congregation have also been encountered at St Edmund's Church (Wessex Archaeology 2012), where twelve undated graves and two tombs were recorded. Pathological details were considered unremarkable and both sexes were represented; nevertheless, this small collection included both adult and infant burials, recalling the level of infant mortality that undoubtedly persisted in the past.

Traces of Salisbury's former residents were also recovered during a watching brief following completion of work at the site of the former Anchor Brewery in Gigant Street (Barber 2005). Two inhumation burials, both extensively disturbed, were lifted from a Quaker burial ground adjacent to a meeting house that was active between 1712 and 1827. Further details of this 'lost' burial ground and the density of burials are unknown; perversely, its use undoubtedly destroyed archaeological traces of the medieval city just as it was itself extensively disturbed, without record, by the construction of the brewery in the 1940s.

Large numbers of residents, from all levels of society, succumbed to plague, which visited the city most frequently in the summer months; Chandler (1983) noted that 172 burials alone were added to St Edmund's churchyard in September 1563. Individual artefacts can also draw attention to this aspect of Salisbury life, stimulating further study using documentary sources. An archaeological watching brief at No. 24 Endless Street (Wessex Archaeology 2019c) observed the removal of a 19th-century brick tenement boundary that was founded on recycled material that included limestone ashlar blocks and gravestone fragments. One gravestone was inscribed with the names of Mary and her spouse, Andrew Randell. Genealogical searches revealed no trace of Andrew Randell but discovered records showing that Andrew Randoll married Mary Burr on 28 October 1727 at St Edmund's Church. Sadly, they both died within four weeks of one another in November and December 1753. They were followed soon after by '2 infants', both also bearing the name Randoll, although it is not certain precisely how they were related to Andrew or Mary. Chandler (1983) noted that smallpox was especially virulent in the 18th century, with a severe epidemic in Salisbury in 1752, which may have accounted for the rapid demise of this family. Furthermore, St Edmund's Church was extensively refurbished by Gilbert Scott in 1865–7, which may provide an intriguing mechanism by which recycled rubble, including unwanted gravestones, was transferred to Endless Street.

Professions

These residents were the lifeblood of Salisbury, contributing to the story of the city by their diverse professions. The range of building construction epitomises this diversity, where the wealthier elements acquired the choice tenement locations while the less well-off may have filled the remaining blocks – features that characterise Trinity Chequer, a chequer populated by residents of mixed status. Among Salisbury's wealthiest residents were a select band of merchants (Hare 2020) who traded extensively with the coast, importing a wide range of products including raw materials for dyeing and cloth processing, together with raisins, oil, wine and soap. These principal components of the city economy, many related to the import and export of products connected to wool, leave no archaeological traces and those responsible for creating this wealth must be identified by the location of their homes and composition of their discarded refuse. Artefacts related to wool industries, from which Salisbury derived so much of its medieval wealth, are, not surprisingly, poorly represented by excavated objects. However, Chandler noted (1983, 110) that weavers and fullers occupied all parts of the city by 1400, with concentrations of weavers to the east of Catherine Street and around St Ann Street. Fullers were more prevalent towards Castle Street and near St Edmund's Church. Excavated evidence for this profession has been more forthcoming; fulling tanks, possibly linked to specialist felt making, were present at No. 51 Brown Street (Chapter 2, W227). Dyers occupied the areas bordering the river with merchants concentrated around the Market Place. Documentation had improved by the 17th century and Chandler was able to reconstruct the spread of professions more accurately. Weavers remained within all parts of the city but featured a concentration to the south of Milford Street, which included Trinity Chequer.

These congregations featuring specific crafts undoubtedly intermingled with other trades, crafts and occupations; a survey of 1455 listed countless changes in owners, occupants and professions (Chandler 1983). This trend can be seen archaeologically by variations in craft by-products created by successive occupants at No. 51 Brown Street.

Tanners, leather workers and horn workers also thrived; tanners accounted for 14% of the labour force in Salisbury in 1399/1400 (Chandler 1983). These trades can be recognised by distinctive craft residues, as indicated by a pit filled with horse skulls in St Edmund's Church Street (Wessex Archaeology 2013). Probable horn-working debris, linked to the production of knife handles or drinking vessels and possibly the production of neatsfoot oil used by leather-dressers (Harman 1996, 89; MacGregor 1985, 119; Serjeantson 1989, 139) is known from No. 51 Brown Street. This archaeological evidence may be compared with documentary sources indicating that tanners occupied parts of the New Street Ward, which extended to St Ann Street, in 1400 (Chandler 1983). This may have formed a convenient link with the cattle market at Barnard's Cross, in the south-east corner of the city. Tanners maintained a presence in this part of the city until at least 1667 although records show that they were also resident in the Castle Street area and beyond, towards the periphery of the city (Higbee 2016), suggesting some degree of fluidity within the population.

Other professions could be located using street names; Love Lane, which extends south from Gigant Street and undoubtedly acquired its name from prostitution, is located close to Trinity Hospital, which was itself reputedly constructed on the site of a former brothel (Pugh and Crittall 1956b). Prostitution was relatively common in many medieval towns and cities and was tolerated as a means of moderating other forms of violent physical and sexual exploitation.

More practical issues may have influenced the location of other industries; Chandler (1983) noted the concentration of bell and utensil foundries on the east side of the city to minimise the effects of the prevailing wind as a fire hazard. This area effectively filled a gap between the city chequers and the city ramparts. The site of the foundry owned by John Barbur, who died in 1404, was located at the corner of Milford Street and Guilder Lane. Excavations (Algar and Saunders 2012), during construction of the Inner Ring Road, showed that the site was initially occupied in the late 13th or early 14th century by potters (Algar and Saunders 2014), who built a kiln on the land. The subsequent foundry, which probably commenced production soon after 1350, manufactured bells and domestic vessels, including tripod cauldrons, and continued in production into the late medieval period. Traces of a furnace were also noted, including the remains a bell-casting pit that extended across the tail of the city rampart, indicating that this earthwork had become obsolete during the later life of the foundry. These industries, potting and metalworking, both benefited from being down-wind of the city and may also have utilised fuel supplied from woodland to the south-east of Salisbury (Algar and Saunders 2014). It is unclear whether mould fragments from casting metal that were found in a levelling layer at Nos 49 and 51 Brown Street relate to a separate centre of production or, more probably, were brought in from the known foundry in Guilder Lane. Chandler (1983) emphasised the significant contribution made to the city's economy by specialist metalworkers, including goldsmiths, ironmongers, needlers, braziers, cutlers and armourers, who were all active in Salisbury by the 14th century.

Archaeological excavations have shown that metalworkers, who created distinctive waste products including highly vitrified slag and hammerscale, were not restricted to the city fringes. Smithing debris was recovered from 13th–14th-century deposits at two locations in New Street (Butterworth 2005a) where residue from a hearth, with an attached flue, may have indicated the presence of specialist copper workers. More extensive traces of iron working – containing debris from hot forging and welding, including hearth bases and hammerscale – of 18th century date were found along the frontage of Rollestone Street (Cotswold Archaeology 2017; Garland et al. 2021).

Ordnance Survey mapping indicated that the industry had persisted, albeit at an adjacent property in Three Swans Chequer, into the 19th century. Smaller quantities of iron-working debris, including hammerscale, slag and coal, were also found at the Milford Street/Gigant Street site (Currie and Rushton 2005), where it was considered to be medieval in date. Some of these episodes may have marked short-term intervals in the residential use of the site while in other cases the industry may have been more prolonged. These threads linking archaeological and documentary evidence confirm that heavy-duty industry, including metalworking, persisted in the city from the medieval period into more recent times, as the discoveries of crucibles from Milford Hill House (see Chapter 3) demonstrate.

Sadly, much of the evidence for those trades that produced small quantities of industrial by-products is limited. This makes conclusions entirely speculative, as with material related to pin making from the River Avon near Bridge Street, which Algar (2012, 238) suggested may have indicated that pin makers were active in this part of the city.

There are several references to masons living outside and to the east of the cathedral contemporary with construction work in the Close during the early 13th century. Archaeological excavations have also contributed to illuminating this trade by recovering stone-working debris, including Purbeck marble chippings, from a shallow ditch beneath the foundations of the cathedral bell tower (Wessex Archaeology 2009). Dumps of stone-working debris were also recorded in the Plumbery (Butterworth 2005c) adjoining the south wall of the nave and illustrating the character of the cathedral as a building site. This evidence depicts an area containing temporary workshops including the masons' lodge, carpenters' shops, smiths' forges and plumbers' shops. Similar localised workshops probably extended across the city, preparing and finalising timber frames for domestic buildings in carpenters' shops before they were erected on-site.

The story becomes less confused during the post-medieval period, by which time records are more reliable and tenements can be located with more accuracy. In this way archaeological excavations within the city have not only confirmed the locations of individual workshops but also supplemented information on the range of products manufactured from those premises. Most notably, these local industries include the workshops and waste heaps of clay pipe makers Joel Sanger, who produced pipes in the first half of the 18th century and who can be located with some confidence at Nos 49 or 51 Brown Street, and James Skeaines (or Skeaimes) who, with William John Morgan, was based in Salt Lane (**Pl. 4.41**) in the mid-19th century (Mepham 2016b).

Plate 4.41 Salt Lane: clay tobacco pipe waste from the production site of William John Morgan

Brown Street in Salisbury in the year 1500 would have looked much different to what it does today; however, by plotting excavated flint foundations and hearths, which frequently represent the only surviving evidence of these buildings and using surviving examples in Salisbury we can reconstruct the scene. This reveals a street filled with timber-framed houses, with jettied fronts and low tiled roofs. Yet despite looking very similar, in many respects the houses were probably very varied, having been built, rebuilt and modified, often on the same ground plan, since the foundation of the city in 1225. These are not the houses of wealthy merchants who lived in grand buildings based around the city centre but were occupied by people with diverse occupations, many based on wool.

Here we strip away the outer wattle and daub panels to reveal a two-storey building with a range aligned parallel to the street frontage and a service range extending to the rear. We enter the building with a through-passage which allows access to the rear of the house. There are two ground floor rooms and two upper rooms. In many medieval houses the front room would have functioned as a shop where goods were sold; however, in excavations in this part of Salisbury it seems that the front room probably provided the principal living room, heated with a hearth in one corner. The chimney stack was undoubtedly the most durable, fire-resistant feature of the building.

Here we view the rear of the main residence. Immediately behind the house is the well which formed the principal source of water. The 'backlands' often contained small outhouses, each with a hearth suggesting that these buildings may have functioned as detached kitchens, workshops or storage space according to the profession of the occupant. A pig or chickens may have been kept to consume domestic food waste and provide additional meat for the household. Our plot also includes a small kitchen garden. A privy (toilet), covering a chalk-lined cesspit, which would have needed to be cleaned out periodically, has been located at the far end of the plot. Our tenement in Brown Street conveniently backed onto the Town Ditch, into which much of the human waste would have been emptied.

We can also see the kitchen, the principal source of food production. We have located the kitchen in a building that was detached from the main house to minimise the risk of fire, although this arrangement was variable with kitchens frequently located in the main building. The owner enjoys a balanced diet and cooks many of the products that are available today including wild foods, such as seasonal fruits and berries, flour for bread, home-grown vegetables flavoured with herbs and spices all washed down with home-brewed ale. Some food is salted or dried for consumption later in the year. The cooking centres around an open hearth with its oven in which foods were baked.

Located in the service range at the back of the house we find a storeroom. This unheated room is used for keeping raw materials used by the weaver as well as finished examples of the cloth being produced in the workshop above. Other, more domestic items are also stored here including barrels of ale, of varying strengths, that the whole household will drink in preference to water from the well which was frequently contaminated from adjacent cesspits. In the corner of the room is a simple box bed where one of the household servants sleeps.

The parlour served as the principal room of our house. We can see that it contains a basic set of furniture including a table, chairs and benches. The table is set for dinner with wooden platters and bowls, drinking cups and ceramic jars and jugs. The earthen floor has been swept clean but contains trampled debris from the hearth.

Weaving could not take place without spun yarn so it is likely that the female members of our family would have spent at least some time preparing wool for the loom. These processes involved carding, to align the fibres, and spinning, to create the yarn. These vital tasks were undertaken by the women and it is likely that our household contained at least a spinning wheel. Our family has elected to place the spinning wheel in the bed chamber, which was, at the time, not a room set aside purely for sleeping and privacy. It is likely that several members of our family would have all slept in the same room.

Our weaver has placed his workshop with its loom in the south-facing upper room of the service range. The room also contains rolls of finished cloth and yarn that will be converted into cloth. Salisbury was renowned for its production of broadcloth weaves, most notably the Salisbury ray, a distinctive striped tweed, which was produced on a broadcloth loom. The loom required two men to operate it and an assistant to keep them supplied with yarn. Weavers were small businessmen. As such, our weaver probably owns the property and shares the street with other weavers who were numerically the most common group of male clothworkers.

The Local Landscape

The new city was founded within an established agricultural landscape that was dominated geologically by Chalk. Small farming communities, many of Anglo-Saxon foundation, were located on the lower slopes of river valleys or seasonal winterbournes. These manors traditionally occupied linear blocks of land, which featured cultivated strip fields adjoining the settlement with permanent grazing on the higher Chalk downs. Much of the local economy was based around wool, the marketing of which helped to elevate and maintain the wealth of the city. Chandler (1983) has described the organisation of wool supply through Salisbury. Much of this was initially for immediate export, but after 1400 movement slowed, and wool was retained and converted into more profitable cloth production within the city. Such was the impact of weaving on the city's economy that Salisbury became renowned for the production of Salisbury ray, a striped broadcloth with the appearance of tweed. Land to the south-east of Salisbury formed the western tip of the London Basin, which comprised a mixture of woodland and heath. This contrasting landscape also provided valuable natural resources for the city that were not replicated on the Chalk. Traces of their exploitation is evident from the charcoal and mineralised seeds extracted from excavated soil samples in the city.

The contrasting roles performed by rural and urban communities have been highlighted in the varying levels of affluence and lifestyle of rural communities, as exemplified at Gomeldon, and those enjoyed by urban residents. Both communities had access to similar markets, however, as Mepham has identified (see Chapter 3). Salisbury residents developed an affinity with higher-quality items, as illustrated by the quantities of tableware recovered. Rural communities, in contrast, were marked by functional household vessels related to food preparation and storage. The pattern is repeated in the assemblage composition of animal bones, where luxury species, including swan and heron, while not ubiquitous, were more prevalent from excavations in Salisbury (see Higbee, Chapter 3) than from Gomeldon (Musty and Algar 1986).

The new city was also located within the catchment of the royal hunting park and palace at Clarendon (**Fig. 4.2, 30**). This establishment (**Pl. 4.42**) represented not only a seat of royal power and competitor to the Church but also a convenient market for luxury goods and products, including fine wares from the kilns at Laverstock, and other desirables that became available in the city. The estate was, during the city's foundation, the largest royal deer park in Britain, covering 1737 ha (4292 acres) and was at the peak of its power in the early 14th century (James and Gerrard 2007), when the new city was developing. However, as Salisbury prospered, Clarendon entered a period of slow decline. Direct archaeological evidence from successive excavations that can be used to demonstrate a clear relationship between the respective owners of the city and palace, church and state, is indeterminate, although certain classes of material from the city may have been derived from activities at Clarendon.

Red, roe and fallow deer bones have all been recovered from excavations in Salisbury; Higbee (see Chapter 3) has postulated that these might have been offered to wealthy patrons who may have participated in or been connected to members of the hunt. James and Gerrard (2007) noted that red and roe deer had both declined in numbers by the 15th century, although fallow deer continued to flourish at Clarendon. It is possible that venison was obtained from other sources, although the connection with Clarendon is unavoidable; it has been estimated (*ibid.*, 62) that between 200 and 400 carcasses may have been produced annually. The park also produced large quantities of rabbits from carefully managed warrens. James and Gerrard (*ibid.*, 59) noted that rabbits were reared at Clarendon on an industrial scale, calculating that annual production may have reached 15,000 each year in the late 15th century. Furthermore, they observed that following the Black Death, improved levels of general affluence made rabbit more accessible to a wider proportion of the population. They concluded that this provided a commercial opportunity that may, in part, be reflected by the rabbit bones recovered from most excavations in the city.

Plate 4.42 Ruins of the Great Hall, Clarendon Palace, overlooking Salisbury in the distance

The park also contained extensive areas of woodland. It is not clear to what extent this resource provided material for the larger properties in the city, but timber from the park is recorded as having been supplied to the Dominican friary for the construction of their church in 1297 (Pugh and Crittall 1956a). Saplings were also provided to enclose the precinct, while oak stumps are also recorded, presumably for firewood. Hazel, beech and ash were coppiced or pollarded on a large scale. James and Gerrard (2007) considered that this was sufficient not only to meet the domestic demands of the kitchens and requirements of the estate but also provided a valuable retail commodity, some of which may also have found its way onto Salisbury fires. This source may have extended to producing lathe-turned bowls, such as that found in waterlogged deposits at the site of the former Dominican friary (**Pl. 44**, below; McNeil 2012, fig. 60), which were used extensively for the table and food preparation.

Environmental Evidence

Much of current knowledge on the use of these woodland resources for fuel and food has been derived from archaeological techniques to extract environmental detail, contained in carbonised and mineralised plant remains, from sediment samples. These techniques have advanced greatly since the excavations of the late 1980s and 1990s and provide details of diet, supplementing evidence of meat consumption represented by bones. They also highlight the use of cultivated and wild plants that might have grown in the city or the surrounding countryside and extend to the availability of imported foodstuffs. Sampling strategies on individual excavations have been determined largely by the availability of well-stratified deposits. These deposits represent a range of contexts including floor surfaces at the Anchor Brewery (Barber 2005) and No. 39 Brown Street, with hearths (Cotswold Archaeology 2017), cess pits (Harding 2016; Rawlings 2000; TVAS 2014a), middens (Barber 2005) and refuse pits (TVAS 2014a) from a range of other locations. The results have been variable and insufficient to differentiate levels of social status within the community; nevertheless, they have reflected consistent aspects of domestic life for people in medieval Salisbury.

Samples from floors and associated hearths at the Anchor Brewery site were among those that produced the most comprehensive results, which can be replicated elsewhere in the city. In addition, they provided the most vivid picture of living conditions within a building, results that were duplicated in samples from No. 39 Brown Street. Charred remains, predominantly derived from fire debris, suggested that the hearths were primarily domestic features, located within the parlour or kitchen, with no supplementary industrial function (Gale 2005). Fuel was derived from a range of deciduous species including oak, hazel, birch, ash, thorn and willow. The analysis from one hearth noted large quantities of charcoal from heather and gorse. These species, which were derived from acidic heathlands to the south-east of the city, functioned as bedding, flooring, fodder and broom-heads but, when discarded, burned quickly and produced great heat. Gale considered that timber was probably supplied to the city as faggots or cordwood from woodlands, which were of great economic value for structural framing and were extensively managed. The environmental residues (Hinton 2005) also contained cereal grains, including wheat, barley and oats, which were grown in the surrounding countryside. They provided staple ingredients for bread, pottage, and brewing but could also be used for animal fodder. Charred weed seeds were also represented, reflecting species common to grassland, cultivated land and fodder. Floor debris from the Anchor Brewery also contained dietary evidence indicating consumption of wild plants and fruit, including hazelnuts, sloes, crab apples, strawberries and wild celery.

Mineralised food waste was more completely preserved in excreta from cess pits, most notably five excavated examples from Ivy Street/Brown Street. The results (Hinton 2000) indicated that the residents of this medieval property consumed a range of fruits, predominantly wild varieties, including plums, sloes and cherries, and apples, both wild and cultivated, as well as blackberries, raspberries and strawberries (**Pl. 4.43**). More exotic species included grapes and figs. The diet was supplemented by a range of vegetables, salads and cereal products and flavoured with black pepper, coriander, fennel, dill and celery. The flow of these luxuries into the city may have formed part of the merchant economy; Chandler (1983) noted that Thomas Hele, a merchant in 1542, listed within his assets imported spices including ginger, dates, nutmeg, cloves and mace. Residues also contained species that may have been exploited for their medicinal properties, including henbane and hemlock, suggesting that residents remained fully aware of the properties of these plants. Hinton (2000) concluded that these dietary traces corresponded with samples that have been examined from other parts of medieval Britain.

Plate 4.43 Magnified examples of environmental materials, including raspberry, apple and elderberry seeds and wheat chaff of the type found in Salisbury's cesspits

This dietary evidence has been supplemented by an animal bone assemblage that documents the consumption of a wide range of red meat; cattle and sheep from the surrounding area, with pork, which was probably raised in the city, supplemented by game (venison, hare and rabbit) and fish brought from the coast. Swan, heron and turkey indicate the presence of affluent residents. White meat also appeared on the menu, including poultry, which also supplied eggs, and fish, as salted cod, pickled herring or smoked conger eel, which were delivered from the Southampton market.

These species were supplemented with oysters, which were probably brought to Salisbury from Poole Harbour, the closest source. Shells, representing both preparation and consumption waste, have been found in the city. These bivalves, along with other marine shell, occur frequently but not apparently in large numbers in medieval Salisbury (Wyles pers. comm.). They may have augmented the diet rather than providing a major component, in contrast with coastal locations, such as Poole and Southampton, or sites on rivers, including London, where oyster beds were prevalent. These locations, marked by large dumps of shell, document where oyster consumption was widespread in all levels of the population throughout the medieval and later periods.

Very little evidence survives in the archaeological record for the consumption of liquids by Salisbury residents, although it is likely to have centred on ale, for general use, with limited demand for wine by the wealthy. Much of the evidence is indirect, including barley as a basic ingredient for brewing as well as the large number of hostelries and inns listed throughout the history of the city. Drinks were probably taken throughout much of the medieval period from wooden bowls, although leather tankards or horn cups may also have been used. Wooden bowls featured prominently in all forms of medieval life, providing vessels for a wide range of functions including not only food preparation and consumption but also medicinal uses. Wood (2005), in a detailed study of wooden bowls and associated vessels, has stressed the important role they served in all levels of society, with representative collections having been recovered from waterlogged deposits in Winchester, London, York and Southampton. These organic vessels were undoubtedly used extensively, but invariably fail to survive; many were used as kindling or simply rotted. However, fragments of a lathe-turned ash bowl (**Pl. 4.44**; McNeil 2012, fig 60), found in waterlogged deposits at the Dominican friary in Fisherton Street, highlight the use of these rarely found artefacts. Ash, which thrives on chalk, was used extensively for producing turned wooden bowls from the 12th to 15th century (Wood 2005, 42). Similar forms are likely to have been included among the most common vessels in households in the city for much of the medieval and post-medieval periods.

Ceramic jugs were specifically designed for the serving of liquid and formed a vital part of the output from the Laverstock kilns. Vessels linked more specifically to the drinking of alcoholic beverages and socialising may be inferred from diagnostic sherds of pottery, of the type represented by the spout from a 16th-century puzzle jug from Vanner's Chequer (Mepham 2016a). These jugs, which were designed to challenge the ingenuity of the drinker to imbibe from a perforated jug without spilling the contents, were most effective during advanced inebriation. More readily identified tankards that were designed specifically for drinking ale appeared in Salisbury during the 15th and 16th centuries when 'Tudor Green' and Raeren stoneware drinking vessels were first documented in the city. Consumption of imported wine can be confirmed by the appearance of glass bottles in the mid-17th century. This beverage was a major import into Salisbury via Southampton, as evidenced by the Brokage Books (which survive for 1430–1566, documenting the tolls charged on goods passing through the Bargate), although much of it was probably sold in the market for consumption elsewhere.

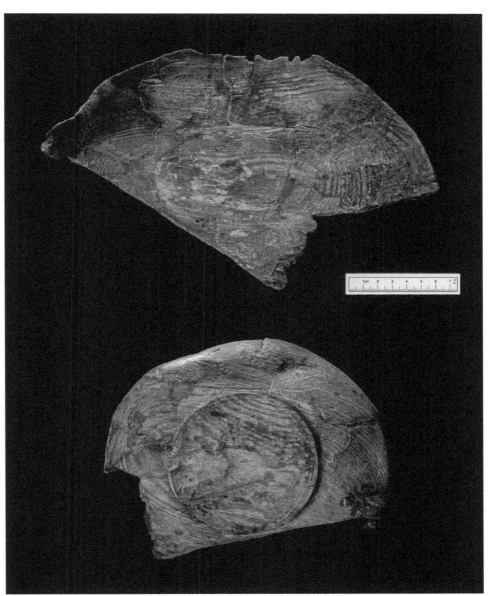

Plate 4.44 Wooden bowl from waterlogged deposits at the Dominican friary; interior view (top) and showing turned foot-ring (below)

Conclusion

The reporting process to publish the results of back-log excavations from the 1980s and 90s has now been completed, releasing a body of data for further, more detailed research. This obligation to disseminate information has also provided an opportunity to review the results of all subsequent excavations undertaken in the city. The combined resource has made it possible to approach the development, population, economy and visual appearance of the city from a previously untapped archaeological perspective. The results have confirmed the disparity of social classes and professions who lived side by side and the contrasts with their rural neighbours. Many of the descriptions undoubtedly apply to features of medieval life in cities across all parts of Britain; however, there are others that may characterise Salisbury more specifically. The account is not definitive but provides a preliminary study that will undoubtedly be corrected, improved or confirmed by future studies using additional results of excavation coupled with more detailed documentary evidence. The city remains a fluid, expanding agglomeration of people that developed from a small primary settlement. The story of that city remains not merely an example of medieval planning with a rich heritage but also a home to a modern population that can draw on its past to plan for the future.

Appendix 1

Clay Pipe Makers' Marks

Mark	No.	Position	Comments
Fox in heart-shaped frame	3	Heel	Later version of fox mark, dated *c.* 1650 (Atkinson 1970a, figs 1–3). Maker unknown, but thought to have worked in Amesbury during early–mid-17th century (*ibid.*, 179).
WI in circle	1	Heel	Maker unknown; examples dated *c.* 1650 (Atkinson 1970a, 184).
Gauntlet (1)	4	Heel	Glove with thumb, used by the Gauntlet family of Amesbury (*c.* 1640–80). Less common of the two Gauntlet marks recorded here (Atkinson 1970a, fig. 1, 6). Gauntlet pipes, being of high quality, were widely copied, but these examples are frequently burnished and probably genuine Gauntlet products.
Gauntlet (2)	25	Heel	'Monkey's paw' form of Gauntlet mark (crude gloveless hand); *c.* 1640–80 (Atkinson 1970a, fig. 1, 12). Examples here are also probably genuine Gauntlet pipes.
IB in heart	1	Heel	Possibly a local maker working *c.* 1650–70 (Atkinson 1970a, 184).
WC or WG	1	Heel	No local marks of this type known, although a William Gauntlet(t) is known to have lived in Amesbury (Oswald 1975, 198). Initials WG also recorded on Bristol pipes dating *c.* 1660–70 (Atkinson 1970a, 184); this pipe bowl dates *c.* 1670–80.
RM in heart, stars above initials	1	Stem	Mark recorded from Salisbury and Winchester, dating *c.* 1690 (Atkinson 1972, 152, fig. 1, 22).
Thomas Hunt (script)	1	Heel	Thomas Hunt known as a Marlborough pipemaker, working *c.* 1667–96, during transition from bowls with marked heels to spurred pipes marked on the stem. The first heeled pipes with this mark probably date *c.* 1640 (Atkinson 1965, 90, fig. 1, 7); the mark appears to be a facsimile of Hunt's actual signature (Atkinson 1972, 155).
THO/HVNT in shield	1	Stem	New-style spurred pipes made by Thomas Hunt from *c.* 1685 (Atkinson 1965, 90, 92–3).

Mark	No.	Position	Comments
GAB/RIE.../AIL	1	Heel	Mark of Gabriel Bailey (Oswald 1975, 198). This maker apparently took over the Gauntlet business in Amesbury in the late 17th century (Atkinson 1970a, 185). Bowl seen here dates to third quarter of the 17th century.
Fleur-de-lis	1	Stem	Mark dated c. 1690–1700 (Atkinson 1972, 154, fig. 1, 31).
THO/HILL	8	Stem	Thomas Hill died in 1710 and had probably worked for at least 20 years. He lived and presumably had his workshop at Fisherton Anger (Atkinson 1970a, 186, 188 no. 4; 1980, 69–70).
W/HIGGENS/SARVM	1	Stem	Atkinson dates this mark to c. 1700. Maker likely to have been related to the more commonly represented Ed. Higgens and appears to have been in business for only a very short time (Atkinson 1980, 69).
RICH/ARD.S/AYER	1	Stem	Richard Sayer's products are known from Marlborough, Winchester, Basing, London and even America as well as Salisbury (perhaps because of their high quality). There appear to have been at least two makers of this name working at East Woodhay, Hampshire, from at least 1685–1716 (Cannon 1991, 25; Higgins 2011, 11)
THO/SMI/TH	8	Stem	None of the marks entirely legible, but appear to be similar to Atkinson 1970a, fig. 2, 16. Only one mark on a pipe with the bowl surviving, dating c. 1700–20. Smith is recorded as a local maker, at work c. 1700 (Atkinson 1970a, 187); he appears in records as a pipemaker in Fisherton in 1703 and at his death in 1736 (J Wright pers. comm.).
W/BARNS	1	Stem	William Barnes worked at East Woodhay, Hampshire; he took an apprentice in 1723. His marks are also recorded from Marlborough, Swindon, Winchester and Newbury (Atkinson 1972, 153; Cannon 1991, 22).

Mark	No.	Position	Comments
WILL/HARDEN	11	Stem	Will Harden is recorded as a local maker, at work between c. 1700–20 (Atkinson 1970a, 186).
ED/HIGG/ENS	15	Stem	This maker married in Salisbury in 1698 and was still in the city in 1710. His pipes are also common in Cirencester, and he may either have had pipeworks in both places or moved to Salisbury from Cirencester around the time of his marriage (Atkinson 1980, 69).
MIC/KEL/WAY	1	Stem	Different readings of the stamp have identified this maker as either Michael Kelway (Atkinson 1970b, 213, fig. 5, 6) or Michael Way (Atkinson 1972, 152). Examples of the stamp are known from Shaftesbury and may have been made there c. 1700–20. No documentary evidence for either name.
IOL/SANGER; IOEL/SANGER	135	Stem	Sanger's pipes, including at least one waster, were particularly common from W227, which may have been close to his workshop. A number of dies are represented, and many of the pipes are polished. Joel Sanger was working c. 1710–40 (Atkinson 1972, 149).
Tudor Rose	1	Stem	Atkinson suggests that pipes with this mark were made at Southampton; examples found there dated c. 1720–40 (Atkinson 1972, 154, fig. 1, 33).
Flower in circular frame with zigzag border	1	Stem	Unparalleled stamp. Zigzag borders were popular among the Marlborough pipemakers, although as borders to names rather than symbols. Date in first half of the 18th century suggested.
W/SAYER	11	Stem	This pipemaker probably worked at West Wellow, Hampshire during period 1720–50. His pipes are widespread and occur at Southampton and Winchester as well as Salisbury (Atkinson 1970a, 187; 1972, 153).

Mark	No.	Position	Comments
THO/MAS/SON; THO/MAS/SEN	4	Stem	This maker probably worked in Salisbury during the period 1730–50 (Atkinson 1970a, 187; 1972, 154).
WS under a crown	1	Stem	Unknown maker, probably mid-18th century; examples of the mark are known from Salisbury and Winchester (Atkinson 1972, 156).
Double-headed eagle	1	Stem	This stamp poorly-impressed, but possible parallel is known, dated 1720–40 (Atkinson 1972, fig. 1, 15).
J/G	1	Spur	Unknown maker. Mark stamped on underside of a substantial spur; fragmentary bowl is 18th-century or later.
A/E or A/C	1	Spur	Unknown maker, 18th-century or later.
W/M	1	Spur	The mark of either William Morgan (working at least 1840–44/8) or his son William John Morgan (working at least 1841–59), both of Salisbury (Mepham 2016b, 158–9).
J/S	1	Spur	The mark of James Skeaines (or Skeaimes), based in Salt Lane, Salisbury. Originally from Southampton, he moved to Salisbury sometime between 1839 and 1858 and became the partner of William John Morgan; later he took over his business, working 1858–67, the last recorded pipemaker in the city (Atkinson 1970a, 188; Mepham 2016b, 158).
J. CLEEVER GAMBIER A PARIS POSENER & CO / LONDON F GOODALL/ GOSPORT	1	Stem	Joseph Cleever was working in Southampton in the period 1867–95 (Oswald 1975, 171). Not a common mark, and not apparently recorded in the city previously; an example is known from Bath (Walker 1970).

Mark	No.	Position	Comments
GAMBIER A PARIS	1	Stem	This French firm produced decorated pipes imported into this country in large quantities in late 19th century (Van Esveld 2018).
POSENER & CO / LONDON	1	Stem	Elaborately decorated pipe with incomplete bowl. Two pipemaking businesses of this name recorded in London: Adolph Posener & Co (1878–99) and David Posener & Co (1866–94) (Oswald 1975, 142).
F GOODALL/ GOSPORT	1	Stem	Frederick Goodall operated in Gosport 1878–1907 (Fox and Hall 1979, 22, cat nos 127–31).

Bibliography

AC Archaeology 2009 *An Archaeological Excavation Undertaken at the Petersfinger Park and Ride Site, Salisbury, Wiltshire*. Chicklade, unpubl rep SW126824

Akerman, J Y 1854 An account of excavations in an Anglo-Saxon burial ground at Harnham Hill, near Salisbury, *Archaeologia* 35(2), 259–78

Albarella, U 2006 Pig husbandry and pork consumption in medieval England, in C M Woolgar, D Serjeantson and T Waldron (eds), *Food in Medieval England: Diet and Nutrition*, Medieval History and Archaeology Series, 72–87. Oxford, Oxford University Press

Albarella, U and Davis, S 1996 Mammal and bird bones from Launceston Castle: decline in status and the rise of agriculture, *Circaea* 12(1), 1–156

Albarella, U and Thomas, R 2002 They dined on crane: bird consumption, wild fowling and status in medieval England, *Actazoologica Cracoviensia* 45 (special issue), 23–38

Algar, D 1970 Rescue and research work in the Salisbury Area, in Excavation and Fieldwork in Wiltshire, 1969, *Wiltshire Archaeol Natur Hist Mag* 65, 207–9

Algar, D 2012 Bone and Antler, in Saunders P (ed.) 2012, 237-9

Algar, D and Saunders, P 2012 Church bells and cast copper-alloy vessels, in P Saunders (ed.) 2012, 67–85

Algar, D and Saunders, P 2014 A medieval pottery kiln in Salisbury, *Wiltshire, Wiltshire Archaeol Natur Hist Mag* 107, 146–55

Allan, J P 1984 *Medieval and Post-Medieval Finds from Exeter 1971–1980*. Exeter Archaeological Rep 3. Exeter, Exeter City Council and the University of Exeter

Ashbee, P 1966 The Fussell's Lodge long barrow excavations, 1957, *Archaeologia* 100, 1–80

Atkin, M 1985 Excavations on Alms Lane, in M Atkin, A Carter and D H Evans (eds), *Excavations in Norwich 1971–78, Part II*, 144–260. Norwich, East Anglian Archaeol Rep 26

Atkinson, D R 1965 Clay tobacco pipes and pipemakers of Marlborough, *Wiltshire Archaeol Natur Hist Mag* 60, 85–95

Atkinson, D R 1970a Clay tobacco pipes and pipemakers of Salisbury, Wiltshire, *Wiltshire Archaeol Natur Hist Mag* 65, 177–89

Atkinson, D R 1970b Clay tobacco pipes found in Shaftesbury, *Proc Dorset Natur Hist Archaeol Soc* 91, 206–15

Atkinson, D R 1972 Further notes on clay tobacco pipes and pipemakers from the Marlborough and Salisbury districts, *Wiltshire Archaeol Natur Hist Mag* 67, 149–56

Atkinson, D R 1980 More Wiltshire clay tobacco pipe varieties, *Wiltshire Archaeol Natur Hist Mag* 72/73, 67–74

Barber, B 2005 The development of Trinity Chequer: Excavations at the Anchor Brewery site, Gigant Street, *Wiltshire Archaeol Natur Hist Mag* 98, 165–212

Barnwell, P S and Palmer, M (eds) 2019 *Working-class Housing: improvement and technology*. Donington, Shaun Tyas

Barton, R N E 1992 *Hengistbury Head, Dorset. Vol. 2: the Late Upper Palaeolithic and Early Mesolithic sites*. Oxford, Oxford University Committee for Archaeology Monogr 34

Barton, R N E, Ford, S, Collcott, S, Crowther, J, Macphail, R, Rhodes, E and van Gijn, A L 2009 A Final Upper Palaeolithic site at Nea Farm, Somerley, Hampshire (England) and some reflections on the occupation of Britain in the Late Glacial Interstadial, *Quartär* 56, 1–29

Bates, M R, Wenban-Smith, F F, Bello, S M, Bridgland, D R, Buck, L T, Collins, M J, Keen, D H, Leary, J, Parfitt, S A, Penkman, K, Rhodes, E, Ryssaert, C and Whittaker J E 2014 Late persistence of the Acheulian in southern Britain in an MIS 8 interstadial: evidence from Harnham, Wiltshire, *Quaternary Sci Rev* 101, 159–76

Benson, R and Hatcher, H 1843 *The History of Modern Wiltshire by Sir Richard Colt Hoare. Old and New Sarum, or Salisbury*. London, John Bowyer Nichols

Bersu, G 1940 Excavations at Little Woodbury, Wiltshire, *Proc Prehist Soc* 6, 30–111

Biddle, M 1967 Excavations in Winchester, 1967. Sixth interim report, *Antiq J* 48, 250–85

Biddle, M 1975a. Excavations at Winchester 1971. Tenth and final interim report: part 1, *Antiq J* 55, 96–126

Biddle, M 1975b Excavations at Winchester 1971. Tenth and final interim report: part 2, *Antiq J* 55, 295–337

Blair, J, Rippon, S and Smart, C 2020 *Planning in the Early Medieval Landscape*. Liverpool, Liverpool University Press

Bonde, S and Maines, C 2012 The Technology of medieval water management at the Charterhouse of Bourgfontaine, *Techno Culture, Int Q Soc Hist Techno* 53(3), 625–70

Bonney, H 1964 'Balle's Place', Salisbury: a 14th century merchants house, *Wiltshire Archaeol Natur Hist Mag* 59, 155–67

Brown, D H 2002 *Pottery in Medieval Southampton c. 1066–1510*. Southampton Archaeology Monogr 8, CBA Res Rep 137

Brunskill, R W 1994 *Timber Buildings in Britain*. London, Victor Gollancz

Butterworth, C 2005a Excavations at Old George Mall, Salisbury, *Wiltshire Archaeol Natur Hist Mag* 98, 236–46

Butterworth, C 2005b Notes on small-scale archaeological excavations in Salisbury: Elim Chapel and 69 Greencroft Street, *Wiltshire Archaeol Natur Hist Mag* 98, 247–9

Butterworth, C 2005c Archaeological recording at the Plumbery, Salisbury Cathedral, *Wiltshire Archaeol Natur Hist Mag* 98, 281–4

Cambrian Archaeological Projects 2001 *Church House, Salisbury, Wilts. Archaeological Evaluation*. Unpubl rep 171

Cannon, P 1991 Evidence of tobacco pipe making in East Woodhay & District, *Trans Newbury Dist Fld Club* 14 (1), 16–27

Cave-Penney, H 2005 Archaeological investigations in Salisbury, *Wiltshire Archaeol Natur Hist Mag* 98, 285–96

Chaffey, G and Fitzpatrick, R 2015 St Edmund's College, Salisbury: new evidence for medieval origins and post-medieval development at the Council House, Bourne Hill, *Wiltshire Archaeol Natur Hist Mag* 108, 143–58

Chandler, J 1983 *Endless Street. A History of Salisbury and its People*. Salisbury, Hobnob Press

Chandler, J 2013 From Salisbury Bus station to Massachusetts: an unexpected journey, *Sarum Chronicle* 13, 117–28

Chandler, J 2015 Vanner's Chequer: a new light on a corner of medieval Salisbury, part 1, *Sarum Chronicle* 15, 7–18

Chandler, J 2016 Vanner's Chequer, part 2, *Sarum Chronicle* 16, 101–15

Chandler, J 2021 Historical background including documentary evidence, in Garland *et al.* 2021, 156–8

Clark, J G 2019 The Small-Town Friaries of Later Medieval England, in D Harry and C Steer (eds), *The Urban Church in Later Medieval England*, 277–300. Donnington, Shaun Tyas

Clarke, B and Baker, W (eds) 2020 Excavation and fieldwork in Wiltshire 2019: 30–36 Fisherton Street, (Phase 2), Salisbury, *Wiltshire Archaeol Natur Hist Mag* 113, 328

Cotswold Archaeology 2017 *Salisbury Bus Station, Endless Street, Salisbury, Wiltshire. Post-excavation Assessment and Updated Project Design*. Andover, unpubl rep CA17491

Courtney, P 1997 Ceramics and the history of consumption: pitfalls and prospects, *Medieval Ceram* 21, 95–108

Crittall, E (ed.) 1962 The Market Place, in *A History of the County of Wiltshire*, Vol. 6, 85–7. London, Victoria County History

Crummy, N 1988 *The Post-Roman Small Finds from Excavations in Colchester* 1971–85, Colchester, Colchester Archaeol Rep 5

Cunliffe, B 1964 *Winchester Excavations 1949–1960*. Winchester, Winchester City Council

Currie, C K and Rushton, N S 2005 An archaeological excavation at the rear of 36 Milford Street/34 Gigant Street, Salisbury, *Wiltshire Archaeol Natur Hist Mag* 98, 213–35

Daniell, C 1997 *Death and Burial in Medieval England 1066–1550*. London, Routledge

Dawes, J D and Magilton, J R 1980 *The Cemetery of St Helen-on-the-Walls, Aldwark*, The Archaeology of York: the medieval cemeteries, Vol. 12/1. London, Council for British Archaeology for the York Archaeological Trust

Davies, S M 1984 The excavation of an Anglo-Saxon cemetery (and some prehistoric pits) at Charlton Plantation, near Downton, Wiltshire, *Wiltshire Archaeol Natur Hist Mag* 79, 109–54

De'Athe, R 2012 Early to middle Anglo-Saxon settlement, a lost medieval church rediscovered and an early post-medieval cemetery in Wilton, *Wiltshire Archaeol Natur Hist Mag* 105, 117–44

Dittmar, J M, Mitchell, P D, Cessford, C, Inskip, S A and Robb, J E 2021 Medieval injuries: skeletal trauma as an indicator of past living conditions and hazard risk in Cambridge, England, *American J Phys Anthropol* 175, 626–45. https://doi.org/10.1002/ajpa.24225 (accessed 15 October 2021)

Draper, J with Copland-Griffiths, P 2002 *Dorset Country Pottery: the kilns of the Verwood district.* Marlborough, Crowood Press

Durman, R 2007 *Milford.* Sarum Studies 1. Salisbury, Hobnob Press

Eagles, B, Algar, D and Saunders, P, 2014 Two graves near Old Sarum: further insight into early Anglo-Saxon settlement around Salisbury, *Wiltshire Archaeol Natur Hist Mag* 107, 77–90

Eames, E 1988 The tile kiln and floor tiles, in James and Robinson 1988, 127–67

Eames, E 1991 Tiles, in P Saunders and E Saunders (eds) *Salisbury and South Wiltshire Museum Medieval Catalogue Part 1*, 93–139. Salisbury, Salisbury and South Wiltshire Museum

Egberts, E, Basell, L S, Welham, K, Brown, A G, Toms, P S 2020 Pleistocene landscape evolution in the Avon valley, southern Britain: optical dating of terrace formation and Palaeolithic archaeology, *Proc Geol Assoc* 131 (2), 121–37. https://doi.org/10.1016/j.pgeola.2020.02.002 (accessed 15 October 2021)

Every, R 2005 Ceramic building material, in Barber 2005, 188–9

Fitzpatrick, A P 2011 *The Amesbury Archer and the Boscombe Bowmen. Bell Beaker Burials on Boscombe Down, Amesbury, Wiltshire.* Salisbury, Wessex Archaeology Rep 27

Fox, R T and Hall, R B 1979 *The Clay Tobacco Pipes of the Portsmouth Harbour Region 1680–1932.* Privately printed

French, C, Scaife, R, Allen, M, Parker Pearson, M, Pollard, J, Richards, C and Welham, K 2012 Durrington Walls to West Amesbury by way of Stonehenge: a major transformation of the Holocene landscape, *Antiq J* 92, 1–36

Gale, R 2005 Charcoal, in Barber 2005, 197–200

Garland, N, Nichol, M and Chandler, J, 2021 A summary report on medieval and post-medieval activity at Salisbury Bus Station, Endless Street, Wiltshire, *Wiltshire Archaeol Natur Hist Mag* 114, 148–68

Gilchrist, R and Sloane, B 2005 *Requiem: The Medieval Monastic Cemetery in Britain.* London, Museum of London Archaeology Service

Gill, M 2021 Re-assessing the Rocks Hill Long Barrow, near Old Sarum, *Wiltshire Archaeol Natur Hist Mag* 114, 34–41

Grinsell, L V (1957) Archaeological Gazetteer, in R B Pugh and E Crittall (eds) *A History of the County of Wiltshire*, Vol. 1(1), 21–279. London, Victoria County History

Hall, R A, MacGregor, H and Stockwell, M 1988 *Medieval Tenements in Aldwark, and Other Sites*, The Archaeology of York: the medieval walled city north-east of the Ouse, Vol. 10/2. London, Council for British Archaeology for the York Archaeological Trust

Hamilton-Dyer, S 2000 The faunal remains, in Rawlings 2000, 45–51

Hamilton-Dyer, S 2005 Animal bone, in Barber 2005, 200–4

Harding, P 2008 Wishaw (Site 20), in A B Powell, P Booth, A P Fitzpatrick and A D Crockett, *The Archaeology of the M6 Toll, 2000–2002*, 398–423. Oxford/Salisbury, Oxford Wessex Archaeology Monogr 2

Harding, P 2016 Excavations in Vanner's and Griffin Chequers, Salisbury: a study of urban development, *Wiltshire Archaeol Natur Hist Mag* 109, 143–72

Harding, P and Barton, N 2021 The Upper Palaeolithic of Churchfields, Fisherton: 160 years in the making, *Antiq J*, 1–14. https://doi.org/10.1017/S0003581521000299 (accessed 17 March 2022)

Harding, P and Bridgland, D R 1998 Pleistocene deposits and Palaeolithic implements at Godolphin School, Milford Hill, Salisbury, *Wiltshire Archaeol Natur Hist Mag* 91, 1–10

Hare, J N 1991 The growth of the roof-tile industry in later medieval Wessex, *Medieval Archaeol* 35, 86–103

Hare, J 2020 Some Salisbury merchants in the reign of Henry VII, *Sarum Chronicle* 20, 55–64

Harman, M 1996 The mammal bones, 89–102, in M Shaw, The excavation of a late 15th- to 17th-century tanning complex at The Green, Northampton, *Post-Medieval Archaeol* 30, 63–127

Haskins, C 1909 The Church of St Thomas of Canterbury, Salisbury, *Wiltshire Archaeol Natur Hist Mag* 36, 1–12

Hawkes, J (nd) *Excavations in Salisbury 1984–1990.* Salisbury, unpubl rep

Hawley, W 1912 Report of the Committee for Excavations at Old Sarum, *Proc Soc Antiq London*, Second Series 24, 52–65

Hawley, W 1913 Report of the Committee for Excavations at Old Sarum, *Proc Soc Antiq London*, Second Series 25, 93–104

Hawley, W 1915 Report of the Committee for Excavations at Old Sarum, *Proc Soc Antiq London*, Second Series 27, 230–8

Headland Archaeology 2019a *Land South of Netherhampton Road, Salisbury, Wiltshire. Archaeological Evaluation*. Unpubl rep, https://doi.org/10.5284/1055197 (accessed 15 October 2021)

Headland Archaeology 2019b *Land North of Netherhampton Road, Salisbury, Wiltshire. Archaeological Evaluation*. Unpubl rep, https://doi.org/10.5284/1055397 (accessed 15 October 2021)

Higbee, L 2016 Animal bones, in Harding 2016, 165–6

Higgins, D A 2011 Clay tobacco pipes, in R Brown and A Hardy, *Trade and Prosperity, War and Poverty: An Archaeological and Historical Investigation into Southampton's French Quarter*. Oxford, Oxford Archaeology Monogr 15, specialist download F2. http://library.thehumanjourney.net/48/1/SOU_1382_Specialist_report_download_F2.pdf (accessed 9 October 2019)

Higgs, E 1959 Excavations at a Mesolithic site at Downton, near Salisbury, Wiltshire, *Proc Prehist Soc* 25, 209–32

Hinton, D A 1992 The finds of metal, bone and wood, in I Horsey, *Excavations in Poole 1973–83*, 146–7. Dorchester, Dorset Natur Hist Archaeol Soc Monogr 10

Hinton, P 2000 The plant remains, in Rawlings 2000, 39–45

Hinton, P 2005 Plant remains, in Barber 2005, 193–7

Hobbs, S and Chandler, J 2012 Salisbury Domesday Books, *Sarum Chronicle* 12, 81–6

Hollinrake Archaeology 2011 *An Archaeological Watching Brief at No. 4 Vicars' Close, Wells*. Unpubl rep WVC 11

Hope, W H St J 1910 Report of the Committee for Excavations at Old Sarum, *Proc Soc Antiq London*, Second Series 22, 190–201

Hope, W H St J 1911 Report of the Committee for Excavations at Old Sarum, *Proc Soc Antiq London*, Second Series 23, 501–19

Hope, W H St J 1914 Report of the Committee for Excavations at Old Sarum, *Proc Soc Antiq London*, Second Series 26, 100–19

Hope, W H St J 1916 Report of the Committee for Excavations at Old Sarum, *Proc Soc Antiq London*, Second Series 28, 174–83

James, T B and Gerrard, C 2007 *Clarendon. Landscape of Kings*. Macclesfield, Windgather Press

James, T B and Robinson, A M 1988 *Clarendon Palace. The History and Archaeology of a Medieval Palace and Hunting Lodge near Salisbury, Wiltshire*. Society of Antiquaries Res Rep 45. London, Thames and Hudson

Jacques, D, Phillips, T and Lyons, T 2018 *Blick Mead: Exploring the 'First Place' in the Stonehenge Landscape*. Oxford, Peter Lang Publishing

Jervis, B 2012 Cuisine and urban identities in medieval England: objects, foodstuffs and urban life in thirteenth- and fourteenth-century Hampshire, *Archaeol J* 169, 453–79

Keene, D 1985 *Survey of Medieval Winchester*, Winchester Studies II, 2 vols. Oxford, Clarendon Press

Kelly, E R (ed.) 1875 *The Post Office Directory of Hampshire, Including The Isle of Wight; Wiltshire and Dorsetshire*. London, Kelly and Co

Kidson, P 1993 The historical circumstances and the principles of the design, in T Cocke and P Kidson (eds) *Salisbury Cathedral. Perspectives on the Architectural History*, 35–91. London, HMSO, Royal Commission on the Historical Monuments of England

Langlands, A 2014 Placing the burgh in Searobyrg: rethinking the urban topography of early medieval Salisbury, *Wiltshire Archaeol Natur Hist Mag* 107, 91–105

Langlands, A, Sly, T, Barker, D S and Strutt, K D, 2018 *Report on the Geophysical Survey at Old Sarum, Wiltshire, April and July 2016, and April and July 2017*. The Old Sarum Landscapes Project Research Report No. 3, https://doi.org/10.5284/1047137 (accessed 15 October 2021)

Leech, R 1997 *The Topography of Medieval and Early Modern Bristol: part 1*. Bristol Record Society's Publication Vol 48. Bristol, Bristol Record Society

Leeds, E T and Shortt, H de S 1954 An Anglo-Saxon cemetery at Petersfinger, near Salisbury, Wilts, *Antiquity* 28 (111), 177–9

Leivers, M and Moore, C 2008 *Archaeology on the A303 Stonehenge Improvement*. Salisbury, Wessex Archaeology

LMMC 1940 London Museum Medieval Catalogue

Loader, E 2003 Ceramic building material, 159–64, in P Harding and A Light, Excavations in Fordingbridge, 1989 and 1997: the former Albany and Greyhound Hotel site, *Hampshire Studies* 58, 130–76

MacGregor, A 1985 *Bone, Antler, Ivory and Horn: the technology of skeletal materials since the Roman period*. London, Croom Helm Ltd

McNeill, J 2012 Objects of wood, in Saunders (ed.) 2012, 200–211

Mepham, L 2000 Pottery, in Rawlings 2000, 29–37

Mepham, L 2005 Pottery, in Barber 2005, 183–8

Mepham, L 2012 Pottery, 126–9, in R De'Athe, Early to middle Anglo-Saxon settlement, a lost medieval church rediscovered and an early post-medieval cemetery in Wilton, *Wiltshire Archaeol Natur Hist Mag* 105, 117–144

Mepham, L 2016a Medieval and post-medieval pottery, in Harding 2016, 153–7

Mepham, L 2016b Clay tobacco pipes, in Harding 2016, 157–64

Mepham, L 2018 Town and country: the production and distribution of Laverstock wares, *Medieval Ceram* 39, 17–28

Mepham 2000 The pottery, in Rawlings 2000, 29–37

Mepham, L and Underwood, C (nd) The pottery, in Hawkes (nd), 23–44

Musty J W G 1963 Excavations near the Bishop's Stables, Cathedral Close, Salisbury. *Wiltshire Archaeol Natur Hist Mag* 58, 452–3

Musty, J 1973 A preliminary account of a medieval pottery industry at Minety, north Wiltshire, *Wiltshire Archaeol Natur Hist Mag* 68, 79–88

Musty, J and Algar, D 1986 Excavations at the deserted medieval village of Gomeldon, near Salisbury, *Wiltshire Archaeol Natur Hist Mag* 80, 127–69

Musty, J, Algar, D J and Ewence, P F 1969 The medieval pottery kilns at Laverstock, near Salisbury, Wiltshire, *Archaeologia* 102, 83–150

Musty, J, Algar, D, Gerrard, C and Hadley, J 2001 Pottery, tile and brick, in P Saunders (ed.), *Salisbury and South Wiltshire Museum Medieval Catalogue Part 3*, 132–212. Salisbury, Salisbury and South Wiltshire Museum

Musty, J and Rahtz, P 1964 The suburbs of Old Sarum, *Wiltshire Archaeol Natur Hist Mag* 59, 130–54

Nenk, B 2012 Floor tiles, in Saunders (ed.) 2012, 269–81

O'Connor, T 1982 *Animal Bones from Flaxengate, Lincoln* c. *870–1500*, The Archaeology of Lincoln 18(1). London, Council for British Archaeology

Orbach, J, Pevsner, N and Cherry, B 2021 *The Buildings of England: Wiltshire*. London, Yale University Press

Oswald, A 1975 *Clay Pipes for the Archaeologist*. Oxford, BAR 14

Ottaway, P 2017 *Winchester: An Archaeological Assessment – St Swithun's 'City of Happiness and Good Fortune'*. Oxford, Oxbow Books

Ottaway, P and Qualmann, K 2018 *Winchester's Anglo-Saxon, Medieval and Later Suburbs. Excavations 1971–86*. Winchester, Winchester Museums Service and Historic England Reports

Pearce, J E, Vince, A G and Jenner, M A 1985 *A Dated Type-Series of London Medieval Pottery Part 4: Surrey Whitewares*. London, London and Middlesex Archaeological Society Special Pap 6

Pettitt, P with Chan, B 2020 Upper Palaeolithic: the crested blade, in M Parker Pearson, J Pollard, C Richards, J Thomas, C Tilley and K Welham, *Stonehenge for the Ancestors: Part 1. Landscape and Monuments*, 290. Leiden, Sidestone Press

Pluskowski, A (ed.) 2007 *Breaking and Shaping Beastly Bodies: animals as material culture in the Middle Ages*. Oxford, Oxbow Books

Poole, K 2010 Bird introductions, in T O'Connor and N Sykes (eds), *Extinctions and Invasions: a social history of British fauna*, 156–65. Oxford, Windgather Press

Powell, A B 2006 A possible site for the Hospital of St John the Baptist and St Anthony at Old Sarum, Salisbury, *Wiltshire Archaeol Natur Hist Mag* 99, 213–20

Powell, A B 2015 Bronze Age and Early Iron Age burial grounds and later landscape development outside Little Woodbury, Salisbury, Wiltshire, *Wiltshire Archaeol Nat Hist Mag* 108, 44–78

Powell, A B, Allen, M J, Chapman, J, Every, R, Gale, R, Harding, P, Knight, S, McKinley, J I and Stevens, C 2005 Excavations along the Old Sarum Pipeline, north of Salisbury, *Wiltshire Archaeol Natur Hist Mag* 98, 250–80

Pugh R B and Crittall E (eds) 1956a The Dominican Friars of Salisbury, in *A History of the County of Wiltshire*, Vol. 3, 331–3. London, Victoria County History

Pugh R B and Crittall E (eds) 1956b Hospitals: St Nicholas, Salisbury, in *A History of the County of Wiltshire*, Vol. 3, 343–56. London, Victoria County History

Rahtz, P and Musty, J 1960 Excavations at Old Sarum 1957, *Wiltshire Archaeol Nat Hist Mag*, 57, 352–70

Rawlings, M 2000 Excavations at Ivy Street and Brown Street, Salisbury, 1994, *Wiltshire Archaeol Natur Hist Mag* 93, 20–62

Reynolds, S and Manning, A 2013 Damascus and Emmaus Houses, 58 Barnard Street, Salisbury, *Wiltshire Archaeol Natur Hist Mag* 106, 275–7

Reilly, K (nd) The animal bone, in Hawkes (nd), 54–67

Rich-Jones, W and Dunn Macray, W (eds) 1891 *Charters and Documents Illustrating the History of the Cathedral, City, and Diocese of Salisbury in the Twelfth and Thirteenth Centuries*, Vol. 97, Rolls Series. London, HMSO

Richards, D 2020 Salisbury's Blackfriars. The rise and fall of a medieval institution, *Sarum Chronicle* 20, 81–96

Richards, J D, Heighway, C and Donaghey, S 1989 *Union Terrace: Excavations in the Horsefair*, The Archaeology of York: the medieval defences and suburbs, Vol. 11/1. London, Council for British Archaeology for the York Archaeological Trust

Rippon, S and Holbrook, N (eds) 2021a *Roman and Medieval Exeter and their Hinterlands from Isca to Excester*. Oxford, Oxbow Books

Rippon, S and Holbrook, N (eds) 2021b *Studies in the Roman and Medieval Archaeology of Exeter*. Oxford, Oxbow Books

Roberts, C A and Cox, M 2003 *Health and Disease in Britain: from prehistory to the present day*. Gloucester, Sutton Publishing

Rogers, K H 1969 Salisbury, in M D Lobel (ed.), *Atlas of Historic Towns*, Vol. 1. London and Oxford, Lovell Johns-Cook, Hammond and Kell

Royal Commission on Historic Monuments (England) (RCHME) 1980 *Ancient and Historical Monuments in the City of Salisbury*, Vol. 1. London, HMSO

Royal Commission on Historic Monuments (England) (RCHME) 1993 *Salisbury. The Houses of the Close*. London, HMSO

Royal Commission on Historic Monuments (England) (RCHME) 1999 *Sumptuous and Richly Adorn'd. The Decoration of Salisbury Cathedral*. London, HMSO

Saunders, P 2009 *Channels to the Past: the Salisbury drainage collection* (2nd edition). Salisbury, Salisbury and South Wiltshire Museum

Saunders, P (ed.) 2012 *Salisbury and South Wiltshire Museum Medieval Catalogue Part 4*, 269–81. Salisbury, Salisbury and South Wiltshire Museum

Saunders, P and Algar, D 2015 Medieval Salisbury: new light on its eastern defences, *Wiltshire Archaeol Natur Hist Mag* 108, 119–32

Saunders, P and Algar, D 2017 Excavations of a medieval brazier's well in Milford Street, Salisbury, *Wiltshire Archaeol Natur Hist Mag* 110, 191–202

Saunders, P and Algar, D 2020 The Anglo-Saxon cemetery at Petersfinger, near Salisbury: an additional grave and associated settlement, *Wiltshire Archaeol Natur Hist Mag* 113, 202–12

Schofield, J (ed.) 1987 *The London Surveys of Ralph Treswell*. London, London Topographical Society Pub 135

Schofield, J 1991 The construction of medieval and Tudor houses in London, *Construction Hist* 7, 3–28

Schofield, J 1995 *Medieval London Houses*. New Haven and London, Yale University Press

Schofield, J and Vince, A 2003 *Medieval Towns. The archaeology of British towns in their European setting* (2nd edition). London, Continuum

Serjeantson, D 1989 Animal remains and the tanning trade, in D Serjeantson and T Waldron (eds), *Diet and Crafts in Towns*, 129–46. Oxford, BAR 199

Smith, R W 1997 *Excavations at Emwell Street, Warminster: the early economy and environment of a Wiltshire market town*. Salisbury, Wessex Archaeology Rep

Spencer, B 1990 *Salisbury Medieval Catalogue Part II: pilgrim souvenirs and secular badges*. Salisbury, Salisbury Museum

Stead, I M 1998 *The Salisbury Hoard*. Stroud, Tempus

Stevens, E T 1870 *Flint Chips*. London, Bell and Daldy

Stevens, F 1934 The Highfield pit dwellings, Fisherton, Salisbury, excavated May 1866 to September 1869, *Wiltshire Archaeol Natur Hist Mag* 46, 579–624

Stevens, K F and Olding, T E 1985 *The Brokage Books of Southampton 1477–8 and 1527–8*. Southampton, Southampton Records Ser 28

Stone, J F S and Charlton, J 1935 Trial excavations in the east suburb of Old Sarum, *Antiq J* 15 (2), 174–92

Strutt, K, Sly, T and Barker, D 2014 *Old Sarum and Stratford-Sub-Castle Archaeological Survey Project: A Project Overview*. Unpubl rep

Sykes, N 2007 Taking sides: the social life of venison in medieval England, in Pluskowski (ed.) 2007, 149–60

Tatton-Brown, T 1997 The Church of St Thomas of Canterbury, Salisbury, *Wiltshire Archaeol Natur Hist Mag* 90, 101–9

Thames Valley Archaeological Services (TVAS) 2014a *47 Endless Street, Salisbury, Wiltshire. An archaeological excavation*. Unpubl rep ESS 13/85

Thames Valley Archaeological Services (TVAS) 2014b *Former Highbury and Fisherton Manor Schools, Highbury Avenue, Salisbury, Wiltshire. Excavation of a Quaternary geology test pit*. Unpubl rep HSS 13/101

Thomas, R N W 1988 A statistical evaluation of criteria used in sexing cattle metapodials, *Archaeozoologia* 2 (1.2), 83–92

Van Esveld, A 2018 Paris, the home of Gambier, J *Académie Internationale de la Pipe* 11, 1–18, https://www.gambierpipes.com/wp-content/uploads/2020/05/Paris-House-of-Gambier-AIP.pdf (accessed 19 October 2021)

Vince, A G 1983 *The Medieval Ceramic Industry of the Severn Valley*. Unpubl PhD thesis, Univ Southampton

Vince, A G, Lobb, S J, Richards, J V and Mepham, L 1997 *Excavations in Newbury, Berkshire 1979–1990*. Salisbury, Wessex Archaeology Rep 13

Walker, I C 1970 A clay tobacco pipe from Bath, *Proc Somerset Archaeol Natur Hist Soc* 114, 100

Walker, T L 1836 *The History and Antiquities of the Vicar's Close Wells, Somersetshire*. Pugin's Examples of Gothic Architecture, Third Series, Part 1. London, J Moyes

Wessex Archaeology 1987 *Goddard's Garage, Salisbury, Wiltshire. Archaeological excavation*. Salisbury, unpubl rep W196

Wessex Archaeology 1992a *Excavations in Salisbury: 1984–1990 archive reports*. Salisbury, unpubl rep

Wessex Archaeology 1992b *Region 3 (The Upper Thames Valley, the Kennet Valley) and Region 5 (The Solent Drainage System)*. Salisbury, Southern Rivers Palaeolithic Project rep 1

Wessex Archaeology 1994 *Bishop Wordsworth's School, Salisbury, Wiltshire*. Salisbury, unpubl rep 37497

Wessex Archaeology 1996a *Former General Infirmary, Fisherton Street, Salisbury, Wiltshire. Archaeological evaluation*. Salisbury, unpubl rep 39900.1

Wessex Archaeology 1996b *Former Infirmary Site, Cranebridge Road, Salisbury, Wiltshire. Archaeological evaluation*. Salisbury, unpubl rep 41196.01

Wessex Archaeology 2000 *21A Highfield Road, Salisbury. Archaeological evaluation*. Salisbury, unpubl rep 47797.1

Wessex Archaeology 2003 *Land Adjacent to Bourne Hill Council Offices, Salisbury, Wiltshire. Archaeological desk-based assessment*. Salisbury, unpubl rep 54280

Wessex Archaeology 2004 *Land Adjacent to Bourne Hill Council Offices, Salisbury, Wiltshire. Report on archaeological evaluation*. Salisbury, unpubl rep 56890.03

Wessex Archaeology 2005 *20 North Street, Salisbury, Wiltshire. Archaeological evaluation*. Salisbury, unpubl rep 58870

Wessex Archaeology 2006a *Harnham Flood Defence Scheme: Middle Street Meadow and Harnham Recreation Ground, Salisbury, Wiltshire. Archaeological evaluation report*. Salisbury, unpubl rep 62340.02

Wessex Archaeology 2006b *Land at Old Sarum, Salisbury, Wiltshire. Interim report on the archaeological excavation*. Salisbury, unpubl rep 61681.02

Wessex Archaeology 2007a *Land Adjoining 120 Fisherton Street, Salisbury, Wiltshire. Archaeological evaluation report*. Salisbury, unpubl rep 65540.01

Wessex Archaeology 2007b *Old Sarum Airfield, Salisbury, Wiltshire. Archaeological evaluation (Areas A and B)*. Salisbury, unpubl rep 66010.11

Wessex Archaeology 2009 *Salisbury Cathedral, Wiltshire. Archaeological evaluation and assessment of results*. Salisbury, unpubl rep 68741.01

Wessex Archaeology 2012 *Salisbury Arts Centre, St Edmund's Church, Bourne Hill, Wiltshire. Archaeological watching brief report*. Salisbury, unpubl rep 84440.01

Wessex Archaeology 2013 Former ATS Site, *28 St Edmunds Church Street, Salisbury, Wiltshire: archaeological watching brief report*. Salisbury, unpubl rep 85490

Wessex Archaeology 2014a *Salisbury Bus Station, Salisbury, Wiltshire. Results of an archaeological trial trench evaluation*. Salisbury, unpubl rep 106740.02

Wessex Archaeology 2014b *7–11 Brown Street, Salisbury, Wiltshire. Archaeological evaluation and excavation report*. Salisbury, unpubl rep 100950.04

Wessex Archaeology 2014c *Salisbury Market Place, Salisbury, Wiltshire. Archaeological watching brief report*. Salisbury, unpubl rep 89120.01

Wessex Archaeology 2014d *191 Devizes Road, Salisbury, Wiltshire. Archaeological evaluation report*. Salisbury, unpubl rep 103640.02

Wessex Archaeology 2014e *Land to the North, West and South of Bishopdown Farm, Salisbury, Wiltshire. Post-excavation assessment and updated project design*. Salisbury, unpubl rep 101630.01

Wessex Archaeology 2015 *Old Sarum Airfield (Area C), Salisbury, Wiltshire. Archaeological evaluation report*. Salisbury, unpubl rep 66013.03

Wessex Archaeology 2016 *Salisbury Museum, West Walk, Salisbury, Wiltshire. Archaeological excavation for the Festival of Archaeology*. Salisbury, unpubl rep

Wessex Archaeology 2017a *Land at United Kingdom House, Castle Street, Salisbury, Wiltshire. Archaeological evaluation report*. Salisbury, unpubl rep 117180.02

Wessex Archaeology 2017b *Land off Rollestone Street, Salisbury, Wiltshire. Archaeological evaluation report*. Salisbury, unpubl rep 116150.03

Wessex Archaeology 2017c *Salisbury Museum, The King's House. Test pit excavation for the 2017 Festival of Archaeology*. Salisbury, unpubl rep SMU17.1

Wessex Archaeology 2018a *Salisbury Museum, The King's House. Test pit excavation for the 2018 Festival of Archaeology*. Salisbury, unpubl rep SMU18.1

Wessex Archaeology 2018b *Milford Hill House, Salisbury, Wiltshire. Archaeological evaluation*. Salisbury, unpubl rep 100171.01

Wessex Archaeology 2019a *30–36 Fisherton Street, Salisbury. Archaeological watching brief*. Salisbury, unpubl rep 206041.03

Wessex Archaeology 2019b *Land at Elmfield House, Petersfinger Road, Salisbury, Wiltshire. Archaeological evaluation report*. Salisbury, unpubl rep 220030.03

Wessex Archaeology 2019c *24 Endless Street, Salisbury, Wiltshire. Archaeological watching brief*. Salisbury, unpubl rep 223070

Wessex Archaeology 2020 *St Thomas' Church, Salisbury, Wiltshire. Ground penetrating radar report*. Salisbury, unpubl rep 229770.02

Wessex Archaeology 2021 *12 The Close, Salisbury. Archaeological evaluation*. Salisbury, unpubl rep 248650.02

Wood, M 1965 *The English Medieval House*. London, Dent

Wood, R 2005 *The Wooden Bowl*. Ammanford, Stobart Davies

Wordsworth, C 1902 *The Fifteenth Century Cartulary of St Nicholas' Hospital, Salisbury, with other records*. Salisbury, Brown and Company

Wright, J 2017 *Brickmaking in Fisherton and Bemerton. Salisbury's almost forgotten industry*. South Wiltshire Industrial Archaeology Society Historical Monogr 22

Wright, J 2020 Salisbury's Black Friars, *Wiltshire Archaeol Natur Hist Mag* 113, 226–38

Yeomans, L 2005 Spatial determinants of animal carcass processing in post-medieval London and evidence for a co-operative supply network, *Trans London Middlesex Archaeol Soc* 55, 69–83

Yeomans, L 2007 The shifting use of animal carcasses in medieval and post-medieval London, in Pluskowski (ed.) 2007, 98–115

Documentary sources

Sale Catalogue, 1903, for the sale by auction of The Friary (Bell) Foundry Works, Friary Road, Salisbury, Wiltshire; Wiltshire Museum, Devizes, DZSWS:SC.25.31

Deeds of the Weavers' Hall, Endless Street, and other property of the warden and commonalty of Weavers in Endless Street, Rollestone Street and Hog Lane, Salisbury; Wiltshire and Swindon Archives, Chippenham, WSA 1214/33

Lightning Source UK Ltd.
Milton Keynes UK
UKHW052044241122
412785UK00003B/62